LOOKA HERE!

Living in New Orleans in the 1940's, 50's, and 60's

Mike DiGiovanni

First printing: July 2018

Printed in the United States of America

Published by **WAR**Arts

ISBN: 978-0-993358-5-8

ACKNOWLEDGMENTS

I am deeply indebted to the following people for making this book possible.

To my wife Debbie, for teaching me some of her fabulous writing techniques. She also helped me with spelling, navigating my computer, and she gave me honest criticism.

To my brothers Paul and Gerard, for reading the first draft of LOOKA HERE! and verifying some of the dates and facts. They both encouraged me a lot.

To my friend Mike Rovere, for making many time-consuming corrections, and writing the opening and closing paragraphs.

To my friend Larry Lee for listening to, and liking, all my stories as I wrote this book.

To my long-time friend and martial arts teacher Jim Wagner, for his helpful suggestions, the cover design, photo placement, and providing me with his technical know-how on publishing.

TABLE OF CONTENTS

INTRODUCTION

LOOKA HERE!

"Looka here!" I'm guessing y'all never heard that phrase before and don't know what it means. That's because it comes from the Deep South where I was born, where life was very different from the rest of the United States, even different from other southern states. "Looka here!" is what someone from the Deep South might say to let you know they're gonna tell you a story or something important that is worthy of your attention. I would say "Looka here!" when ya'll might say, "Listen up!" I am writing this book so you can see and feel how life was for me, a second generation Italian American, living in New Orleans in the 1940's, '50's, and '60's.

Na Ah gotta tell my story just like Ah lived it back in New Orlans. Ah want ya'll to see and feel what um feelin' as we go back in time. In order to accomplish that Ah'll hafta tawk just like Ah did back then. But first Ah betta teach ya'll a lil' about how to talk rite. We don't pronounce er, g, r or th at the end of words MOST OF THE TIME. So looking=lookin', walking=walkin', with=wid 'n'=and 'n' Ah=I. Ya get da picture? Na Ah'll try to smooth it out for ya as we go along, but this might be kinda hard for me 'cause Ah don't tawk like dat anymore. So, Looka here!

Chapter One

EARLY YEARS

NEW ORLANS 1938

Ah entered this world on a warm September day way back in 1938. Ah suppose it took the usual amount of time for my little brain to kick into gear, but Ah like to think that Ah became aware of my surroundins a li'l sooner thn others. Ah shared my house with my mother, father, brother, and a whole bunch of roaches.

My earliest memories are of my mother (we called her Ma). Her cookin and the care she gave us provided a secure family feelin'. She combined Italian and Cajun dishes that could rival any restaurant in the area.

Ma's parents were born in a poverty-stricken area of Sicily. Her father's family came to Alabama seekin the American dream. Instead they ended up workin in the steel mills in Birmingham. They found themselves in a hostile environment. The locals resented the influx of Italian immigrants 'n' were hostile to them. There were incidents that caused her a of lot pain resultin' in low self-esteem that remained with her for the rest of her life. She only told us about a few things that happened to her. Ah think it was too painful for her to relive those memories. Every now 'n' then, she did share a few things with us like: bein' called a WOP (Without Papers), dago, garlic eater, greese ball etc. Ah didn' understand what some of those terms meant, but Ah did figure out they were racial slurs. Another incident that she could never forget happened in about the ninth grade, the last year of her schoolin'. (She couldn' finish high school, 'cause she had to get a job to help out with the family's finances.) Ma was very athletic when she was in school 'n' Ah'm proud of her. She ran track 'n' even pole-vaulted (it's kinda hard for me to imagine Ma pole vaultin'). Anyways, she was a fast runner. In one particular race she crossed the finish line just a little bit ahead of the other girls. It was a close race all the way. Ma clearly won, but the officials gave the first place ribbon to the favored blond girl. Ma referred to her as one of "those Baptists." She never got over this injustice. There were a few other incidents, ‘n’ even stories of the Klan burnin’ crosses in front of Italians’ houses, but like Ah said she wouldn’ talk about um. So ya see Ah grew up hearin’ about, witnessin’, ‘n’ experiencin’ racial prejudice from both sides.

Alabama was not alone in the anti-Italian department. States from the Deep South to as far north as New Jersey ’n’ New York resented the influx of Italian immigrants. In the 1890’s anti-Italian sentiment was ragin’ in America. This led to one of the largest mass lynchins’ in U. S. history. In 1891, New Orlans police chief David Hennessy was assassinated. This occurrence led to the arrest of about one hundred Italians. Only nineteen were indicted, but this didn’ stop a large angry mob from stormin’ the jail ‘n’ hangin’ eleven of the nineteen after a jury found them not guilty. Fav other prisoners later died from wounds they suffered in the attack. The U. S. government paid Italy $25,000 dollars to repair and restore broken relations between the two countries. Problems between locals ’n’ Italian immigrants continued for many years. As late as the 1920’s people would still taunt Italians by sayin’, “Who killa da chief.”

One day my Father (we called him Pop) came home from gramma school ‘n’ asked his Sician uncle, what “Who killa da chief ment?” This demeanin’ phrase angered his uncle. He could not allow this bullyin’ to continue. He sent Pop over to the kid’s house with a message for his father, “Send your son out to the street to either take back what he said, fight my nephew to settle it, or umma gonna killa you!” The kid came right out; they fought. Pop kicked his butt and, as far as Ah know, Pop wasn’ teased again. Na that’s the way to handle injustices! There’s no need to limit free speech. Someone once said, “I may not like what you’re saying, but I’ll defend your right to say it with my life. You have a right to say and do whatever ya want, but your rights end where my nose begins.”

Even though we were dirt poor Ma always had wonderful meals for us. Family life centered around those delicious meals. She could make a healthy, tasty meal out of food scraps. Ma was also one of the first people in our area to become health-conscious. Ah don’t know how she knew so much about nutrition or where she got her information, but she was on the cuttin’ edge of health-related issues. Durin’ the early fifties, we were one of the first families to get a juicer.

Pop was hard workin’, kind, ‘n’ understandin’. His approach to life situations were the opposite of Ma’s. He didn’ hold onto things. Pop always had empathy for us ‘n’ others. He worked seven days a week, 365 days a year, deliverin’ ice. Think about that the next time ya don’t wanna go to work ‘cause ya got a hangnail or somethin’. Ya see, in our part of the world there were no refrigerators or in-home telephones, 'cause people couldn' afford um. Television wasn' even around yet. Pop had a third grade education, could barely read the newspaper, 'n' could hardly sign his name. Yet he was able to add columns of numbers in his head 'n' he coulda' taught psychologists about people. Pop loved people 'n' they loved him: everyone; Wineheads, bums, poor blacks 'n' whites, people from all walks of life loved 'n' respected him. As you can, tell Ah also loved 'n' respected him. Feedin' his family was Pop's top priority. He worked seven days a week for thirty-fav' years.

He never took days off—vacation or sick days. Ah can remember Ma havin' to tie his shoes for him 'cause his back hurt so bad he couldn' bend down. He still went to work delivering 25 to 100 lbs. of ice all day long. Come rain, heat or cold, Pop went to work. He would always say, "dose people gotta have ice or dere food's gonna get bad." This was the beginnin' of my education on work ethics, responsibility, commitment, 'n' a never-give-up attitude. It was not uncommon for men 'n' women, young 'n' old alike, to go out of their way to thank him for keepin' their milk drinkable whether they could pay or not. Years later Pop opened a Mobil gas station, 'n' ya know the core of his business was his former ice customers. Ah can still hear um sayin' "Mr. Paul Ah always buy ma gas from you 'cause when Ah was out of work you let me owe you for da ice." Ah want you to know most of those people came back 'n' paid him every penny they owed, even if it was years later. As you can tell Ah'm proud of my Pop. Ah still get a lump in my throat when Ah talk about him. This ordinary man is my hero, my mentor, my teacher, but most of all, he is my Pop 'n' Ah still miss him. Pop taught me that respect has to be earned before you can demand it.

Another person that had a big influence on my life is my big brother Paul. He is only sixteen months older than me, but the polar opposite of me. He's tall, Ah'm short. He was loud, Ah was quiet. Ah could play quietly for hours; Paul needed more excitement 'n' adventure. Often this quest for adventure got us into trouble. Paul was always there when Ah needed him. Our schools 'n' neighborhoods were tough places. A little guy like me needed some backup.

Once when we were very young a bunch of us wandered off lookin' for some excitement (Ya see, there were no playgrounds or parks in the area). We ended up on a busy street way out of our neighborhood. Some of the older kids found some pine cones, 'n' without thinkin', we started throwin' um at cars. Ya know how it is, before long we were all throwin' pine cones. Doncha' know, the very first cone Ah threw went right through an open pickup truck window 'n' hit da driver right in his face. He slammed on his brakes, turned on the next corner 'n' started chasin' us with his truck. Ah took off like a bat out of hell. Ah don't know, but maybe this is why Ah can run so fast. Ah ran several blocks before duckin' into an alley. Pretty soon a coupla' others joined me. The older boys started sayin' that we could end up in Milne home, the juvenile detention center. Thank God we didn' get caught. Ah learned a valuable lesson that day. Don't follow along when ya know the group is doin' somethin' wrong. If ya do make the mistake of followin' um, run like hell!

THE BAD SANTA

Na Ah don't know at what age we became skeptical about kid things like Santa Claus, the tooth fairy—ya know kid stuff. It started with Santa Claus. Ya see, in a lot of Italian families there's a tradition regarding Santa Claus that was brought over from Italy. We had two Santa Clauses: a nice one for good little boys and girls and a mean one for bad kids. If you were bad, the mean one would give you a really hard spankin'. Na don't get all down on Italians, a lot of other European countries had similar traditions. Anyways, one year Paul got a spankin' from the mean Santa. Ah watched the whole thing. Na ya think this isn' enough to have ya on a psychiatrist couch for the rest of your life, 'r what? That was the end of Santa Claus for us. We shed all the kid stuff 'n' moved on.

Unlike today, in the' 40's and 50's boys settled their differences by fightin'. Bare fists and boxin' gloves were the only weapons used. Kickin' or usin' any other weapon was considered cowardly. Ah can remember one fight that happened when Ah was in the third or fourth grade. One of my classmates and me got into a scuffle. Ah threw him down, then someone broke up the fight. Well about a week later Ah went to get a haircut and doncha know Ah ran right into this kid. We started pushin' and shovin' each other again. Some grown ups in the barber shop saw us, brought out boxin' gloves 'n' refereed the fight. Differences were settled 'n' things went back to normal.

As Ah said before, my brother Paul is a lot bigger than me. Ah mean a lot bigger! We were both athletic 'n' now both of us were lookin' for adventure. Sometimes Ah provided the excitement 'cause Ah kinda had a quick temper that sometimes got me in over my head with bigger boys. Havin' one of the toughest guys in the school for a brother helped, 'n' Ah suspect Paul enjoyed gettin' into a good fight, so things usually worked out to everyone's satisfaction.

SIGHTS N SOUNDS OF THE CITY

Now ya know a lil' about my family. Let's go on a journey back in time. Ah want you to see the sights, smell the aromas, 'n' hear the street sounds of New Orlans jus' like Ah did in the 40's, 50's, 'n' later 60's.

Early in the mornin' ya could hear rattlin' from mule-drawn garbage wagons. Later the rag man sang out "Rags, rags, bring me your ol' rags." The vegetable truck rang a bell. Finally, my favorite, the watermelon man. He would cry out "Watermelon, watermelon, Ah got watermelon red to the raain." My Pop was also part of this street symphony. He would drive slowly through the streets of his ice route singin' out, "Ahiiieeceman! Ahiiieeceman!" Ah didn' think much about it then, but in a few short years, I too became a part of this choir.

We lived in a very old house at 3115 Maris Street. Ah gotta tell ya, from a very young age Ah could feel a strange presence in that house. Ah found out later, it was indeed haunted! Na you can be skeptical if ya wanna', but Ah know f' sure, there was a spirit lurkin' around. Once when Ah was takin' a nap in the afternoon, Ah was kinda awake and kinda asleep. Suddenly, Ah saw a black nun beckonin' for me to come to her. As you can imagine, this scared da bejeebies out of me. From then on, Ah could never sleep without a light on.

Years later Ah did some research and found out there used to be a black nunnery near the location of my old house. Coincidence? There's a long history of black nuns in New Orlans' dating back to 1730.

Several times Ah heard someone say my name. When Ah went to see who called, Ma would say, 'Ah didn' call you." On some occasions when Ah heard someone call me, Pop would be nappin'. Some years later, Ah did some research on black nuns in New Orlans 'n' learned they had a nunnery in my ol' neighborhood. Ah passed by the store 'n' bought me some night lights. Na ya know ya woulda done the same thing.

Our street had about fifteen kids close to my age livin' on one block. Life for the most part was fun on Maris Street. (Except for my spooky ol' roach infested house). Days were filled playin' games like save the country, red rover send someone over, hunta hay, 'n' stick ball. We had to play all of our games in the street 'cause—like Ah said—there were no parks in this area of town. Actually there were very few neighborhood parks anywhere. Maris Street was longer than most streets and, like all New Orleans streets,

Maris Street suffered from a lack of maintenance. Our neglected gravel street would develop giant pot holes. Ah can still hear some of the grown ups saying “The city ain’t gonna fix dis street so we gotta do it ourselves.” The fix was puttin’ oyster ‘n’ clam shells in the holes. Cars drivin’ over the shells ground them up and—wala—problem solved. Imagine slidin’ for a base while playin’ stick ball; yeah u’rite, it was a very painful experience! In the evenins’ grown ups would sit out on their front steps ‘n’ talk. All of the houses were hot ’n’ humid most of the time. There was no air conditionin’, so families sat on the front steps to cool off. Those box steps provided a platform for neighbors to chat. New Orlans people are naturally friendly ‘n’ they love to socialize/gossip. On weekends most grown ups would visit with family ‘n’ friends, play cards, or just talk. Boy Ah could write a whole book about the ghost stories Ah overheard when Ah was a kid. Stories about people seein’ ghosts throwin’ rocks at each other in the now famous cemeteries. Others saw images of a little girl that had died many years before. My younger brother Gerard still has a picture that clearly shows this girl’s ghostly form. And get this; some people swear they saw the devil sittin’ on a rooftop cursin’ at people. No wonder Ah was scared most of my life. My parents told some pretty good stories about our own house on Maris Street. This is why Ah could never sleep in the dark. Yeah, in New Orlans the boogie man is F’ real!

WW II

It was about this time that Ah became aware of America’s involvement in WW II. This was a time when the entire Nation came together to help the war effort in every way they could. We had to win this horrible war. Everyone had to do their part. In our neighborhood it meant standin’ behind our fightin’ men, makin’ the necessary sacrifices and doing everything we could to support the war effort. Meat ‘n’ gas were rationed. A lot of other foods were scarce or not available at all. Most of the time stores didn’ have any coffee. As a substitute, people used Postum, a tasty hot beverage without caffeine. Today Postum is sold in health food stores as a healthy alternative for coffee. Most people didn’ mind the sacrifices. Ah don’t remember anyone whinin’ about the war. This was a time when wars were fought to win, or you didn’ fight at all.

Ah remember bein’ very scared that my beloved Pop would have to leave us and go off to war. Na, for a sensitive chile like me the very thought of my Pop goin’ away was almost unbearable. Many nights Ah cried when he came to kiss me goodnight. Ah was too young to explain my feelings so Ah just cried. After months of agonizin' over whether or not Pop would be drafted into the Army, we received a letter from the draft board statin' he didn' have to go. He got a hardship referral because he had two small children 'n' was our sole support. However, he had to give up his ice route 'n' go to work in an aircraft factory. Pop got a job at Consolidated-Vultee Aircraft Factory located near Lake Pontchartrain. Their contribution to the war was the iconic PBY Catalina aircraft. Pop was one of 6,200 employees at the plant. Like Ah said, everyone had to do their part.

Ah also remember blackout drills. A loud siren would blow signalin' that all lights had to be turned off. Ah didn' like it. Darkness coupled with the loud siren made that ol' house seem even spookier to me. Ah'm still not comfortable bein' alone in a dark house, specially an old one. Anyways, small airplanes would fly over us, if they saw a light on a flour bag would be dropped on the house. The next day a block warden would issue a ticket to that house. Ah can't remember anyone on our block ever gettin' a ticket. Everything concernin' the war effort was serious business.

At night we would all gather around our radio and listen to the war news. We cheered, we prayed, 'n' we waited anxiously. Ya gotta know at this point, we weren't sure how this war would end. However, we were sure 'n' united on one thing: there could be no compromise. We had to get an unconditional surrender from our enemies. NO COMPROMISE!

One day while listenin' to the radio my Uncle Tony told us "One of these days you'll be able to see the people that are talkin' on the radio. A lot of people are talkin' about a new gadget called television. This device is somethin' like a radio, but you can actually see the people, just like at the movies." Ah thought, boy that would be great, but naah, that couldn' happen. It just didn' seem possible. At this time, all visual news came from newsreels at the movies.

A short time later, Ma and I were on Canal Street on one of her marathon shoppin' trips, when all of a sudden horns started blowin'. Some people were screamin', others were throwin' paper out of the windows. We didn' know what da heck was goin' on. Finally Ma asked a cop, "What's goin' on?" He exclaimed, "The war's over! Germany surrendered!"

We found out later, that the entire war was not quite over. It was only over for Germany. Japan hung on, so on August 6, 1945 the United States dropped an atomic bomb on Hiroshima. They still hung on; so then on August 9th we dropped another atomic bomb. This time we hit Nagasaki. Finally, on September 2, 1945 Japan signed their unconditional surrender aboard the USS Missouri. Americans could finally breathe easy. It's estimated that if the war had continued it would have cost us another 160,000 American lives.

After the war, there was joy and relief on Maris Street. Life seemed good. Excitement was in the air. Our country, our neighborhood, our families were safe and secure again. We could move on with our lives. Na Ah didn' know it at the time, but my life was soon goin' to have some big changes. We would be leavin' Maris Street. There would be no more street games. The sights and sounds of the city would become a distant memory, only brought to mind by some tourist writin' or talkin' about their excitin' vacation in New Orlans.

Ya see, after the war Pop's aircraft factory job came to an end. In our area refrigerators were replacing ice boxes in most homes; Pop's ice route didn' exist any more. Sure there were lots of jobs, but not so many for a man with only a third grade education. So Pop tried his hand at runnin' a fillin' station. The only one that he could afford was in Chalmette, a little town near the Lower Ninth Ward. Chalmette is located about seven miles East of downtown New Orlans in St. Bernard Parish. The fillin' station sold sandwiches to a nearby school. Ma had to make the sandwiches, so Paul 'n' I had to go with them to the station. We made the seven mile drive from Maris Street to Chalmette every day. It seemed like a road trip to me.

FAMOUS BATTLE SITE

Chalmette was as Cajun as can be. Cajuns are ethnocentric and by nature skeptical of outsiders. They always treated us like outsiders. Ah could feel it. They just didn' trust us. This was enough to cause a sweet young kid like me not to like um.

Pop's service station happened to be located just across the street from where the battle of New Orlans was fought. Ah had no idea that Ah was playin' on hallowed ground, 'cause nothin' had been renovated yet. Those priceless, historic ruins were left in disrepair for years.

Someone had started a rumor that the British buried gold somewhere in the area before they made their hasty retreat. No one ever found gold, but that didn' stop the locals from diggin' holes everywhere, destroyin' much of this historic site. They even dug up some grave sites and demolished most of the remainin' structures. Ah played hide and seek in the remains of General Jackson's headquarters buildin' that was still on the neutral ground (median). Time had taken its toll on the site and it was finally removed.

What a shame?

There were also rumors that the whole area was haunted, 'n' um here to tell ya Ah could swear Ah heard weird noises comin' from the battlefield at night. Were they real? Who knows? Years later, when Ah worked for the Southern Railroad Ah ended up workin' right next to the battlefield. We were always there right about midnight…you talk about scared! Na Ah know Ah heard battle cries comin' from the battlefield. Still don't believe me? Ah tell you what, go pass by dere at midnight 'n' listen, den ya gonna know f' sure.

SEGREGATION

The fillin' station business didn' last long, so Pop bought another ice route in the Upper Ninth Ward of East New Orlans. Pop's ice route was about eighty miles from the Mississippi State line. The area was mostly swamps. Almost all of the people were dirt poor, black 'n' white alike; they couldn' afford refrigerators. Ice was a necessity. Na ya need to understand, the South was segregated at this time, New Orlans was no exception.

In the 40's and 50's blacks and whites were separated in every way. There were separate schools, movies, motels, and restaurants. The plan was to have separate but equal facilities for both races. Some white restaurants had a window on the outside for colored people. Also, black people had to ride in the back of public buses behind a sign that read, "For colored patrons only." Once, Ah had an experience with this law. You see, Ah was very dark and my hair was curly (and Ah mean really curly). Well, this bus driver told Ma Ah had to sit in the back of his bus. Ma lost it. She gave him a verbal lashin' then grabbed my hand and took me off that bus. Ah didn' know what da heck all the fuss was about. Ah knew Ah didn' do anything wrong. We caught another bus, Ma told the driver what had just happened, then she sat her lil' curly haired chil' right up front. Yeah, we didn' have a problem on this one. What an eye opener. This experience made a lastin' impression on me. Encounters of this nature sure make ya think about things from a different angle.

Later, we moved to the section of town where Pop's ice route was. Our new apartment was in a house located in the middle of three acres of land bordered by a motel on the West side and a trailer park to the North. The East side had thick thorn bushes that made the whole area inaccessible to everyone except us. We made tunnels under the briar bushes 'n' built wooden bridges across swampy places. This was our fort, our safe place, except for the snakes! Beyond the briar patches there was an insane asylum. We often heard eerie screams comin' from the buildin'. One evenin' just about dusk, we were sittin' in a mulberry tree talkin''n' just kinda coolin' off a li'l, when suddenly we heard a maniacal laugh comin' from behind a clump of briar patches! Ah jumped down runnin' as Ah hit the ground. Ah'm tellin' ya Ah was kickin' up a dust cloud as Ah ran down the road. Ah'll never forget that laugh Ah can hear it as Ah write this. The back of the property rolled right up to the edge of another swamp. City sounds were replaced with swamp sounds. The street vendor choir was replaced by croakin' frogs, chirpin' crickets, and a variety of songbirds. Our apartment was small; Ah'm talkin' really small. The entire place consisted of: one bedroom, one bathroom, a tub, no shower, no stove, no telephone, and no front door. A curtain served as our door.

The house was very old, three stories tall, isolated, and spooky. Ma still cooked wonderful meals on a two-burner electric hot plate. Na Ah could deal with all of that. What affected me most was that the house was infested with roaches and mice. Ah didn' mind the mice so much, but the roaches freaked me out. Many nights Ah was startled awake to find roaches crawlin' on me. Most of the time Ah ended up stayin' awake the rest of the night. The family that owned this estate lived downstairs. Mr. Cochrane was the head of the house. He was by far the meanest man Ah ever met. There were rumors that he shot someone in Alabama. Ah kinda think they were true cause when Ah was in high school he did shoot a guy. This guy was trespassin' on Mr. Cochrane's property when he asked the trespasser what he was doing. The guy answered, "Killin' frogs." They exchanged words, then Mr. Cochrane shot him! Mr. Cochrane wasn' all bad cause after he shot the guy he drug him up to his house, put a blanket over him, 'n' tried to stop the bleeding. The guy lived, 'n' sued Mr. Cochrane when he recovered.

Next was Ludy (just back from the war), not quite, but just about as mean. Na Ah actually saw Ludy shoot people with rock salt, for pickin' figs. (A shotgun shell loaded with rock salt won't kill ya. It jus' stings 'n' burns like hell). Then there was Leslie, a cop, 'n' a pretty good guy. Finally there was Jack. He was just about our age. This kid was neck 'n' neck with his father in the meanness department. My brother 'n' I both knew attitude adjustments would be needed. One day Jack 'n' I were arguin' about somethin'. Soon fists were flyin'. Ah was much quicker than Jack, but within a few seconds, Ah realized that this really wasn' one of my smarter decisions.

Ya see, Jack was a year older than me, much bigger, 'n' meaner than a snake. Needless to say the fight wasn' goin' very well for me. Thank God my brother Paul was there. He quickly jumped in savin' me from needin' my face reconstructed. Paul was both quicker and stronger than Jack. He was gettin' in some really good shots. Na Ah told you Jack was mean. He grabbed a box of salt 'n' threw salt in Paul's eyes. They ended up on the floor. Jack's brother finally broke up the fight. Ah did mention that Jack was mean didn' I?

However, since there were no other kids around we learned how to get along. Eventually Jack became one of our best friends. We were always competitive but our friendship remained for life. Before long another kid moved into the area. He was just about my age, a little taller 'n' a lot heavier. Johnny lived in a small house on the other side of the swamp about a half mile or so from our house. As Ah said, Johnny was a little taller than me, but still smaller than Jack 'n' Paul. This meant that it was up to me to establish the pecking order. We had to fight it out for our position. (Kinda reminds ya of a wolf pack, don't it?) Johnny was not afraid to fight, but his fightin' skills...not so hot. The fight didn' last long. A few well placed punches, 'n' it was over for now. But Johnny didn' forget. The pack's positions were in place and order was restored.

Ah still missed my ol' friends, from Maris street, Ah also missed the games, 'n' activity of the city. Ah guess Ah missed everything from my ol' neighborhood except the haunted house. Livin' on the edge of a swamp was often lonely. This had a big effect on me, cause to this day Ah still don't like bein' alone.

BURNED AT THE STAKE

The next few months were filled with a blend of lazy hot summer days mixed with some excitin' adventures engineered for the most part by us. For example, we made sling shots usin' old shoe tongues 'n' sliced up inner tubes. These were used for target practice, killin' snakes 'n' wardin' off kids tryin' to intrude on our swamp. Ah was involved in several territorial rock fights, not worth mentionin' at this time.

Robin Hood movies were very popular with kids our age. Whenever Ah could obtain the ten cent entrance fee and seven cent bus fare Ah would go to the daytime matinee. These movies—well ah guess all movies—really influenced us 'n' many of our ideas came right from the movies. Our desire to own bows 'n' arrows came straight out of Robin Hood movies. Ah fancied myself becomin' an expert with this ancient weapon. We tried to make our own weapons, but we didn' have the right kind of wood or tools to make very effective ones. So we did what kids throughout the ages have always done: we begged our parents to give us bows and arrows for Christmas. To our surprise we got them. Unfortunately, Johnny ended up with a nasty arrow wound to his arm.

We always tried to make our games as realistic as possible, copyin' movie scenario's. While Johnny was healin' from his arrow wound we thought it would be safer to switch to Cowboys 'n' Indians for a while. Well one day while playin' the game, we thought we'd make it a lil' more realistic. We decided to burn a Cowboy at the stake. Let's see, where could we find a Cowboy? Johnny had a Cowboy gun so he had to be a Cowboy. We grabbed Johnny, tied him to a wooden post on our house, got some sticks and put them around Johnny and the post. Then without even thinkin' we lit them. (Ah told ya, we sought realism!) Sure enough, the fire got out of control. We couldn' put it out! We started yellin' (Johnny was yellin' loudest). Jack's Mom heard us. She grabbed a hose and put out the fire. She probably saved Johnny 'n' the house. Yeah, we probably didn' think that one through.

THE SWING

As we grew, we ventured further 'n' further from our house. We found this gatherin' place called "the swing." Older kids from the area gathered there durin' the day 'n' into the night.

Some older guys built a platform high up in a very large oak tree then they went a short distance to the Industrial Canal to get a rope. This fav' mile waterway connects Lake Pontchartrain to the Mississippi River, allowin' cargo ships and barges access to river wharves. There were always a lot of barges tied up along the shore line. When ropes were needed, we headed for the canal. Getting' a good rope required some creativity. Someone had to shinny out onto a barge, untie the rope and throw it into the water. This caused one end of the barge to swing out into the canal current, makin' the other rope on the front end really tight and stiff. Finally, the guy on the barge shinnied back to shore, pulled the untied rope out of the water, and made a hasty getaway. All of this had to be done in about thirty minutes because the watchman came by every half hour. We managed to get two ropes for our own yard. They were put to good use. We tied them far enough apart for us to swing from one rope to the other, just like Tarzan in the movies.

In the swing area, a rope was tied to a large branch some distance from the platform. Then the platform was used for a launchin' pad to swing out from. As the person came back towards the platform, someone would jump from the platform to the rope. We kept doin' this until it was too far out for anyone to jump to it. Needless to say there were a few broken bones and a lot of shattered egos.

Another thing we did in the swing area was mud fights. The whole area was swampy so mud was readily available. We chose teams, gathered mud and went at it. Mud fights were usually good ol' fun until someone would put a rock in the mud. This caused a lot of great fights! One of the best barefisted fights Ah ever saw was at the swing. Both of the guys were high school age. One of them lived in a camp by Lake St. Catherine. His camp (house) was so far from school he had to ride a train to and from school. This guy's whole family were fishermen. They depended on the lake for their survival. There was no welfare or food stamps for them. In most cases, the government didn' even know these fishermen existed. The other guy's family had a dairy farm in Little Woods near Lake Pontchartrain. Both of them worked and looked like men. Anyways, they had some kinda problem (probably about a girl). One day they met up at the swing and exchanged a few words. They didn' do the usual monkey dance—arm waving chest poundin' stuff. One of them just said, "Let's settle this right now!" Two older guys stepped in. One said he would act as the timer, the other offered to referee the fight. Both fighters agreed to fight fav', three minute bare-knuckle rounds, with a one minute rest between rounds. They also agreed to shake hands 'n' leave in opposite directions, immediately after the fifth round. There were only a few rules: bare knuckles, nothin' in or on the hands, no kickin', bitin', or wrestlin' allowed. Wow, what a fight! Ya couldna' paid money to see a betta' fight. The fight was nip 'n' tuck until the middle of the fifth round. By then both fighters were pretty banged up. Finally Rene, the Lake Catherine guy, pooped out. He had to say "Ah quit." He just couldn' go on. After the fight, Rene said, "We gotta' do this again sometime." Then they left per their agreement. Ah was a fourth grade kid at this time, but Ah still remember the life's lessons Ah learned that day. Ah learned that honor, courage 'n' pain build character. If differences were still settled like this, there would be no need for gangs and bullyin' wouldn' even exist. Think about it, drive by shootin', stabbin', and gang beatins' are cowardly acts. In my opinion, anyone that does those deeds is lower than pond scum. There's no honor, courage or character involved in gang activity or bullyin'.

Mud fight wars gradually evolved into BB gun war games. All of us had those daisy BB guns that were popular at the time. BB gun battles required more rules than mud fights, so we made up some that Ah thought were pretty responsible and mature. No shootin' in the face was the main rule. No brainer right?

These games progressed and evolved further into organized events with teams, protective equipment, and referees. They became so popular that Dixie magazine presented them as the cover story one week. So, what's the real history behind paintball war games? Um just sayin'.

OUR HOUSE BURNED DOWN

One hot summer day, Jack, Paul, Johnny, 'n' I, got tired of of the usual indoor games we were playin'. We needed somethin' a little more exciting. We were often stuck indoors for a coupla' hours tryin' to avoid the unbearable heat or an afternoon downpour. One of us had discovered that you could put a wooden match in the barrel of a BB gun, shoot it at an angle against a wooden wall, 'n' it would light. Then you could try to hit someone with the lit match. Ah was the only one that got a pretty bad burn. A lit match landed on my neck 'n' stuck to it. Ah still have a mark on my neck from that burn. One afternoon we grew tired of the match game so we decided to go outside to play. Ma was at the store usin' the pay phone. Pop 'n' Paul were workin' on the ice route. No one was home except Jack, his older brother Ludy 'n' me. All of a sudden Ah saw smoke comin' from the inside of the house! Ah raced back to the house where Ah saw Ludy tryin' to put out the flames. It was too late. That ancient ol' house went up in flames, like a match box. All Ah could do was run. Everything we owned burned. All we had were the cloths on our backs. Ah didn' even have shoes on. Pop had to buy us clothes that same day. This caused us to sink deeper into poverty 'n' changed our lives again. But with a lot of help from friends 'n' family, we survived.

After the fire, we were forced to move in with relatives. First, we stayed at my Ant's house in Metairie, MET-uh-ree, Louisiana. We only stayed there about two weeks 'cause they had fav', ("five") kids, 'n' it got kinda crowded. Then we moved in with my Grandparents. They lived in the little town of Kenner, Louisiana. Na Kenner is only about twenty miles West of New Orlans, but it seemed like a far away foreign country to me. Everything was different from the Ninth Ward. They wore different clothes, talked funny, Ah mean, these kids spoke with such a twang, Ah could hardly understand um (nothin' like da clear speech style of da Ninth Ward). Some cities have districts or boroughs. New Orlans is divided into eleven Wards. Each Ward has a distinct dialect.

Kenner was like a typical small Southern town, kinda like someplace in Alabama. The locals didn' even speak the same language that Ah spoke. Na um not gonna sit here and tell ya that they didn' know how to speak, but Ah sure didn' understand um. For example whenever Ah greeted someone with the typical New Orlans wah ya at? they didn' know what da heck Ah was talkin' about. You see we always thought the standard how are you? With the standard answer i'm fine, even if your house just burned down, was shallow. When someone from New Orlans, especially from the Ninth Ward, asks wah ya at? They really wanna know what's happenin' in your life. Is your family well, ya job o k. if not, let's talk. Can Ah help? Wadda ya need? All of this from the simple greetin', wah ya at? Na if you didn' feel like sharin', you could always answer "Like the bear, makin' tracks but Ah ain't gettin' no where." Or ya could say, "It's ar'write". So, anyways, Ah really didn' like anything about Kenner.

LOOKING DEATH IN THE MOUTH!

Ah decided to enjoy my surroundings as much as Ah could. After all, Ah got to spend a lot of time with my grandparents. Grandpa Troncale was born in a poverty stricken area of Sicily. He left Sicily with his family when he was about thirteen years old. They landed in Mobile, Alabama and then migrated up to Birmingham Alabama to work in the thrivin' steel industry. Italian immigrants found jobs alongside the large black labor force. Grandpa's family managed to pay off their passage debts. Most of them sought opportunities in the flourishing tobacco industry. Some of them became wealthy, but by then, my grandpa was married and had four kids. He decided to take his family out of the hostile environment in Birmingham and move to New Orlans. Na let me tell you a little about Grandma Troncale. She was very smart and a strict disciplinarian. She earned and demanded respect. If ya didn' listen' to her, ya got a stout ear or hair pull. Na ya probably wonderin' what does all of this have to do with lookin' death in the mouth. Hang on, 'n' Ah'll tell ya, um layin' out my characters for ya.

Grandpa loved to fish in the countless bayous that were a stone's throw from his house. He always took us with him when we weren't in school. Na Grandpa could sit there fishin' 'n' smokein' his pipe, all day long. He wasn' at all the way Italians are portrayed in movies and television. Grandpa was the calmest person Ah ever knew. He taught me more about fishin', huntin', pickin' wild berries, and snakes, than anyone else. On one of these fishin' trips he allowed us to use his single shot bolt action 22 rifle. For safety reasons, he only allowed us to have birdshot rounds for ammunition. Ya see birdshot has tiny little b. b's that can kill smaller birds and snakes, but wouldn' be fatal if humans were accidentally shot.

While Grandpa was fishin' Paul and I decided to explore our new surroundings. Every swamp has its own beauty. This one had the most impressive lush growth of Cypress trees Ah'd ever seen. Moss covered trees towered above the dark murky swamp floor. The ageless Cypress tree knees looked like little gnomes sticking there heads up out of the black swamp water. A Cypress swamp has indescribable beauty. Ya gotta see it to believe it. Ah was captivated by the beauty and felt compelled to go deeper and deeper into the swamp. Soft mud and Cypress knees made walkin' in the waist deep water difficult, still Ah trudged on. Ah had to see what was behind that next tree. We were not greenhorns in this environment; we knew how easy it is to get lost in a swamp, so we cut notches on trees marking our path.

Walkin' in a swamp is kinda like bein' in a combat zone; danger could be lurkin' anywhere.

We always took turns, when only one rifle was available. It was my turn. Ah was walkin' gingerly tryin' to find snakes before they found me. They weren't hard to find. There was an abundant supply of the venomous little devils around.

Let me tell you a lil' about cottonmouth moccasins. There seems to be some disagreement about their temperament. Ah'm here to tell ya true stories that actually happened to me, not some laboratory test. Moccasins are nasty creatures. Their bite can lead to hemorrhaging in the circulatory system, causin' a whole host of problems, including death. They can be aggressive and they will attack. Ah believe they are bad news. There are only four kinds of moccasins that Ah'm afraid of: big ones, small ones, live ones, and dead ones!

Ah saw a moccasin sunnin' on a log some distance away. Impulsively, Ah fired at him. Some of the bird shot found its mark, but it wasn' enough. Ah only managed to piss off the ill tempered little bugger. He slid off the log and swam right at us. Na we really had a problem. Ya can't run in waist deep water. We only had a single shot rifle, birdshot ammunition, and the snake had to be real close to ensure a kill with one shot. Yeah, 'n' ya better not miss. Paul had the bullets, so he snatched the rifle from me and quickly inserted a round in the chamber. Then he said, "Get behind me (ya know, he didn' have to say that twice; Ah was already there). Ah peeped around

Paul and watched the snake swim towards us. When he got within strikin' distance, Ah saw the open white mouth 'n' painful lookin' fangs. Paul fired right into the open mouth and blew his head off. We had to take a moment to settle down and then continued explorin' and huntin' until the sun was directly overhead, tellin' us it was time to make our way back to Grandpa. Ah scrambled up the levee 'n' sat down next to my Grandpa tryin' to soak up some of his calm aura. When Ah looked down at my ankles Ah found about a half dozen leeches attached to them. Grandpa calmly helped me remove um. We caught a great big snappin' turtle on the way home and had turtle soup for supper that night.

This snake story puts me in mind of another one that happened some years later when Ah was a switchman on the Southern Railroad. One of our job sites was in Chalmette behind the sugar refinery. Our work area had very little dry land for us to work on. The only elevated places around were our railroad tracks and the giant scale we used for weighin' boxcars filled with raw sugar; everything else was swamp. Our job was to weigh the cars, make up a train, then take them to the main yard in New Orlans for further distribution. On one occasion Ah was workin' the evenin' shift from 2:30 til 10:30 at night. My partner was about a half a mile up the tracks 'n' Ah was walkin' slow, dilly-dallyin' alongside the tracks. Suddenly Jim's frantic screams for help snapped me out of my boredom. Ah could see him scufflin' with somethin' on the side of the tracks so Ah ran towards him as fast as Ah could. When Ah got there ah found him battlin' with the biggest moccasin Ah'd ever seen. That sucka musta been at least four feet long and weighed about fav or six pounds. Jim was hittin' this huge snake with the only weapon available: a cattail reed. The cattail kept breakin' on the snakes muscular back. Na da snake's really irate 'n' starts vehemently strikin' at us. Ah grabbed reeds in both hands 'n' started poundin' that bad boy as hard as Ah could. The trick was not to let him curl up 'n' leap full length at me. That nasty devil was determined to sink his venomous fangs into my leg, Ah was resolved not to let um. Ah kept hittin', dodgin', 'n' shufflin' my feet. Ya talk about perfectin' your footwork, this'l do it f' sure! One of us grabbed reeds while the other hit. When the reeds broke, the other one jumped in.

The battle was over as quickly as it began. It seemed like Ah'd been battlin' this monster snake for hours when in real time it was only about three minutes before my assailant finally lay still. Ah looked at his muscular body 'n' had a small measure of respect for his fightin' spirit. Na don't start feelin' sorry for the snake. In a life or death battle there can only be one winner. Besides um sure that this guy was a direct decedent of the snake

Eve spoke to in the Garden.

After lookin' at him for awhile Ah realized that alive or dead, this snake would scare the hell out of anyone. So Ah decided to play a li'l joke on the guys back at the main yard in New Orlans. Ah found an empty boxcar with an open door, picked up the snake with a stick and my gloved hand, then Ah placed the snake right in the doorway 'n' made him look like he was ready to strike. Ah thought this'l really scare um. Ah went on about my work 'n' soon forgot about the snake. Well along about eight o'clock that night Ah ran across the open door boxcar 'n' thought Ah'd check on my snake. Ah looked in and discovered that the snake was gone! Na there was a pissed off snake lurkin' around somewhere. Ah spent the rest of the night imaginin' that he was behind every bush with his mouth open waitin' for me. Ah can't remember ever tryin' to play a practical joke on anyone after that. Na Ah gotta get back to my story's timeline.

DID THE ROACHES FOLLOW US?

Pop managed to find us a little two bedroom shack near the swamps. My problem with this house was it had as many roaches as the one that burned down. Ah thought, didn' millions of roaches die in the fire? Wha'd the survivors do? Follow us?

This house was small; agin' we're talkin' really small. It had two small bedrooms, bath with a tub, no shower, and of course there was no phone or TV. However, it did have a small two burner gas stove, and a tiny icebox. Ah have an antique one just like it today.

We were back in East New Orlans, on the edge of a swamp again. There was a run down tourist court some distance away on our East side, on the West side the owner's house sat on about four acres of land. They had a boy my age, but that's the only thing we had in common. He was used to the good life and kinda spoiled like some rich kids are. Na um not judgin' or questionin' his parents parentin' style, but if ya choose to live in East New Orlans, ya gotta coonass up a little bit. This kid, (Jawn), thought that he could push me around 'cause his family owned our shack. Well ya know that wasn' gonna happen. We got into a fight one day, well kind of a fight, Ah hit him in the stomach one time, endin' the fight. He went home and told his father. My Pop also found out about the fight, and was kinda worried 'cause we really needed that house. After Ah told Pop what happened, he understood. Boys had unwritten rules that had to be followed. Jawn's father couldn' believe that his son lost a fight to me. Ya see, Jawn was taller and a lot heavier than me. So Jawns father put him in trainin', he tried to teach his annoyin' kid how to fight. Ah think his father worked with him for about six weeks, Then he arranged a rematch. This time his Father had us fight with boxin' gloves on. All of their efforts were for naught. The results were the same. A jab to the face, cross to the body and the fight was over. Ah kinda felt bad for Jawn and his Father, but this fight settled it. Ah didn' want to be mean, but Jawn really couldn' or wouldn' do anything we did. Ah mean he never wanted ta hunt snakes or nothin'. Don't cha know, Jawn really didn' learn anything, he grew up 'n' became an annoyin', very rich fat snob. Ya might know, he owned a used car lot.

MAKING THE BEST OF IT

Behind us there were about three acres of trash filled land. This is where we 'n' those before us had to throw our trash 'cause there was no trash pick-up in this section of town. Past the trash was a seldom used road, some rail-road tracks, and a huge swamp. This was it. We had to make the best of da situation. Let's see; we had three acres of trash, railroad tracks, trains, and a swamp. What ten and eleven year old boys wouldn' be happy with all dat?

Once again we had to provide our own entertainment, 'n' invent ways to have fun. One of our favorite pastimes was climbin' up a thin, tall willow tree. When we got high enough our weight would cause the tree to bend, givin' us an excitin' ride down to the soft swamp mud. Ma would hose us down with a water hose before lettin' us in the house. We also caught rides on slow movin' freight trains. We would scramble up the ladder. Once on top of the box car we ran across one car and jumped to the next. When this got borin'—or more likely when we got run off by some railroad man—we hunted snakes with our sling shots. Years later Ah was the railroad man runnin' kids off. Probably sayin', "Don't you kids realize how dangerous it is to play on railroad cars? What's wrong with young people these days?"

Closer to home, we could always shoot rats with our BB guns. There were a lot of um. They thrived in the mounds of trash behind our house. One day some black kids thought we were shootin' at them 'n' started throwin' rocks and stuff at us. This started a small war. We were holdin' them off pretty good with our BB guns when from out of nowhere, a rock slammed into my jaw. The sound inside of my head was sickenin'. Ah can't remember what ended the fight, but Ah do remember havin' to work my jaw back into its socket. We made our way through the trash piles 'n' went back to our house. Ma noticed the cut on my face and really got upset. Ah told her that Ah fell down. Yeah Ah know, but she woulda been upset if ah told her the truth. Ah couldn' chew right for months. This was only one of the many rock wars Ah was involved in. It stands out in my mind, cause my jaw still clicks from time to time.

About this time we managed to get a single shot 22 rifle. This new tool gave us the opportunity to hunt bigger game. Na Ah didn" mind huntin' rabbits, squirrels, or poule d'eau, but skinnin' and cleanin' um was a different story. Ah soon discovered that rabbits didn' look as pretty on the inside as they did on the outside. Poor pop, he loved animals almost as much as people. Many a time he couldn' finish his spaghetti dinner 'cause one of us had proudly shown him one of our skinned rabbits. We tried to make belts with our cache of snakeskins, but couldn' master the tannin' process.

Evenings were spent listenin' to the radio, shows like Fibber Mcgee 'n' Molly, Bob Hope, the Lone Ranger, and the Creaking Door were my favourites. The Creaking Door was the scariest of all. It kept me awake at night. It didn' matter much 'cause Ah was already awake. Those friggin roaches were still buggn' me. Ah figured out a way to get a li'l revenge on them, Ah shot the little ******* with my BB gun. Ya see we didn' have closets, so we had to put our winter clothes in cardboard boxes that were stacked in our bedroom. At night when roaches crawled out onto the boxes Ah shot them. Ah never gave up on tryin' to reduce their population, even if it was only one roach at a time.

Chapter 2

ADOLESCENSE

OFF TO WORK

We were starting to grow up. This meant that it was time to start helpin' out with the family's finances. On Saturday's in school months and three or four days a week in summer Ah helped Pop on his ice route. The work was hard, but Pop's company and the people knowledge Ah gained proved to be valuable to me for the rest of my life. Pop made sure that Ah didn' injure my young back by not allowing me to carry over fifty pounds of ice at a time. Ah couldn' work as hard as Paul so Ah got fifty cents a day; Paul got a whole dollar. My goal was to be allowed to deliver 100 lb. pieces so Ah could make the big bucks too. Paul saved his money and bought a bran' new bike at the end of summer. Ah had to settle for a nine dollar used one, 'cause my parents had to help me pay for it. No matter, now we could venture out further from home.

We heard about this swimmin' hole that was about ten miles away so naturally we decided to check it out. It was worth the dangerous exhaustin' bike ride. We had to ride our bikes on a major highway the whole way. Ah couldn' believe my eyes when Ah saw how big the pond was. There was even a rope tied to a tree branch so ya could swing out over the water and drop in. Except for havin' to crawl out every time a moccasin swam by it was a fun day. We returned to the pond about a week later 'n' were told by some local guys that one of their friends had been bitten by a moccasin while swimmin' on the other end of the pond. They informed us that the pond had become a nestin' place for moccasins and it was infested with them. They also warned us about a hostile gang of older black guys that were attackin' white kids. Ah was very disappointed. The pond was beginnin' to lose it's appeal. No sooner had the guy finished his warnings, here comes a gang of BIG black guys. As soon as they saw us they came right after us, yellin' racial slurs, 'n' threats. They outnumbered us at least two to one 'n' Ah knew they had knives. We were lucky to get out of there before we became a news story. Ah grabbed my bike and made a hasty retreat. You need to understand that racial prejudice went in both directions. Sadly, Ah saw and experienced it from both sides. Ah never went back to the pond.

Ah ended up makin' friends with some kids that lived about fav miles up the highway. We had wheels, we had our guns, and we had friends. Life was good again.

THE LONG BUS RIDE

There were no schools in our area, the closest one was C.J. Colton, an hour long school bus ride away. Colton school was in the Lower Ninth Ward on St. Claude Avenue. Every day Ah went from the edge of a swamp to the heart of town. C.J. Colton was familiar to me cause Ah started there in the third grade. Ah was now in the fifth grade, had a lot of friends and felt secure in the area. Getting' to school was another story. Ya can't keep a bunch of grammar school kids cooped up on a bus for over an hour 'n' not expect stuff to happen. Fights were pretty common, but friendships were lastin'. Ah tried to stay out of trouble 'n' succeed most of the time, only had a coupla little altercations. However, one fight really stands out in my mind. It was between my brother Paul and this kid from Texas. They had fought a year or so before, but someone broke up the fight before there was a clear winner. This kid went back to Texas for awhile. Well, when he came back they met up on the school bus. As soon as they saw each other they exchanged words, then fists. Na the bus driver had to be from the Ninth Ward 'cause he simply stopped the bus and let them get off the bus to fight it out. All of us watched from the bus windows. The fight wasn' goin' well for the Texan. So he pulled out a pocket knife and cut Paul on his shoulder. In an instant the bus driver and some older boys broke up the fight. Paul had a small cut on his shoulder. The bus driver pulled out his first aid kit and bandaged him up. The Texas kid was kicked off the bus, and banned from it. Ah never saw him again; he musta changed schools. That was the end of it, no cops, no school officials, no anger management. Problem solved, and it didn' cost the taxpayers anything. What a different world. Jus' think about what would happen if this fight happened today.

IT AIN'T HAPPY DAYS

About this time some people from someplace out of town moved in. They coulda' jus' been from outside the Ninth Ward or they might'a even been Yankees. Ah really didn' care. They were a nice family. Ah don't think they researched the area enough 'cause they opened up a malt shop right off the highway. These nice people probably thought it would be somethin' like a Happy Days place in a Beaver Cleaver neighborhood. Wrong. This was East New Orlans. The Fonz woulda been beat up every day. Right after the place opened, we turned it into a jumpin' teen hangout, New Orlans style. Most of the time, we hung out in the malt shop, but sometimes outdoor activities offered more excitement. For example, we played bike tag. Bike tag went like this: you chose up sides then started ridin'. The other team had to touch or pass someone up. When someone touched or passed a person that person was out. The team getting' all the other players out won. Simple right? But how about if you cut in front of a slow movin' truck or car, then your opponent couldn' pass or touch you. Maneuvers like this added an air of excitement to the game. As you can imagine this caused horror, havoc, and a whole lot of anger on the road. There were a few other traffic stoppers that Ah thought were funny at the time. One was squirtin' lighter fluid on my bike fenders, lightin' it, then ridin' down or across Chef Highway at night. Can you imagine seein' a flamin' bike goin' down the road on a dark night. If ya had a few drinks ya might think you're seein' things. As luck would have it some grown up's saw us and told Pop about our shenanigans. Ah'd never seen him so mad. He was furious. He took our bikes away and made us work on the ice route every day for a month, without pay! Ah would like to offer a belated apology to any drivers that may have suffered any physical or mental problems that Ah may have caused.

We continued to do a lot of huntin'. There was still boo coo open space around. Rabbits 'n' lots of birds were all over the place. We only had one single shot 22 rifle at this time. Get this, Ah could hit a rabbit on the run with one shot. Fortune smiled on us when my Uncle Jimmy sent Paul a double barrel 410 shotgun from California for his 12'th birthday. That summer Paul saved up his ice route money and bought a bran new 12 gauge shotgun, then he gave me the 410 so we both could hunt either together or apart. Nice gun. To this day, Ah think that was the best gun Ah ever owned. We spent endless hours huntin' in those days. Mind you, we always hunted alone, no adults. We followed all of the local safety rules 'n' were very careful. Ah can't figure out how someone can point a gun at somebody, pull the trigger, 'n' then say it was an accident. Gun rule number one: NEVER point a gun, loaded or empty, AT anyone. Always IDENTIFY your target and beyond. Anyways, it was not uncommon for us to hunt all day, come into the malt shop with our guns, show the owner that they were empty, place them in a corner, then go about the business of havin' fun with our friends. One day Paul decided that things were a little dull around the malt shop, so he decided to generate some excitement Ninth Ward style. He opened up two 410 shotgun shells, poured the shot out, then loaded them into the gun (if you're not familiar with shotgun shells this makes them like a blank), then he got a friend to help him. This guy pretended to disrespect Paul's girl. Paul and his friend pretended to get into a fight. Paul grabbed the gun. The guy ran out the door with Paul in hot pursuit, BAM BAM Paul fired both barrels. The guy yelled, rolled on the ground, 'n' pretended to be dead. People were screamin', the malt shop owners were in shock, others ran. Then the guy gets up laughin'. The neighbor whose lawn this took place on didn' think it was funny. He called the cops. The malt shop owners didn' think it was so funny either. Come on now; that was funny. Soon after this the malt shop owners put their shop up for sale, probably had enough of East New Orlans. Na Ah know that a lot of gun rules were broken, but Ah still think it was funny.

We thought the neighborhood needed a little break, so we settled down for a'while. A short time later, we moved again.

GENTILLY WOODS

Pop's hard work finally started payin' off for us. Havin' saved for years, he finally had enough money for the down payment on a house. There was a very large section of land bein' developed about ten miles west of us, still in the Ninth Ward but a lot closer to Canal Street and other shoppin' areas. Ah also didn' have to ride the school bus anymore. There was a school within walkin' distance of our new house. The whole development now called Gentilly Woods was so big it was like a city within a city. There was one section for whites and one for blacks. The current history website doesn't mention that the original development was indeed segregated. Remember segregation was in full swing at this time. So, um not gonna rewrite history. Um gonna tell it just like it was, warts 'n' all.

Pop bought a $15,000 three bedroom house with a large yard. The whole subdivision looked like a Beaver Cleaver neighborhood. We were one of the first families to move in. The first thing ah noticed was NO ROACHES! Yay! Na the nice clean surroundings were quiet and pleasant, but it was a big lifestyle change for me. Ah missed a lot of things about my old neighborhood by the swamp. The kids my age seemed kinda borin' and whimpy. Sure the house and neighborhood was squeaky clean, but it was lacking in excitement. No malt shop, no bike tag, 'n' Ah'm sure none of these kids would set their fancy bikes on fire 'n' ride um on a busy road at night. Ah felt out of place in my new neighborhood. Kinda like the Beverly Hillbillies in Hollywood.

They were still clearin' the land for the black section that would be behind us. So we got our shot guns and went huntin'. Rabbits were all over the place. We bagged two or three every time. It seemed to me that every time Ah walked back home with my shotgun slung over my shoulder and rabbits hanging from my belt, people stared and pointed at me. What… didn' all boys hunt? Ya might know some people complained about the shootin', but we didn' quit until the land was cleared and construction started.

Ah was now in about the sixth grade, feelin' out of place and missin' my old friends. Ah needed to do somethin' so Ah went out for the school track team. Track became my lifeline for excitement and self esteem. Ah soon became the fastest kid in Gentilly Terrace Grammar School. Yeah um braggin', but Ah was! Ah guess runnin' away from snakes and chasin' trains to hop a ride had some merit. One Saturday a month the city sponsored a track meet, invitin' kids from all schools to compete. This was a good way to get experience and see how ya stacked up against the best of the best. Also, you were on your own, no coaches, parents, or cheerleaders. Ah went simply because Ah loved to run. Ah had to ride three separate busses to get to the stadium, but it was worth it to me. Ah met the renowned track coach "Tad" Gormley at the stadium that was named after him. Mr. Gormly donated his own time to these Saturday track meets. One of the things that he taught me was how to get off to a fast start. Mr. Gormley often said "Athletes are not born with athletic ability; success comes from hard work. Real power must come from inside of you, if ya don't have the spirit to compete, even great ability can be wasted." There were no medals or ribbons. Ya got your name in a small section of the sports page if ya placed. That was it. Only those that loved track and competition showed up. Ah was proud to be one of 'um.

Ah met up with an ol' friend from East New Orlans at every meet. One Saturday he didn' show up, so Ah went around asking people if they'd seen Curtis. One of the guys asked " didn'ch' hear,? Curtis got killed last Tuesday." Ah was numb. My brain couldn' process the information. This was my first encounter with the death of a young healthy friend. How could this happen to such a good kid. He helped take care of his severely handicapped sister and he also helped with the family's finances. Why is he dead? Ah still couldn' grasp it. Ya see, Curtis was a few years older than me. He was fifteen and had just got his driver's license. He was sittin' in the family car waitin' for his mother to get off work when a drunk driver plowed into the back of her car, killin' Curtis. That was it! Curtis was dead 'n' the drunk was still alive. This incident heightened my awareness of the injustices in our legal system. Ah will never forget the devastation that drunk caused, Curtis's father never got over his son's death. He started drownin' his pain with booze. Years later after Ah got out of the Army Ah managed a bar for awhile. All too often, Curtis's father would be drinkin' heavily at the bar. It was heartwrenchin' watchin' this broken man still grievin' for his son. Ah would go over to him 'n' say, Mr. Lesch doncha' think ya had enough booze tonight? Why doncha' go on home?" He'd always say you knew my son Curtis didn'ch. He was a good boy. Ah'd always answer, "Yes sir he sure was, 'n' Ah still miss him too."

MILNE HOME

Ah also loved football 'n' wanted to play on a team. The only team around was Milne boys home. Milne home was an interestin' place. For some reason (probably economic), they made it into a juvenile detention center 'n' a place for older boys that couldn' get adopted. The center didn' have enough inmates in the younger, lighter weight divisions to field football teams so they let outsiders join the teams. Ma was skeptical about her little darlin' (me), bein' around all those juvenile delinquents, but my Grandma convinced her that it would be OK. She told Ma, "If he behaves himself he'll be as good as they are." Ah think she was kiddin' don't you? Ah told Ma that Ah knew some of the guys from school anyway.

Makin' friends with the inmates was easy. They were my teammates. We practiced and played some tough games together sharin' the glory of winnin' and agony of defeat. In this atmosphere ya had to earn respect. Football got me the respect Ah needed. Ah learned a lot about these guys. They could be loyal friends just like any other teammate. Some of these friendships turned out to be helpful later when Ah ventured out into the Vieux Carre' (voo ca ray), Ah was only twelve or thirteen years old when Ah found my way down to Pirate's Alley for excitement and shootin' pool. Pirate's Alley got its name because the famous pirate Jean Lafitte hung around there when he was in the area. My older friends from Milne convinced the pool hall owner to let me play even though ah was way under age. They watched out for me like Ah was family. Ah probably was the only family that most of um had. There was a sayin' back in my time (sounds like ancient history don't it; Ah guess it was), if you could shoot pool real good, ya musta had a misguided youth. Ah was still in my youth 'n' Ah could run the table pretty often, however, Ah thought Ah had pretty good guidance. On the other hand, sports teaches you superb life's lessons necessary for success. Discipline, teamwork, loyalty, and fortitude are inherent in sports and life. Pop was the best life's lessons mentor Ah ever met. Gettin' street wisdom usually requires some hard knocks. Ah had a few street lessons at Milne. Ya see, we always played barefooted even when there was frost on the ground. The Times-Picayune newspaper even wrote a big article about this. Well one day Ah left my only pair of shoes in the locker room. Doncha know when Ah went to get um after practice, they were gone. Ah had to ride the bus home without shoes. The next few weeks Ah had to go to school wearin' a pair of raggedy ol' shoes. To this day Ah never let my stuff out of my eyesight.

Practice at Milne was never borin'. There was always somethin' excitin' happenin'. For example, it was not uncommon for an attempted escape to happen while we were practicin'. Whistles would blow and then the entire staff (includin' our coach) would start lookin' for the inmate. Another interestin' thing was the way fights were settled. The combatants were brought to the home plate area of a baseball field, given boxin' gloves, and the fight was on. There was always a male staff member on hand for the referee. They had to continue fightin' until one of them said, "Ah give up!" Ah'd like to see schools implement this policy today. Ah bet there'd be a whole lot less bullyin' and violence.

Now you can understand why we won a lot of games jus' because of our name. When other teams and their parents realized where we came from they became fearful of us. A coupla elbows to the face (we didn' have face masks), a few hard tackles, 'n' the game was ours. In my last year at Milne we won every regular season game. This gave us the opportunity to play for the championship of the entire Southeast region, includin' parts of Mississippi. We were matched up with a military academy from Biloxi, Mississippi. This team was well coached and disciplined. Our name didn' scare um at all. Have you ever heard anyone say that they got the piss knocked out of them? Well um here to tell you it can happen. Ah got hit so daw gone hard Ah had to run off the field right to the bathroom. Ah came back into the game literally pissed off! Ah tried my best to get even. Ah smashed into everyone as hard as my eighty-five pounds of ferocity could muster. We ended up losin' a tough hard fought game. Coach was very proud of us anyway. By the way, this game attracted a very large crowd includin' my whole family. Coach wanted to reward us by getting' us lettered jackets, but Milne couldn' afford them.

Someone in the community suggested that we have a paper drive. Money from the paper drive plus some donations got us the jackets. These jackets were bright green with Milne written right across the front. Ah was proud to wear my jacket, even though some parents moved their kids away from me on the bus.

I'M GONNA BE A CHAMP SOMEDAY

Ah was now going into the seventh grade, 'n' somehow Ah heard about this new type of experimental school. It was the first Jr. High in New Orlans. At this time, junior high grades were seventh, eighth and ninth. Perfect! Ah felt like Ah needed a change. Yeah, Samuel J. Peters was the school for me. The problem was this school was clear across town. It took over an hour on three city buses to get there. Once again Ah was in a new environment. S.J. Peters was in the middle of the city. The kids there were city kids, and Ah was in a different ward. If you visit New Orlans, you'll notice that as you travel from ward to ward everything changes. People from different wards each have a distinct accent, dress code, and attitude. A lot of the mid-city kids were disrespectful to teachers, adults, and people in general. This kind of behavior seemed strange to me, and Ah didn' like it. They thought they were cute and tough. They were neither; just punks. Pop taught us to have respect for everyone. Ah naturally migrated towards the athletic kids and soon made some friends. Track season was a long way off so Ah decided to try another sport: boxin'! Ah remembered that some of my old friends from Colton school had taken up boxin'. Most notable were Ralph Dupas and Willie Pastrano. Ralph Dupas became the number one contender in the lightweight division. He lost a hard fought title bout for the lightweight world crown. Ralph then moved to the junior middleweight division and on June 29'th 1963 he won the wbc/wba world titles. About this time Ralph's racial identity was bein' questioned. It's hard for me to understand how mean some people can be. You see at this time black athletes were not allowed to compete against white athletes in Louisiana. The Louisiana boxin' commision was contemplatin' barrin' Ralph from fighting white opponents. All of Ralph's fans and friends—myself included—wrote protest letters to the boxin' commision. To my knowledge, the matter was never settled. However, at some point the law was changed.

Another grade school friend, Willie Pastrano, was a light heavyweight and wound up becomin' the light heavyweight champion of the world! These guys were friends from grade school through high school, and beyond.

Get this. Ralph turned pro' at the ripe old age of fourteen. Ah wanted to be part of the gym that produced fighters like Ralph and Willie. Ah had visions of bein' a champion someday. Na this gym was in the heart of the French Quarter. It was owned by Saint Mary's church, it was called Saint Mary's Italian. Perfect place for a kid with Di Giovanni for a last name. Pop drove me down there the first time, 'n' Ah joined the gym. Ah was now a member of the distinguished Saint Mary's Boxin' Club. Ah immediately felt at home there, 'cause Ah already knew Ralph, Willie, and some guys from Milne. These guys helped me get started, in the sweet science of boxin'. It was here that Ah met the legendary boxin' trainer Mr Whitey Esneault. In spite of his fame he only wanted to be known as Mr. Whitey. He trained several world champions but his real legacy was of all of us other fighters he trained and taught who never became champions. We found self respect and purpose in the lessons we learned from Mr. Whitey. He looked and sounded just like Mickey, Rocky's trainer in the movie. He had a gruff voice, but a heart of gold.

After months of trainin' Mr. Whitey said to me. "Hey kid there's a standby spot for a possible fight on a new TV show called the Pepsi Cola Amature Hour. Ya want it?" Ah jumped at the opportunity. "Yes sir!"
It seemed like Ah had trained and waited a lifetime, before Ah was finally on a bus headed for the TV studio. Ah rode on the bus with my sparrin' partner, the guy Ah was gonna fight if there was a disqualification of one of the bouts. As we rode past the winos, prostitutes, and pimps, Ah thought Ah might have to fight this guy in just a little while. How do you reconcile fightin' a friend? Fighters are trained to win fights regardless of who their opponent is, includin' sparrin' partners. These are just some of the thoughts that were buzzin' around in my head. We finally arrived at the TV station, found our dressing room, then waited. Sure enough, one of the fighters for the main event was disqualified because he had fought less than a week before. This was against the amateur rules. Mr. Whitey came in 'n' said, "Get ready ya'll are gonna fight the main event." Na ah know my heart skipped a few beats. Can you picture it? This was a young fourteen-year-old boxer's dream. Ah mean the main event on a televised fight! Mr. Whitey lectured us about goin' all out. After all, we were representin' Saint Mary's boxin' on live TV.

Years later when Ah saw the first Rocky movie my mind raced back to

Mr. Whitey. Same voice, same lecture. Ah got a lump in my throat 'n' tears in my eyes. Reality set in when someone yelled "OK kid. You're on." It was time to take that long walk down to the ring. Boxin' is different from most other sports. Once ya enter the ring, it's just you and him. No teammates. No backup. You're it. Ah felt like Ah'd walked a mile, when out of the blue a lady from the audience jumped up and yelled to me, "Don't do it kid! You're too young! You'll get your face messed up!" Ah kept walkin'. Ah was thinkin' to myself, Miss. Ah grew up in roach infested shacks on the edge of a swamp, swingin' on ropes hung from trees, playin' bike tag on a major highway, dodgin' snakes, 'n' Ah survived BB gun wars without any major injuries. If Ah survived all that, this fight surely wouldn' cause any extensive damage. Ah mean, this guy wouldn' have any weapons, just boxin' gloves.

Once in the ring starin' at the TV camer's for the first time in my young life, things started movin' in slow motion. Then Ah heard, "In this corner,"... After that Ah only heard low muffled sounds. Ah looked around the ring and noticed that Ralph Dupas was gonna be the referee. Na the pressure was on. Ah jus' couldn' lose in front of my ol school mate. The ding of the bell snapped me back to the moment. At last the fight was on. As Ah said we were sparrin' partners, so we spent the first round mostly movin' around getting' used to the cameras, crowd noises, and feelin' each other out. At the end of the first round Ah heard Willie yellin', "Mix it up little D. You're on TV. "The cameraman also signaled for more action. That was all Ah needed. The next round, Ah let my fists fly, and Ah tagged him with a good right hand shot to the stomach. He was hurt. He bent over 'n' couldn' catch his breath. Ah had him, but you know what? Ah backed off. After all he was my sparrin' partner and my friend. Everyone in my corner was screamin' "Finish it. Ya got him." The crowd was screamin'. Willie and the guys from Milne were also screamin'. He recovered 'n' caught me with a good right hand shot to the jaw. Say what? So much for friendship. My fighting instincts kicked in. Podna or not, this was gonna be a fight. Ah fought back with everything ah had in my arsenal and Ah caught him with another good shot to the gut. He bent over gaspin' for breath again. 'n' once again Ah backed off. Ah did it this time 'cause Ah thought Ralph was gonna give him a standin' eight count, but he didn'. My corner really went crazy this time. They didn' understand Ah wanted to beat him fair and square, toe to toe, no cheap shots. Finally the bell rang. Na Ah knew the fight was close, but Ah had to fight my own fight. Ah would not sacrifice character for victory. My corner told me, this is the last round. The fight is about even.

You have to go all out in this last round or ya gonna lose. You're the better fighter. Show us what ya got. Dig deep. That's exactly what Ah did. The last round was a real barn burner. We both let our fists fly. Not much movin' around. We stood toe to toe 'n' punched it out. The fight ended up bein' a pretty good main event. By the way, Ah won a split decision. The trophy Ah received for winnin' that fight is one of my most valued sports awards, but like most trophies it now sits on a shelf in my closet. Trophies are mainly for the recipient. This one brings me back to that moment in time when Ah felt like Ah coulda' been a champion. Ah received another reward that touched me deeply. You see, Mr. Whitey got three dollars for each kid that fought. He knew how poor we were, so he gave us the money. In my mind, this made me a professional fighter.

When Ah got home Ah yelled, "Pop, Ah got three whole dollars for just nine minutes work." Ah know Pop was very proud of me, cause he told everyone about the fight (family, friends, ice route customers, people on the street, anyone that would listen). His son was on TV. (Winning this fight also had another benefit, or like we say in New Orlans: lagniappe, (lan yap). No one, Ah mean no one, at Samuel J. Peters ever challenged me.)

Well, the eigth grade finally ended. Now Ah had a whole summer to decide whether to continue boxin' or transfer to high school and go out for football. My decision was partially made for me. Ya see, New Orlans people have a lot of rituals and superstitions. Growin' up in this atmosphere musta made some of this stuff rub off on me. Ah had developed this ritual of goin' into Saint Mary's church 'n' prayin' under the statue of Saint Michael. Ya know, the one where Saint Michael has the devil down on the ground with a spear pointed at him. Ah reasoned Saint Michael was a skilled warrior saint. Ah was named after him. So he's the guy that could help me prevail in fights (come on now, gimme' a break, Ah was just a kid). Well, one day Ah went in to pray 'n' noticed that the spear point was missin' from Saint Michael's statue. Ah took this as a sign. So Ah decided to give football a try. After all, Paul was already on the team at Nicholls high school. Maybe Ah could of made it as a boxer, or maybe Ah did get a sign to quit. Ya never know. Ah guess Ah still have a little New Orlans in me—ya think? Anyways like an old song says, ya gotta be a football hero to get the beautiful girls.

Ah also liked the blue and grey school colors. Everything about this school was different. For example, the band wore Confederate uniforms, 'n' the majorette carried a sword instead of a baton. However, the main reason Ah wanted to go out for football was Ah love the game.

High school was very important to us because few kids from our area would ever be able to afford a college education. The only hope for gettin' a college education was to earn a scholarship. Not very likely for me. Ah mean, Ah only weighed about 130 lbs. soakin' wet. (Ever see those Southeast Conference football players?)

Ah was facin' a long hot summer before Ah could even think about football. Another crucial problem was money. Ah needed it. Ya see, the only way we could play football was to have enough money for our many teen expenses. Pop's ice route slacked off in the winter so money was tight. We needed to get good payin' summer jobs, or football was out of the question. Pop found out that the ice house where he bought his ice from had a summer route open. No one wanted this route because it serviced what we call camps. These houses are built high above Lake Pontchartrain on stilts. On one side of Little Woods Road there were dairies. Across the road, there was a canal, then two sets of railroad tracks. Finally a wooden ramp led to the camps. These ramps could be anywhere from 100 to 300 yards, or more. Now ya understand why this route was open. The work promised to be backbreakin'. But we knew we could make money here because most of the camps were summer rentals. There would be families and friends getting' together for fun, games, and partyin'... New Orlans style. This meant they would have lots of, Ah mean really boo coo beer. So, even if they had a refrigerator, they would need a lot of ice. Laissez les bon temps rouler, let the good times roll. We jumped at the opportunity and took the route. Mr. Jim, the ice house owner, made this deal with Paul and me. We would pay ten cents more than anyone else for every 100 lbs. of ice we sold. The ice house would supply a truck and gas. We knew there was the potential of sellin' a lot of ice so a deal like this was good for everyone involved. Mind you, there was no written contract, just our word and a firm handshake. The work was a whole lot harder than Ah thought, and we were so busy that we could hardly keep up with the demand. So we decided to bring Jack on board as a full partner.

Get this; we were teenagers with our own business! Most boys our age were goin' to the beach, had menial jobs like paper routes or just hung out. We, on the other hand, had to grow up fast. Ah worked seven days a week from 6:30 in the morning til' 2:30 in the afternoon or whenever we finished the route. Each camp bought from 100 to 400 lbs. of ice, and we averaged sellin' about two to three tons of ice a day. Mind you, we had to park our truck on the road then lug 100 lbs. of ice across a road, up the ramp over a canal, cross over two sets of railroad tracks, then trudge down the other ramp to the camp. Ah saw my brother Paul do this with 100 lbs. on his shoulder 'n' another 100 lbs. in his other hand usin' ice hooks. Ah learned stuff that just can't be taught in school. Work ethics and people skills require on the job trainin'. Ah learned valuable things on that ice route in Little Woods. Masterin' people skills is a valuable tool that can be used in most jobs. Many years later, Ah used those skills when Ah hired building maintenance workers. My benchmark was a person's temperament. Ah often explained why Ah favored one person over another like this: mechanical skills are not as important to me as personality cause ah can train a monkey to turn wrenches, but Ah can't change an individual's character. We were doing men's work 'n' most people treated us like men. It wasn' uncommon for customers to give us beer for a tip. Boy, what a treat that was on those hot humid summer days. None of us became alcoholics or anything. Drinkin' a few beers just wasn' a big deal, 'n' we didn' think anything of it.

Remember, this was the 50's, 'n' every place in New Orlans was segregated, even the beaches. There was one beach for whites, 'n' there was another one for blacks. The black beach was called Lincoln Beach. Ah didn' think much about it back then. To me this beach was jus' another customer. Nowadays, people visit this historic landmark that is symbolic of the times. Lincoln Beach was one of our best customers. They would often buy a whole truckload of ice, plus fav' or so kegs of beer. This stop was easy money for us 'cause all we had to do was, back our truck up to their icehouse, lay the 300 pound blocks of ice down, then drag them into the icehouse. Sounds pretty simple, but trust me, it wasn'. We had to dig the ice hooks into these huge blocks of ice and lay them down softly so they wouldn' break into useless pieces. The beer kegs were easy. We just rolled them right into the box. Ah was comfortable at this all black beach because when Ah worked with Pop, we were often the only white people around.

Life on the Little Woods ice route was seldom borin', 'n' to top it off the money was good. We were makin' a lot of money. Ah was pullin' in anywhere from $50 to $200 dollars a day. We ate like kings: spaghetti and meatballs for breakfast, maybe a po boy with some gumbo for lunch, topped off with fried chicken that night.

Ah became very proficient with my working tools. There were only two: an ice pick, and ice hooks. Ah could lay down a standing 300 lb. block of ice with the hooks 'n' cut it into three 100 lb. pieces with my ice pick in about 30 seconds.

Ah could usually find some fun, or, adventure to make my day. Ya see, there were always a lot of girls that vacationed at the camps. They came from all over, in town, across town, 'n' out of town. However, it was kinda hard to get to know them because for some reason their fathers didn' want them to hang out with ice men. Go figure. Well one rainy day we managed to talk some girls into hangin' out with us. We were havin' a nice lunch, talkin' 'n' ya know, actin' like teenage boys around girls. As luck would have it, some of the girls mothers came by and saw us. They started yellin' at their daughters and us. One of the mothers was so irate that she started wackin' Paul with her umbrella. Our fun lunch was over, but the laughs were not. We laughed and teased Paul about this for the rest of the day.

There was also fun to be had in Little Woods at night. Ruby's was the place to be for young and old alike. Ruby's was also one of our best customers. It was without a doubt the most unusual night spot in the city. Ruby's was located about a quarter mile past the end of Little Woods Road. This made it kinda hard to get there. You had to walk down the railroad tracks, cross over them then make your way down the wooden ramp. In daytime, Ruby's was a combination restaurant, grocery store, and ice distributor. People from the surroundin' camps would come with their skiffs and pirogues for groceries and ice. This is where we came in. We supplied Ruby's with the ice. Gettin' ice to Ruby's was quite an undertakin'. It's a good thing we were young. We would load a very big cart with anywhere from 900 to 1200 lbs of ice. This ice cart was so big it had car tires for wheels, high wooden sides, and a long metal pull handle. The heavy loads required teamwork. It took all three of us to get this thing down the tracks. Paul was the only one that could pull without bein' lifted up off the ground. So Paul pulled while Jack and I pushed. This was our most backbreakin' stop, but the money was good. Well, that was Ruby's daytime. At night Ruby's transformed into a combination restaurant, bar, and country/cajun coonass dance hall. Ah can still hear Hank Williams singin', "Goodbye Joe. Me gotta go, me oh, my oh/ me gotta go pole da pirogue down da bayou/ my Yvonne…." Then Fats Domino, "This time um walkin' to New Orlans um walkin' to New Orlans, um gonna need two pair of shoes…." Can ya imagine how exciting this was for a fourteen year old?

One night ah was at Ruby's havin' a good ol time enjoyin' the music 'n' suckin' in as much fun as Ah could when suddenly this guy comes bustin' in shoutin', "There's a bunch of guys from the Lower Ninth Ward linin' up on the railroad tracks sayin' they're gonna come in here and kick some ass." That didn' sound like fun.

Some of our big guys went out to see what was goin' on. The rest of us followed. We were gonna back um up if they needed us. They found out that two Lower Ninth Ward guys were at Ruby's one night, one of them got too friendly with a local's girl. Need Ah say more? They both got an educational beat down. Now they wanted revenge. Our guys were kind enough to oblige them. After a few skirmishes our guys backed up onto the ramp, and formed a human wall across it. The attackers couldn' break through our line, and after a few of um ended up in the lake. They backed off. These guys warn't about to quit. They quickly regrouped, then started rippin' off the neighborin' camps wooden hand rails to use for weapons. We were trapped. There was no way for us to get from Ruby's to our cars, without goin' through this angry mob. One of our older guys, Joe, managed to blend in with their crowd and weave his way to his car. He got his bran' new handgun out of the glove compartment then maneuvered his way back through their bloc. When he got back to our side, he turned around and started pointin' the gun at one guy at a time, darin' them to take Lfeelin' froggy? Jump." Then one of our guys, Buddy, grabs ahold of the gun. Now, Buddy and Joe are fightin' for the gun. You need to understand a li'l about Buddy. He's not like anyone ya know. Ya see, Buddy's lookin' at sane in the rear view mirror 'n' it's way back there. He wanted to just start shootin' these guys. All the while um thinkin', so this is what nightlife is all about. Ah hafta admit, it was kinda' excitin' for a fourteen year old. Thank God, Jimmy, a guy with a cooler head, managed to talk Joe into givin' him the gun. Jimmy turns, faces the crowd and tells them that they have three choic-es, "Come forward, leave, or he was gonna give the gun to Buddy." Time seemed to stand still. An adult broke the silence yellin' that the cops were on their way. This was a good excuse for the Lower Ninth Ward guys to leave and still save face. After they left, Joe decided to test fire his new gun. It wouldn' fire! He didn' have time to test his new gun, so he didn' know that there wasn' a round in the chamber, makin' it impossible to fire. You had to pull the cylinder back and let it slide forward before the gun could fire. He finally got the gun to work. Some of our older guys started takin' turns shootin' at some stumps in the lake. Ah thought, that's enough ex-citement for the night, so Ah got my date 'n' left. Na Ah don't remember all the details, but on the way home Ah probably speculated, "if those big guys woulda' jus' let me get out there, Ah woulda gave um what for." All the while, Ma thought her little angel was jus' hangin' out with friends doin' normal Beaver Cleaver type of teenage things. Ya know what, this was nor-mal in East New Orlans.

NICHOLLS HIGH SCHOOL - REBELS!

Summer finally ended, 'n' my freshman year at Nicholls high school began. Ah had mixed feelins' about school. On one hand, school would be a whole lot easier than luggin' tons of ice to the camps. On the other hand, ah knew Ah would miss the money 'n' excitement of the ice route. Then Ah thought, what the heck, it might be fun bein' a kid for awhile.

Ah had saved enough money to buy all of my own clothes, 'n' still have enough spendin' money to last til the next summer. Now Ah could place all of my attention on football, havin' fun, and school. My priorities were in that order. We had the usual classroom, subjects; you know things like math, English, and history. Na Ah don't know about some of my history. Ya know, Ah was nineteen years old and in the Army, before Ah found out that the South lost the war! And for years Ah also thought that damn and Yankee was one word. No matter, Ah didn' have a dog in that fight anyhow. You see my Grandparents didn' get here until the late 1890's. For those of you that are products of the current school system, this was after the civil war. Ah settled into my high school routines 'n' began to anticipate football tryouts. Ah really wasn' too worried about makin' the team, but maybe Ah shoulda' been. Ah guess Ah didn' realize how small Ah was compared to most football players. Ah only weighed 130 pounds soakin' wet. Ah'd like to say it was all muscle, but that would be braggin'. Ah thought that years of playin' in the swamps, runnin' track, my brief boxin' career, and a gruelin' summer deliverin' ice gave me the stamina, skills, and determination needed to make the team.

Right off the bat Ah had technical problems. First of all, they couldn' find a practice uniform that would fit me. Seems Ah was too small for all of um. Did this mean Ah was the smallest person that ever tried out for football here? Naa, Ah knew ah was big. They finally found one that kinda fit. Rather almost fit. OK, it really didn' fit at all. My uniform pants fell down to my knees. Ah didn' have a belt, so Ah used a piece of rope to hold my pants up. Then Ah found out that the legs were also too big. Ah also had to tie my thigh pads with rope to keep them from floppin' around when Ah ran. Can you imagine how odd that must have looked? When Ah got to the practice field some of the older guys started laughin'. They thought it was funny. Ah didn' think it was so funny. Others said "You're too small. You'll never make this team." You know what? This only heightened my competitive spirit. It made me try harder, a lot harder.

At the end of that very first practice, we ran wind sprints. Ah left all of um in the dust. They wern't laughin' now. They realized that Ah would soon challenge them for their positions. Ah knew that Ah wouldn' forget and would get even with every one of them. Sure enough, that's exactly what happened. In my Junior year Ah was playin' in games while they were sittin' on the bench.

After football season ended Ah went out for track. Na this was more up my alley. Size didn' matter; speed was the only thing that counted. Makin' the track team was a piece of cake for me. Ah consistently placed 1'st, 2'nd, or 3'rd in the 100 and 220 yd. dashes. The broad jump was a little harder, but Ah always managed to place. Even harder, was pole vaulting. Ah only have two medals for that event. Nicholls consistently won most public school track meets. My relay team won every public school race for four consecutive years. We set school records 'n' all. Ah loved runnin' track. There's a euphoric feelin' when ya hit your stride. You feel like you're floatin' along feelin' good. There's nothing like it. (Runners ya know what Ah'm talkin' about. It's the best natural high ya can get. Use sports, not drugs. Your body will thank ya).

FIFTEEN AND DRIVING

Na, jus' when Ah was gettin' used to the fun and games associated with school life, it was almost summer again.

Hot, humid weather signaled that it was time to get back to work, back to the ice route, back to Little Woods. Ah was fifteen years old now, 'n' at this age in New Orlans you could get a driver's license. Pop couldn' take me downtown to take the test because as Ah said before, he worked seven days a week. So, Jack's dad offered to take me. As mean as he was to others he liked Pop, Paul, 'n' me. We were probably the only people in the whole world that he liked (this includes his wife). Ah think he respected my fightin' spirit. Anyways, the driver's tests were pretty much the same as they are now except there were no driver's education classes. Parents had to teach their kids how to drive. Pop was the best teacher Ah coulda had. When Ah was workin' with him he would let me pull the ice truck up about a half a block in first gear. After Ah mastered that he'd let me shift to second gear, then third. The final lesson was learnin' to back up. Ah practiced this maneuver by backin' up to the ice house platform. Drivin' and stoppin' an ice truck loaded with ice is pretty tricky. If you take off too fast, ice will slide out 'n' smash to the ground. If ya stop too hard loose ice would shatter when it hit ice in the front of the truck. So Ah learned to make smooth starts and stops right off the bat. Thanks to Pop, Ah passed the tests on my very first try, 'n' got my license. Now Ah could drive Pops car and Ah could even drive the ice truck. Can you imagine? Ah was a fifteen year old high school kid drivin' a truck loaded with two and a half tons of ice and a dozen kegs of beer. What a different world. This wouldn' even happen in New Orlans today. What happened? Why can't kids drive or hunt alone anymore?

We slipped right back into our ice route routines and soon even the excitin' things in Little Woods became routine. The glamor of bein' treated like an adult and makin' a lot of money quickly wore off. Ah worked hard every day, but when night rolled around, it was play time. Ah shot a lot of pool, went swimmin' in the lake at night, hung out with friends, 'n' on some occasions Ah was able to get into nightclubs and enjoy the music of Sam Butera, Al Hirt 'n' several other notable local musicians.

THE SHELL ROAD GAME

All of those things were fun, but Ah still wanted a little more excitement. So when Ah heard about a game that tested your courage 'n' offered excitement as well ah thought Ah'd give it a try. Na this game is not recommended for the faint hearted. On second thought, Ah really wouldn' recommend it to anyone. The game required an even number of cars. Usually it was two cars, sometimes there were four. One car would remain in Ruby's pawkin' lot while the other car drove a few miles up Paris Road in the opposite direction then made a U-turn. Both cars would wait about fifteen minutes, rev up their engines then peel out. Now both cars are headin' towards each other at breakneck speed. This is where it really got excitin'! Both cars turned off their lights! My heart was poundin' so hard Ah could hear it above the roar of the engine. All Ah could see was the bleached white clam shell surface of Paris Road. No one wanted to give in cause whoever stopped or turned their lights on lost face and the game as well. This was a way of testin' your own courage by deifyin' danger 'n' cheatin' death. There was one other option where both parties could save face. They could swerve around the oncomin' car at the same time. This was not an easy maneuver because clam shells don't provide much or any traction. The night Ah was playin' this game (we called it the shell road game), we ended up in a ditch on the side of Paris Road. A flash of brilliance flashed into my mind that night. Ah decided then and there that the shell road game was not wholesome, healthy, 'n' really didn' have any long term benefits. Ah mean this rite to adulthood could be counter productive. See, Ah was gettin' smarter every day. Ah learned that ya can't let school interfere with your education. Ya gotta learn some things on your own.

Near the end of summer, Paul was ridin' a horse and ended up with a broken leg. This meant that Jack and I had to finish the summer ice route alone. We tried to hire some friends, but they couldn' handle the work. It takes a lot of skill to carry 100 pounds of ice. There are several things ya have to contend with besides the weight. First of all it's cold; second, it's slippery; 'n' third it's hard to balance. We used a large paper sack to shield us from the cold. Experience allowed us to master balancin' our load. Without experience, it's almost impossible to carry ice. Our new helpers would often drop their ice onto the wooden ramp. Then they couldn' pick it up, because it was too slippery. Na these guys were big football players with huge egos. They really didn' want to call out for help, but no matter how hard they tried, they just couldn' pick up the ice. Ah'd walk out there maybe with a li'l swagger in my step, grab the ice 'n' throw it up on my shoulder. Jack didn' let their awkward situation slip by. He teased these poor guys relentlessly. By the end of the day their ego's weren't so big anymore. His favorite dig was, "You big slobs can't pick up dat ice and this little 135 pound kid can. You augh'ta be ashamed of yourself." Yeah, none of them lasted more than a week. Our ol' friend Johnny was the only one that could be of some help.

One day we finished the route early and were headed home when suddenly out of the clear blue sky, Johnny looks over at me, and says "Ah think ah can whip you now. Ah go "wha'd you say?" So he says it again. Jack started laughin', pulls the truck over to the first grassy area he could find, and says "Is this spot good enough for ya'll?" We both agreed. As soon as we got out of the truck the fight was on. This fight wasn' as easy as the one we had a few years back. Johnny was now a good head taller than me, about fifteen pounds heavier, 'n' he was a determined fighter. He just wouldn' give up. After about five minutes of hard fightin' Ah was finally able to land some really good shots. Ah was kinda glad when he finally said "OK Ah quit." We got back in the truck and went home. That same night we went out 'n' shot pool together. Johnny 'n' I remained friends from that day on.

MOVE YOUR CAR!

One hot humid day (if you ever been in the southeast ya know what Ah'm talkin' about) Jack 'n' I were strugglin' to finish the route. (Jack was sick 'n' Ah was dead tired.) Ah was thankful when we finally got to our last stop: Ruby's. Now remember, Ruby's was way past the end of the road. Both of us were pretty miserable by now, and just wanted to get home. Without Paul there to help us we had to lighten the load and make two trips to Ruby's. Doncha know, there was a car illegally parked in the loadin' zone. Jack was already in a foul mood; this pushed him over the edge. All Ah wanted was to get done and go home. Jack decided to take matters into his own hands. He got in the car 'n' released the handbrake. Then we pushed it out of our way. After we finished our last delivery and headed back towards the truck these two fishermen approached us and asked, "Who moved our car?" Na one guy was big, Ah mean really big. The other one; not so big. Jack answered with a kinda perturbed tone, "We did. Why?" Without hesitation the big guy hit Jack so fast and hard that he was stunned. The other one came towards me so Ah got into my boxin' stance, fists up, elbows tucked. Ah was surprised when he stopped in his tracks. Ah guess it was my 130 pounds of rajin' fury that scared um. Right? Ah think the big guy realized right away that he had just hit a sixteen year old kid and his car was illegally parked.

They jumped in their car and sped away. It took a few minutes to try to figure out what had just happened, then we headed right home. When we got to Jack's house his dad noticed his busted lip and asked Jack what happened. Jack told him that some man had hit him. Mr. Cochrane flew into a rage. He screamed, "Let's go find them!" Jack's brother, a New Orlans police officer happened to be there. He jumped up put on his uniform, and got his gun. We headed back to Little Woods. Before we left Mrs. Cochrane pleaded with us not to let Mr. Cochrane get his hands on the gun. We went back to Ruby's pawkin' area, split up 'n' started lookin' for the culprits. We couldn' find the big guy but Ah did see the smaller one walkin' down the tracks. When he saw us his eyes got as big as saucers. Ah said, "That's one of um." We made a circle around him then forced him to come with us. He didn' try to resist. Ah kinda felt sorry for him; he looked like a condemned prisoner. We put him in our car and whisked him off to a police station. The nearest police station was way down in the Lower Ninth Ward, about two blocks from my high school. Some guys from my team happened to be hangin' out in front of the pool hall, saw me get out of the car with a cop 'n' thought Ah'd been arrested. A couple of um came over 'n' offered to make phone calls for me. Ah told um Ah was o.k. 'n' said, "See ya'll later." When our prisoner got into the police station, he clammed up and wouldn' talk at all. After about an hour of questionin' a police captain called us on the side. He said, "Looka here. Ya'll don't have anything on this guy. Ah can't charge him with anything. In fact, he could charge you with kidnappin'. Furthermore, Ah'm disappointed that a police officer was involved in this mess." He went on, "Here's what Ah'm gonna do. Ah'm gonna ask him to forget about it and Ah'm TELLIN' ya'll to forget about it. Now get the hell out of here. Ah'll have an officer drive your prisoner back to Little Woods." Ah was glad that we didn' find the big guy cause there's no doubt about it, Mr. Cochrane would have killed him.

Ah was eager for school to start. Ah mean, sittin' in a classroom, playin' sports, and goin' out at night compared to luggin' around tons of ice, ice wars, 'n' fightin' with adults. A no brainer right? Ah couldn' understand why my classmates complained so much. High school was fun, and football was a lot safer than Little Woods.

Ah started goin' steady in the beginnin' of the school year, so Ah always had a date for all of the school events. Going steady was actually a pretty good arrangement for me. It allowed me to place all of my attention on sports 'n' not all the social activities that require havin' a date.

THIS STORY'S A RIOT

Ah managed to gain a few pounds over the summer which made my football uniform fit a li'l better. My football skills musta improved, cause Ah started gettin' a lot more playin' time. Ah even came in for my brother Paul when he needed a rest. Paul was now the most valuable player on the team, so coach didn' take him out too often. Luckily Ah was able to get in some playin' time in several other positions. Coach even had me play on the line opposite the opposin' team's really big guys. Ah was quick enough to scoot past them before they could move their big beefy bodies. In a few games Ah was even able to scramble through the center's legs and get to the quarterback as soon as he got the ball. This usually worked pretty good throughout the first half. Then they would have their big linemen line up shoulder to shoulder formin' a solid wall of beef. This was never good for me. Ah found out that big guys with trashed ego's can hurt ya. So, after Ah got pounded for awhile coach would mercifully change me to another position that was a lot less harmful to my head and body. Na um feelin' pretty good and probably kinda cocky, you know, the swagger 'n' all. Just about this time, we were scheduled to play our cross town rivals. Coach decided to put me on the line again, and as usual Ah had the big guys seein' red in a very short time, and really enjoyin' it. Thankfully coach pulled me off the line before they could do any permanent damage. (Remember, Ah only weighed about 135 pounds.) Now Ah'm playin' defensive halfback, far away from the angry big guys. Ah still managed to heckle them—from a safe distance of course. Paul was takin' a short break. Anyways this guy throws a block right into my knees after the whistle had blown. My short fuse ignited. When the guy went to get up Ah shot a knee straight into his rib cage, knockin' him over. Now Ah got another big guy pissed off. He jumped up and took a swing at me, (the nerve of that guy!). Ah didn' react kindly. Ah tore into him like a buzzsaw. All 135 pounds of my raging fury didn' scare this guy one bit. We were really goin' at it. In the heat of the battle Ah happened to notice that my opponent was about 6' 3" tall and weighed a good 60 pounds more than me. Ah didn' care (well maybe a little). Ah just kept on bobbin' 'n' weavin', and when ah could reach him, punchin'.

All of a sudden Paul came runnin' off the bench and hit the big guy so hard he knocked his face mask off. (By the way the other team had face masks, we didn't. Our school couldn' afford um.) As if this guy needed another advantage right? At this point, both benches emptied. All of the players from each team entered the melee. The situation got totally out of control. Ah don't know how long we fought, but finally security, police, referees, coaches, 'n' some people from the stands managed to stop the riot. Paul got thrown out of the game and the next game to boot. Somehow in all of the excitement, they failed to get my jersey number. They probably thought, that little guy couldna caused all this trouble. Ah ended up finishin' the game in Paul's place. Next day, a local newspaper devoted a full sports page to this high school riot. One of the sports writers did find out my name. He made public that Ah was the guy who started the biggest riot in both team's history. This had to be a proud moment for my parents. Ah mean with their son's name in the paper 'n' all. Na ah didn' know it at the time, but this incident would come back to haunt me in the future. Ah'll tell ya'll about it later. Aw, OK Ah'll tell you about it now. Jump ahead with me about four years. Ah was just out of the army a short time. Ah'd spent over twenty seven months in Germany and now Ah was makin' up for lost time. My hair was long and Ah looked the part of the bar hoppin' street guy that Ah was. One day, um mindin' my own business, drivin' my girlfriend's car in town, 'n' as luck would have it this cop noticed that the car's brake tag (they only have these in New Orlans) was expired. So he pulls me over and asks for my insurance and registration. Ah had neither. Now Ah really have his attention. "What about your driver's license?" Yeah Ah did have one of those. He takes my licence and stares at it a long time. Then, with a questioning look on his face, he asked "How do you pronounce this name?" Ah answered "Mike Di Giovanni. Sir." (Ya always say sir to New Orlans cops.)

His eyes squinted a bit, “Did you go to Nicholls high school?”

“Yes sir” Ah said expecting somethin’ good to come from this fact. Ah was shocked when he said, ”You’re goin’ to jail!” Ah said “aw come on now. You can’t put me in jail just ‘cause my name is Mike Di Giovanni, can you?” Ah really wasn’ sure. Then he says “don’t you recognize me?” “No sir, Ah promise you officer Ah never saw you before in my life.” He started laughin’, and said “Ah’m the guy you punched in a high school football game a few years back, and on top of that, you caused a riot at my home-coming game.” All the while um thinkin’ back then you had a height ‘n’ weight advantage na ya got a gun, hummm. After makin’ me sweat awhile, he finally said “looka Ah already started writin’ you this ticket. They’re numbered so Ah can’t tear it up, but Ah tell ya what, jus’ go to court on the date that’s on your ticket. Ah’ll be there. Ah can get you out of it f’sure.” That’s jus’ what he did. He turned out to be a really good guy after all. Scared the hell out of me though. Trust me, you don’t wanna go to jail in New Orlans. Now let’s get back to my story.

I’M A GOOD BOY---OFFICER

Football season was over, ‘n’ quite frankly things seemed kinda dull. Track season was still a ways off so Ah filled my time doin’ the usual teen things. All of us shot pool a lot, listened to music, and jus’ hung out. Well one Sunday mornin’ Ma said to me “Michael you haven’ been to church in awhile. Why don’t you go today?”

Ah wanted to be a good boy ‘n’ listen to my mama, so Ah said, “OK Ma, Ah’ll go.”

When Ah got there the church was so crowded Ah had to stand outside ’n’ wait to get in. So um just standin’ there waitin’ to get into church, when Ah heard, “Hey Mike come on over here.” Ah left church to see what was goin’ on. Jack Cochrane and this guy Robbie were sittin’ in a four wheel drive jeep. Robbie was a few years older than us and already had a job in construction. Robbie was one of these guys that always had a mischievous smile on his face, and he was always doin’ somethin’ bizarre. He did things that made me think ol’ Robbie wasn’ dealin’ from a full deck. After the usual greeting, wha y’ at? Robbie said, “Hop in. We’re going off roadin’ in this jeep. Come on hop in. We gotta go.”

Ah jumped at the opportunity for some excitement. Jack and Robbie were in the front seats so without givin’ it another thought ah jumped into the back seat and we were off. We went flyin’ down Chef Highway. Suddenly Robbie swings onto a dirt road, then a levee. Now Ah gotta tell ya a li'l about Robbie. Although he was several years older than us, Ah don't think his brain had fully developed yet. You know what Ah mean. He was the kind of guy that pushed things to the limit of what's sensible. Robbie was obnoxious and seemed to enjoy annoyin' people. After a while, Ah asked "Where'd ya'll get da jeep?"

They both answered at the same time, "We stole it!" What da! Ah was almost in church now Ah'm speedin' down the road in a stolen jeep! Ah could hear myself tryin' to explain to the police. Well you see officer, Ah'm a good boy that listens to his Mama. Ah was in church when... naw that wouldn' work. Might as well enjoy the ride. We were headed across Lake Pontchartrain towards the little town of Slidell. Robbie's weavin' in and out of traffic, cuttin' off cars, flippin' people off, and throwin' things at cars. Ah was beginning to realize that Robbie was really bad news. We went across the fav mile bridge at breakneck speed and entered Slidell. In the 50's Slidell was so small you couldn' find a store open on Sunday's. Jack said he was hungry, so we stopped at the first store we came to. Sure enough, it was closed. Jack wouldn' accept this obvious fact, so he starts bangin' on the door. No one answered. Determined to get food, he pushed his shoulder into the door causin' a glass door panel to brake and fall out. He still didn't give up. He reached in through the broken panel and opened the door. Then Jack went into the store, got some cookies 'n' stuff, put some money on the counter then he left. Again my thoughts went back to explainin' my touchy situation to the police. "You see, officer, Ah was at church, then Ah got in this stolen jeep. Jack got hungry. This led to breakin' into a store.... Why are you looking at me like that officer? It's all true, Ah'm a good boy and ah listen to my Mama. Honest."

We headed back to New Orlans like a bat out of hell. About a half hour later we were back in the city limits. Just as Ah was startin' to feel a little better, we entered my subdivision. Robbie noticed this man putting the final touches on his newly installed lawn. All at once, he starts blowin' his horn, jumps the jeep over the curb onto the lawn. The guy was startled but managed to jump out of the way. Then Robbie started spinnin' the wheels and makin' circles all over the lawn. Ah ducked down into the back seat. Are you kiddin' me, this was only about a mile from my house. Boy was Ah relieved when Ah finally got home. Ah jumped out of the jeep, vowed Ah would never go any place with Robbie again, and went in. Ma said "You couldna been in church all this time. Where ya been"? Ah answered "o just hangin' out, didn' do much."

GOLDEN MEADOW

Jack's girlfriend, Jackie, managed to land a part-time gig singin' with a country band. The music was mostly Cajun with a country song thrown in every now and then. This was Jackie's chance to fulfill her lifelong dream of becomin' a singer. Her band played weekends at Cajun night spots in several little towns near New Orlans. We drove to Barataria, Lafitte or Golden Meadow to support Jackie's band. Golden Meadow is the kind of town that you picture when ya hear about Cajun country in Southeast Louisiana. It had everything you see in movies. The town is situated on Bayou Lafourche about 80 miles south of New Orlans near the Gulf of Mexico. Na you talk about Cajun. Ah've never seen a town as Cajun as this one. Ah saw people dressed in their best clothes pollin' their pirogues down the bayou. Some were goin' out to eat. Others were headin' for a night out on the town. Cajun music reflects the culture. It's lively, fun, and excitin'. Try listenin' to a few songs. You'll become a fan in no time. Golden Meadow is one of the most unique places Ah've ever seen, and Ah suppose our group musta seemed pretty odd to the locals as well. Jack had bruised ribs from football 'n' couldn' walk right. Paul was still on crutches from his horse ridin' accident. And Johnny had a patch over one eye that was damaged in a fight. Ah was the only able bodied person in the group.

Can you imagine what the locals thought of our motley crew? Somehow we managed to overcome their reservations, then we were allowed to join in the fun. Ah listened to some of the older people's stories about their life in bayou country 'n' better understood why they protected their lifestyle from outsiders. Ah hope this little jaunt into bayou country gave you some insight into the Southeast Louisiana bayou country 'n' the Cajun culture.
One night we had car trouble on our way back from Golden Meadow. We wound up getting home at about five o'clock the next mornin'. Pop didn' say anything about us getting' home late. He just said "Change your clothes; you're my helpers today." Lesson learned. Ah could hardly keep my eyes open and Ah was dog tired, but somehow Ah managed to finish the route. Ah was never late gettin' home again. Ah told you Pop could teach psychology to psychologist.

This is the same photo that is on the front cover of this book. Let me tell ya what its about. That's me, on the left, when Ah was 8-years-old. On the right is my brother Paul. He was 9-years-old at the time. We have bamboo fishing poles in our hands, and we're about to go fishing in a bayou (a marshy outlet of a lake or river) near our grandfather's house in Kenner. To me this photo catches the essence of what life was all about during my childhood livin' in New Orlans in the 1940s, and that's why Ah chose it to be on the front cover. That, and it lets ya know what Ah looked like when Ah was a child.

Chapter 3

HIGH SCHOOL

THE IMPOSSIBLE LEAP

Prior to my football team's spring trainin', our coach offered us free tickets to the Sugar Bowl if we would serve as ushers durin' the first quarter. Spring trainin' was always in late January.

Ah'm still confused about this because as you know, January is not spring. Anyways, ya can't get hung up on exact terms cause in New Orlans speak, it may not mean what ya think. Ah willingly accepted the job. My girlfriend Pam was going to perform with a dance group at halftime, and Ah had to be there. What a disaster the whole thing turned out to be. Ah put some people in the wrong seats and almost caused another riot. However, Ah'm not at that part of my story yet. Johnny found out that he could get free tickets for himself and his girlfriend Tootie, but he had to go clear across town to pick them up. Pam and I decided to take the ride with them. As usual, there was a lot of traffic so Johnny took a short cut. We were on a seldom-used road that had a cemetery on one side 'n' a high block wall on the other. This huge wall held back the dirt and railroad ballast that supported a set of elevated railroad tracks. Johnny started playin' around, veerin' the car to the right then whippin' the wheel back the other way, causin' the car to rock back and forth. We were all laughin' and havin' a good ol' time when suddenly Ah heard this deafenin' crashin' sound. The next thing Ah knew Ah was lying next to my unconscious girlfriend in the cemetery. All Ah could hear was moaning. Pam regained consciousness but was still dazed and confused. She was moanin' 'n' sayin' that her ear hurt. When Ah looked at her head 'n' ear, Ah saw blood everywhere. Her ear was almost cut off! The moanin' continued even louder. Ah was still on the ground in the cemetery. It took a few minutes for me to clear my head. Then Ah took a quick assessment of my body. My chin was scraped to the bone 'n' Ah had a few other minor cuts 'n' bruises, but that was it. Boy was Ah lucky r'what? If you coulda' seen that car, you'd wonder how any of us survived. The front fenders were wrapped around a tree almost touchin' each other. It was obvious that the car was completely demolished. Ah still heard moanin' so ah went around to the drivers side where Ah found Johnny unconscious but still moanin'. His face was cut up pretty bad. He had knocked the steering wheel completely off its mount. Then Ah heard Tootie moanin' as well. She came to 'n' immediately complained about her neck hurting. Ah said to her "Ah gotta get help fast." Instinctively, Ah placed her head between the driver and passenger seats to support it. My thoughts were jumbled, everything was fuzzy. Ah hadn' faced anything like this in my life. Ah had to get a grip. Lives depended on it. Then just like when Ah was boxin' everything seemed to start movin' in slow motion. Without any further thought, Ah bolted into action. Ah was at the block wall in an instant. Using every bit of strength 'n' athletic ability in me ah jumped for the top. Everything Ah had wasn' enough. Ah needed more; a lot more. Ah'm tellin' ya a spirit led supernatural effort was needed. Ah couldn' do it alone. Ah was gettin' weaker with every try. God had to help me on the next try! Na you can believe what ya want, but Ah know He helped me make it on the very next attempt. My fingers barely caught the top block. By now they were scraped and bleedin' from the rough edges on the cement blocks. Ah managed to hang on and finally scramble up onto the railroad tracks. Ah was up high, overlookinn' a busy street that was about three or four hundred yards away. My screams for help were so loud that an ambulance driver heard them and stopped. He used a bull horn to yell back to me sayin' he was on another call but would call in the accident. Ah ran back across the tracks to the edge of the wall. It was so high, Ah couldn' jump down Ah had to turn around, slide over the edge on my stomach, hang, then drop. Ah raced back to the wreck 'n' made sure Tootie's head was still secured. Then Ah told Johnny not to move, even though he was still unconscious. Next Ah rolled up a sweatshirt for Pam's head. The silence was deafenin'; time stood still.

While we are waitin for help to arrive let's get back to that wall. After about two weeks, Ah went back with Jack and Paul to show them how high this wall was. We all tried to scale it; none of us could even come close. Over time several others also tried, football players, basketball players, tracksters all failed as well. Ah know God was at that wall with me Ah jus' know it, Ah felt it f' sure. Na Ah know some heathens out there are gonna read this, maybe some are my friends, others relatives, they just ain't gonna believe. But, Ah know f' sure He was there!

The sound of sirens broke the eerie silence. Suddenly the whole area was overrun with ambulances, reporters, police, TV cameras, and a whole bunch of people. The paramedics asked me how Ah knew what to do. Ah couldn' answer that question cause Ah didn't know what to do, but "He did!" They said that if Tootie had moved her neck a fraction of an inch she would have been paralyzed for life. Dere ya go.

GOD CONTROLS THE DETAILS IN LIFE

Medical teams loaded us into ambulances and with the help of police escorts they sped towards Charity Hospital. Once again Ah heard whailin' sirens; it all seemed surreal. Was this really happenin'? Would Tootie and Jawn live? Ah felt alone and helpless. Prayers just started pourin' out of me. Funny how ya turn to God at times like this. The ambulances came to a screechin' stop on the emergency ramp. Gurney's, doctors, and nurses were waitin'. Tootie, Pam, and Johnny were whisked off to emergency rooms. Next thing Ah know, police, TV reporters, and journalists converged on me. Everyone wanted to know what happened.

"Were ya'll speedin'?"

"No sir."

"Was there another car involved?"

"No mam."

"Then what happened?"

"We jus' hit a tree. Ah can't remember much before that,"Ah lied.

Soon Ah was alone again, feelin' low enough to crawl under a snake with a high hat on. Gawd, Ah know you jus' saved me, 'n' already um lyin'. Ah mean with Tootie 'n' Johnny in really bad shape, maybe dyin', Ah just couldn' tell the police that Johnny was foolin' around, rockin' the car back 'n' forth.

The next person Ah saw was Pop. He was as white as a sheet. Ya see there was another car accident that evenin' in which two teenagers were killed. That's where the ambulance Ah called out to was goin'. Pop thought that Ah was one of the teens. He was in shock, just standin' there lookin' at me. Ah went over to him and gave him the warmest hug Ah'd ever given in my life.

My heart nearly stopped when Ah saw a priest go into Tootie 'n' Johnny's rooms to give them their last rites. Nooo, Ah silently screamed. This can't be. We're all goin' to the Sugar Bowl! We were jus' laughin' 'n' havin' fun a little while ago, Ah could still hear the laughter in my head.

Several agonizin' hours passed before Ah found out that they would live. Tootie had some broken vertebrae in her neck. She was in the hospital about a month, then physical therapy for a very long time. Johnny had a broken jaw, broken nose, broken ribs and a punctured lung. Pam had her ear stitched 'n' firmly attached. My shins were scraped, my body was bruised, but it was my mind that suffered most. That deafenin' crashin' sound, 'n' those eerie moans were in my head for a long, long time. Our accident 'n' the one where two teens died were the top stories on the news that night 'n' the next day. F' true, this is not the way Ah wanted to get on television, but there Ah was—big as life, ripped jeans (the force of the crash caused my jeans to rip all the way up the back seam) butt showin', in a cemetery, tendin' to my injured friends.

YOU'RE NOT TAKIN' MY CUSTOMERS!

Before long, hot humid days signaled the start of summer again. It was time to get back to the dog-eat-dog business world. Once again we hustled 'n' were able to get most of the vacation business. One of the local restaurant owners noticed that we were makin' a lot of money 'n' Ah guess he got jealous, so he teamed up with the other ice man that serviced camps in the area. This guy lived in one of the camps 'n' worked his route year round. Most of his customers also lived in camps year round. They knew him 'n' were fiercely loyal to him. However, we still managed to run circles around him getting' most of the vacation dollars. Now Sept, the other ice man (strange name for a strange man), was in his forties 'n' still lived alone with his mama. Ol' Sept wasn' the sharpest tool in the shed. Ya know what Ah mean. Get this. His mother was a witch. A real witch! F' true. On top of that, they both practiced voodoo. Sept never looked at you, he looked through you, 'n' he never talked. Creepy right?

One day Ah was walkin' up and down the camp ramps singin' out i--ee--c--e man, i--ee--c--e man, just like Pop. All of a sudden this witch lady with long stringy gray hair came runnin' towards me. She was yellin' 'n' castin' all kinds of voodoo spells on me. Ah freaked out when Ah noticed what looked like shrunken heads linin' the hand rails of their ramp. There was no mistakin' who she was. She had to be Sept's mama. Ah made a hasty retreat, vowin' never to come near that camp again. Yeah Ah know. Sounds kinda like a fairytale, but it's all true.

Like most wars, this ice war started over an aggressive territorial takeover. Of course, money was involved as well. In our world when somethin' was worth fightin' for you fought to win. Ah mean, once committed, you continued to fight until the enemy was completely defeated. So now the gloves were off. It was go time. We used every advantage we had. We were younger, we could work faster, 'n' we had more endurance than ol' Sept. Also, we could bring our unused ice back to the ice house 'n' get our money back. Sept couldn'. Most important, we were smarter. Aw come on now, Ah'm not braggin'; it didn' take much smarts to be smarter than Sept. Furthermore, we didn' have any strange voodoo rituals clouding our minds. We determined to outmaneuver, outwork, 'n' outwit our competition. Sept always started at the beginnin' of Little Woods Road around nine in the mornin'. Ah knew he was compelled to do this because he was a creature of habit. Also, his regular year-round customers expected their ice at a certain time. So, we started at the beginnin' of the road (around 7:30 AM) 'n' worked towards the middle, servicin' most of the vacation camps. Then we raced to the very end of the road then worked back towards the middle. Usin' this strategy we were able to get most of the vacation customers and dollars. We were makin' a lot of money, more than most jobs in the area. This didn' sit well with Sept or this local restaurant owner. (Isn't it interestin' how envy kicks in when someone else is successful?) Don't be like dat. God don't like it. They teamed up against us. Big grown-ass men battlin' kids.

The restaurant had a huge walk in freezer. Sept would fill the freezer with ice then the restaurant sold ice to nearby camps 'n' people stoppin' by with cars and trucks. This greedy little sucka even hired a helper to deliver the ice. This poor guy probably didn' know what he was gettin' into. He had to use a dolly to haul the ice makin' their whole operation slow and cumbersome. Tryin' to steal even more customers from us, the money-grubbin' restaurant owner made a giant free standin' wooden framed ice for sale sign. He probably thought he was winnin' the battle. Wrong! One mornin' we drove our fairly large ice truck right through the sign. What a show! Wood 'n' sign pieces went flyin' everywhere. We didn' even slow down; jus, kept on goin'. This move was so bold that no one saw us do it. The message was clear: we were serious about keepin' our customers. Our next move was even more aggressive. Whenever we saw their stooge deliverin' ice with his little dolly we rained rocks down on him nonstop until he finally had to jump in the lake. Maybe we went a little too far. Ya think? They musta called the cops. What a bunch of sore losers.

About an hour after one of our rock attacks an unmarked police car pulled us over. Two really large detectives got out, came over and questioned us about the sign and rock throwin'. Go figure. We courteously told them our side of the story. "You see Officer, these guys are stealing our customers. In effect, they're taking clothes right off our backs." We told them of our desperate need for money to get us through school. To my surprise they let us go! They gave us a lecture and stern warnin' to stop assaultin' our competitors. They also told Paul that because Ah was so young, he was responsible for me. And if Ah hit anyone, he was going to jail. First time Ah ever saw Paul nervous. Ya know what? It all worked out. After awhile, their stooge quit haulin' ice for them. It was just too hard for people to carry their own ice out to the camps. After that Scrooge only sold food in his restaurant. He gave up the ice business. However, Sept fired one last shot. One day, Ah noticed that Sept had three voodoo dolls stuck to the side of his ice truck. There were two large ones and one small one. All three were pierced through their hearts with ice picks. Na who ya think those voodoo dolls represented? They kinda freaked me out, but Jack and Paul thought it was funny.

HOW DID I GET HERE?

Somehow Ah got through another summer. It was time to relax in a classroom again. School was a welcome break from witches, ice wars, 'n' voodoo. Ah often wondered if my summers were really that different from other kids' summers. Ah didn' talk much about my summers cause most of my Lower Ninth Ward classmates didn' even know where Little Woods was and none of them ever worked on an ice route. Most of the time Ah just listened to their stories. Can you imagine me tryin' to tell them about runnin' away from a witch, ice wars, or running my own business?

After classes were out Ah went to football practice. Yay! Ah was in my comfort zone around my teammates. Ah love football because it's not just a game. You can learn more life's lessons in a few years playin' football than most people acquire in a lifetime. Our whole American value system is deeply ingrained in the game. Think about these examples and you'll see how they relate. First and foremost, ya learn that hard work pays off. Then there's teamwork, pride, determination and a multitude of other American values entrenched in the game.

Ah was flyin' high at this point; Ah lettered in track 'n' football. Ah was pretty well known throughout the local sports world. (Mostly for good things.) Football players rule in the South. So na um struttin' around thinkin' Ah'm cool, Ah'm cool. Ma was happy 'cause my school grades were better than they'd ever been. Ah was flyin' high. Ya ever read the Proverb, "Pride goeth before a fall?" Ah hadn', but Ah was about to find out about it first hand.

Football spring trainin' rolled around again. This is the time when coaches try out new plays and strategies. My coach was no exception. He had this wild idea about usin' my speed 'n' our great big fullbacks' strength 'n' power. Ah'm going to try to explain this part of my story as best Ah can so even those that don't understand football will get it. Ya see, Coach wanted to try out a few special plays, designed to surprise and confuse our opponents. He put this big hard runnin' fullback in a halfback position. Ah was placed on the line next to the center. The plan was, Ah would step back, come across the line and lead this big guy up the field, givin' him an extra blocker in front of him. (OK if you still don't understand, just pretend you do 'n' read on). We ran into a big problem; one practice that almost ended my football career 'n' my life. You see, the big guy only had to run about two yards. Ah had to step back then run five yards to get ahead of him. Ah took a step back as planned, sped across the line; the big fullback steamed straight ahead at full power. We met just before Ah could turn up field. His huge knee smashed into the side of my helmet. Ah sorta came to, everything looked blurry. Ah was confused. Someone was askin' me questions that Ah couldn' answer. Then everything faded to black. Ah had no memory of even leavin' the practice field. The next mornin' Ah woke up with a tremendous headache. Ah was groggy 'n' still confused. Ah was trying to piece things together. If you've ever been knocked out or woke up from anesthesia you know what Ah'm talkin' about. Still tryin' to clear my head, Ah managed to focus in on Ma standin' at the foot of my bed. Ah asked, "How did Ah get here?" Tears welled up in her eyes and her voice cracked as she asked "Don't you remember? You were hurt at football practice." Ah remembered going to football practice, but Ah didn' remember bein' hurt. Ah had never seen Ma look so scared. Ah knew somethin' had happened but couldn' figure out what. Ah tried to comfort her with some really stupid macho cliches. It didn' work. Moms know when somethin' serious is wrong with their child. Then Ah did another really dumb thing. Ah insisted on goin' to school. Ah wanted to prove to myself 'n' Ma that Ah was OK. Reluctantly, she let me go. This is one time that Ah really shoulda listened to my Mama because Ah passed out in my very first period. My head hit my desk, 'n' Ah was out like a light. Yeah, Ah know you're agrein' with me that it was dumb! That was it. Ah was in and out of consciousness for the next three days.

Some time later they sent me to Tulane University for a brain scan. This was cutting-edge technology back then. Tulane had the best brain doctors in the South. Test results were mixed with both good and bad news. The good news was Ah would recover. Bad news was, they found evidence that Ah'd had several concussions before this one. So now when anyone questions my mental stability, Ah can say Ah've been tested. My doctor told me that most professional fighters don't suffer as much brain trauma in their entire careers. The report also said that further trauma could cause serious permanent damage or even death. As you can imagine, Ah was devastated. There was an empty feelin' again. Ya may have felt it yourself, kinda like sinkin' into a dark pit. Except for occasional bouts with dizziness, Ah felt fine. Summer rolled around again. My fuzzy head cleared 'n' Ah was ready to get back to work. This was the summer when big changes started takin' place. Paul ended up gettin' married right after high school. Na this was not uncommon in our area. In most cases, the life cycle was shortened. It was kinda like live fast and die young. Ah'll tell you more about this later. Paul got married then Jack joined the Navy. This made it impossible for me to handle our ice route by myself. Ah had to give it up.

My need for money didn' go away. Ah had to get another job. Before long, Ah landed a job buildin' chainlink fences. Anchor Fence Company built fences in New Orlans 'n' all of the surroundin' parishes. Na Ah thought the ice route was hard. Buildin' fences was off the charts. Fence buildin' is gruelin' work. We pounded in fence posts by hand then drove metal stakes through post collars to secure them. Finally we stretched the wire. Mind you Ah was still a teenager, however; they didn' cut me any slack. Ah had to either keep up with the grown men or get fired. The relentless heat made the work exhaustin'. Boxes of salt tablets hung on both sides of the truck. Ah had to swallow handfuls of them to ward off dehydration. There were no sports drinks at the time. Ah had to rely on salt tablets to keep me goin'. The only problem with salt tablets was that by the end of the day, you could see and feel the salt crystals on your skin. Ah could feel my young body getting' stronger and gainin' endurance. Ah was back to my old self.

By the time August rolled around strange—yet familiar—feelins' began to surface within me. Excitement 'n' anticipation filled every fiber of my body 'n' mind. Football was in the air and Ah could feel it. Ah felt like there was a giant magnet pullin' me towards the practice field. Here was my dilemma. Ah could go to school for half a day 'n' work the other half or go against the advice of family, friends, and doctors and play my final year of football. What would you do? This was a tough decision for me. Ah spent a lot of sleepless, agonizin' nights tryin' to sort things out. After a few weeks of this, Ah decided to play. Ah had to do it. Everyone was surprised when

Ah showed up for practice. Yeah you rite, maybe not too smart, but did you ever have something ya just had to do? Ah had to prove to myself that Ah could do this. Ah had to see if Ah could defy logic, tempt the fickle finger of fate and still survive.

On the very first day of practice, we lined up for head on tacklin' drills. Who ya think lined up opposite me? Yeah, you guessed it. The big fullback that almost killed me! Ah thought, is this my fate? Ah was facin' the biggest test of my life. It was do or die. Ah slammed into the big guy with every ounce of force and determination in me. Ah did it. Ah took him down and survived. The tacklin' drill went on for about an hour. When it was over Ah made an assessment of my head and body. Ah was relieved to discover that everything was still intact.

Ah went on to score seven touchdowns in my final year of football. My coaches chose me for the best runnin' back award 'n' presented a trophy to me at the annual football banquet. My teammates selected me to represent them as their homecomin' king.

My head musta healed pretty good, 'cause years later, Ah earned a black belt in karate, a silver glove plus teaching credentials in Savate, trained extensively in Jeet Kune Do, Kali, street fightin', 'n' several other disciplines. My instructors were the best in the world, most notable are: Jim Wagner, Burton Richardson, 'n' Salem Assli, to name a few.

Na if ya think um braggin', ya missed the whole point of my story. What Ah'm tryin' to tell ya is that if you persevere you can overcome a lot of obstacles. Ya gotta keep on keepin' on.

Currently Ah'm fightin' the toughest opponent Ah ever faced, one that can't be beat, one that all of you will face. That bad boy is aging. Ya can't beat it, but you can put up a hell of a fight. Ah've been fightin' one thing or another all my life, 'n' Ah'll treat agin' like any other opponent. Ah'll fight it. Ah'm an ol' fighter and will be one 'til the end. That's all Ah know. A warrior spirit comes from somethin' that's deep down inside of you. Ya can't teach it or learn it, but those who possess a warrior spirit will bring it to the surface when it's needed. Ya see, life's gonna knock ya down from time to time. Still, ya gotta get up 'n' get right back in the fight. Timin', power and speed are great assets, but fights are won by beatin' the person, team, or country's spirit. Ya need to defeat their will to fight. A true warrior won't quit. His spirit might bend, but it won't break. We sang a little song that makes all this clear. It goes like this, "Beans and cornbread had a fight, beans knocked cornbread out of sight. Cornbread said man dats all right. Ah'll be back tomorrow night." Ah probably shoulda' been a preacher right?

Now, back to my story. My final track season was the best ever. My school won the public school track meet again and our relay team set records that stood for at least a decade. Then it was over. Ah graduated from high school. A deep sense of loss came over me. Ah was facin' an uncertain future. Up until now, Ah knew what was comin'. Ah could feel the onset of summer and prepared for the ice route. When the air cooled and fall rolled around Ah became excited about school, football, 'n' seein' my crosstown friends. Ah felt like ah was loosin' somethin' and Ah was; it was my youth. Ah was loosin' my youth! College was out of the question. Ah realized Ah couldn' prolong my adolescence. Ah had to go out 'n' make my way in the world. Then it came to me. Ah'll join the Army 'n' see the world.

Ah was currently in the National Guard trainin' on weekends at the now historic Jackson Barracks military base. Ah was already a weekend warrior, why not become a full time warrior? So two weeks out of high school my buddy Ronnie and I went downtown and joined the Army. Ah knew there was a great big world out there just waitin' for me. But, there was this kinda funny feelin' in the pit of my stomach. Ya know like a pendin' disaster was about to happen.

This is me (front row, second from the right) with the F.T. Nicholls High School track team during the 1955-1956 school year.

Ah saved the patches from my MILNE football jacket..

Ah'm 16-years-old for this 1956 High School Year Book photo.

Chapter 4

U.S. ARMY (1957-1960)

YOU'RE IN THE ARMY NOW

Family 'n' friends gathered at the airport to see me off. Ah said my goodbyes, boarded the aircraft and soon Ah was headed towards Fort Chaffee Arkansas. The hum of propellers made me aware that Ah was flyin' high above the earth. My mind asked, Michael, what are you doin'? If the good Lawd wanted you to fly, He woulda given you wings! Besides, you've hardly ever ben' out of your neighborhood. Now you're flyin' for the first time, headed for some hick town in Arkansas." Tears began rollin' down my cheeks. A seasoned Army captain saw the tears, he asked, "First time away from home son?"

"Yes sir Ah replied, first time flyin' too."

He continued, "I've been in the Army twenty years and I still get choked up every time I leave home."

Ah'm glad he took the time to comfort me. This was the nicest officer Ah met in my entire three-year tour of duty. Ah relaxed. My mind drifted from home to the adventures Ah knew were waitin' for me. A few hours later we landed at the Fort Smith Arkansas airport. My feet barely touched the ground when this little sergeant started gettin' in our faces screamin' at us, "Form a line assholes; Ah ain't got all day." Ah thought yeah and you ain't got no manners either. This is where it all started. My private war with the Army. Ah was used to being treated with a certain amount of respect. Ya see, where Ah came from you had to back up your words. It's actions that count, not words. This makes for a much nicer society. Na Ah could see right away that these guys weren't gonna play nice. We were loaded into buses and whisked off to Fort Chaffee. As soon as Ah arrived on the base, Ah was assigned to a buildin', bed and foot locker. Then we were dismissed with a warnin', "Bed check is at ten o'clock. Don't miss it! Now get the hell out of my sight. Ah got things to do." His tone of voice indicated he would back up his words. My high school buddy Ronnie and I took off right away. We found a recreation buildin' about a mile away. It had pool tables, so we went in.

We were passin' time playin' pool, when another little loud mouth sergeant screamed "OK you guys let's start cleaning this place up." Where'd they get these guys? Didn' their Mamas teach um any manners? "Grab some brooms and mops, and make those floors shine. Get with it." Na Ah knew this guy didn' know my name or what barracks Ah was in. So Ronnie and I talked in our local neighborhood language. We called it zz's. You simply added zz either before, after, or in the middle of a word, i.e. tazzalk, means talk. With practice, yazzou cazzan master it in a short time. Anyway, we made a getaway plan. We both grabbed mops and mopped in a line straight to the door, then we tossed the mops towards (OK maybe at) the little loudmouth 'n' bolted out the door. Not a very good first night right?

After waitin' three days to get my uniforms, basic trainin' started. Right away, Ah noticed that the army went to great lengths to annoy, frustrate, and aggravate you. The first place they sent me to was the barber shop. Ah had about four guys ahead of me, but this smart ass barber pointed his finger at me and said, "Come on up here boy Ah wanna cut your hair now." That sucka shaved ma head! This didn' make sense to me. Ah mean if ya wanna teach me how to fight, Ah'm 100% on board. But, why ya wanna aggravate me? Ya know what, the Army didn' ask me, even once, for my opinion. There was no doubt in my eighteen year old mind Ah coulda told them how to run their trainin' sessions, but like Ah said, they didn' ask me. Go figure. We learned how to march in formation, field strip, clean, and reassemble our rifles. They finally did teach me all the basic combat skills necessary to survive in battle. Maybe Ah learned a li'l about how to deal with aggravation as well. Many years later ah found that these same basic fightin' skills can be modified and used in modern street fightin' trainin'. We also spent a lot of time learnin' about our rifles. This was sooo boring. Ah cut ma teeth on a gun stock. Ah already knew all of the safety rules, sight picture, arm positions, etc. Finally, it was time to head out to the firin' range. Doncha know they chose three thirty AM to start. On top of that, we had to march fifteen miles to get there. Ah was sleepy, tired, hungry, and a little angry when we finally got to the firing range. Na ya know, they coulda sent some of dem big trucks ovah by my barracks to pick us up if they wanted to be nice about it. So na, after all this, Ah hafta get in the correct mindset for the task at hand. Ya see, Ah always liked to fool around and have a li'l fun to avoid boredom. A few months back Ah was on the firin' range with the National Guard. 'N' like Ah said, Ah spent eight months in the National Guard while still in high school. Well, boredom set in. Ah was hittin' the bullseye every time. Ah wanted to try shootin' at a smaller target to further test my skills and for a li'l excitement. So, when the pit guy held up the metal pointer showin' me where my round hit, Ah shot the pointer, causin' it to vibrate in his hand, scarin' the heck out of him. Ah guess this guy didn' have a sense of humor 'cause after that each time Ah fired a round he waved a flag indicatin' Ah'd missed the entire target.

Needless to say, Ah didn' qualify that day. The regular army was different. Ah had to qualify with my rifle, because if Ah didn' Ah would havta' recycle back to week one of basic trainin'. Thank God, Ah qualified 'n' got the heck out of there. About a week or so later, we went to the obstacle course. This was right up my alley. The entire course seemed like a giant amusement park to me. Ah was havin' so much fun Ah ran the entire course three times before a Sergeant yelled "Get your ass off that course! What's wrong with you boy?" It's time for me to go home."

Another fun thing was boxin'. We passed the time after trainin' by havin' boxin' matches. One evenin' while boxin' this big ol' country boy, my thoughts raced back to St. Mary's boxin' gym. Ah guess Ah got caught up in the moment cause Ah gave that big boy a boxin' lesson. Ah also gained a li'l needed respect from my peers. The rest of basic trainin' was pure misery, consistin' of routine army stuff: marchin', spit 'n' polish etc. Oh, yeah, there was one other thing. Near the end of basic, we had to go through a tear gas chamber; stay in there for a certain amount of time, then remove the protective mask to experience the effects of tear gas. Well Ah didn' think experiencin' smellin' tear gas would make me a better soldier. Ah mean, it's not like Ah hadn' experienced hard knocks or miserable things livin' in East New Orlans. Ah always had to think outside the box just so Ah could avoid the daily routine sufferin'. Avoidin' the gas chamber seemed like just another ordinary task for me. Ah said to myself. "Self. Ya gotta think." And sure enough, a very simple plan became clear to me. The tear gas buildin' was like a house. You went in one door and out another. So, Ah waited until a lot of people bunched up at the door, distractin' the Sergeant; then Ah went around the buildin' 'n' jumped in with the guys comin' out, Ah coughed and pretended to gasp for air like the rest of um. When in reality Ah hadn' even gone into the gas chamber at all.

Once again Ah got homesick. Ah missed hangin' out with my friends as well as the sights 'n' sounds of New Orlans. Reality set in. Ah was in the army now. It was time to pay my dues for the privilege of livin' in the greatest country in the world.

Next thing Ah knew, Ah was crawlin' on my stomach with machine gun rounds whizzin' over my head and dynamite explodin' all around me. All part of the trainin'. There wasn' time for homesickness or philosophical thinkin'.

After the first ten weeks of trainin' Ah got a week's leave at home. It sure was good to be reunited with family 'n' friends again. Most of the discussions were about how much Ah'd changed. When Ah thought about it Ah realized that Ah had changed a whole lot. In a very short time Ah was transformed from a boy into a man. Now at nineteen years old Ah was a man. We always said back on the ice route if we had to wait til' twenty one to be a man we should just give up. Ah guess the Army saw it the same way.

WASHINGTON D.C.

After my brief stay at home Ah bummed a ride with some close friends. Actually they were more like blood brothers. These three brothers were my friends from as far back as Ah can remember. It just so happens that they were headed for the Marine base in North Carolina. From there Ah took a bus to Fort Belvoir Virginia. Ah had two more weeks of Basics. After that, refrigeration school. Yeah, doncha just love school? This was great. Ah could sit in school all day. Afterwards Ah would study or hit the streets at night. Ronnie and I spent every weekend in Washington D. C. The town was jumpin'. On our first night there we heard New Orlans music blastin' out of a nightclub. It was like a giant magnet pullin' us inside. Once inside, we ran right into a guy from our neighborhood in New Orlans. Dominick was stationed on a nearby Navy base. He knew everyone in the club, includin' the band. Ah thought, boy ya can't beat dat wid a stick. All the guys were paisanos'. Dominick introduced us, and we were welcomed with open arms. Everyone sayin' "Ay paisano. How ya doin?" However, there was one more thing before we could enter the inner circle. We had to be tested. Italians stick together, but you have to prove your loyalty and courage. So, this is how you were tested. Let's say Dominick was outside. One of the goombas would come up to you and say Dominick's outside fightin' a bunch of guys. Come on out, he needs help. If you went out ready to fight you were in. Ah got in on the first test. Then it was party time Italian style. Wow, kinda like New Orlans. Excitement was in the air. Ah felt right at home with this group. We partied almost non-stop every weekend. Ya could grab a cupola hours sleep on someone's couch or floor, then party again the next day. The good times were rollin'. Well, one night um dancin'—really tearin' up the dance floor—when another goomba kinda whispers, "Yo

Mike. Dominick's fightin' some marines in the alley."
Ah go "Bra Ah already been tested."

He whispers again'. "Ah ain't kiddin'." So, Ah gave the girl two really cool twirls sendin' her spinnin' towards the back of the room. Then Ah calmly walked out into the alley. Sure enough Dominick was fightin' this BIG marine. Dominick was all over this guy. The big lug couldn' land a punch. Ya see, Dominick was a high rankin' amature fighter back in New Orlans. Frustration soon overcame common sense, 'n' some other Marines jumped into the fight. That was it, the brawl was on. All of us came flyin' into action. In seconds, the whole alley was filled with the sounds of fists hittin' flesh and bone. Soon the fight spilled out of the alley onto the banquette (sidewalk). Ah'm tellin' ya, a brawl is confusin'. The whole scene was chaotic. Ah even hit one of my own guys twice. It seemed like we were fightin' for hours, but actually it was only about a minute or so. Anyway, somebody jumped on one of our big guy's back. He shook him off. This caused the Marine to go flyin' right into the Club's large plate glass window, smashin' it. Glass came rainin' down everywhere. Then Ah saw flashin' lights a cupola blocks away. Dominick yelled, "Meet ya at Cindy's apartment." We split up and ran in different directions. Na here Ah am runnin' down alleys, jumpin' over garbage cans tryin' to get away from the cops. In the midsts of all this chaos, Ah couldn' help thinkin' that jus' a few months ago the only racin' Ah did was in track meets. We managed to get away, spent a nervous night on Cindy's sofa, then early the next mornin' we hitched a ride back to Fort Belvoir where we sat like little angels in our refrigeration class.

My contract with the Army was in exchange for three years of my life. They would teach me the refrigeration repair business. Wo! Suddenly Ah realized Ah was an indentured servant just like my Grandparents were. We had to attend classes Monday through Friday, but from Friday night 'til Monday mornin', we were free to have fun. True to form, when Friday evenin' rolled around, Ah headed back to D. C. with Ronnie. We went straight to the club. When we tried to enter, the doorman stopped us sayin', "Wait a minute. Ah gotta talk to the manager." A coupla minutes later this beady-eyed manager comes over and looks us up and down. "I recognize you two," he says. "Ya can't come in here anymore. You're banned from this club, and all the other Italians (good thing he said Italians n' not WOPS) that you hang out with are also banned. You guys are bad news. You're all troublemakers. That big window you broke cost us a lot of money. If you don't leave I'll call the cops."

There wasn't anything else to discuss. We left. Ah found a pay phone and called Dominick. After Ah told him what happened he said, "Come by Cindy's apartment tonight. There's a party. Everyone's gonna be there. We'll talk then." So at the party we talked about bein' banned from the Club. Joe lost it! Ya see, Joe had been a bouncer at that club for a year and a half. The manager knew him. Joe was a typical New York Italian. He had a fiery hair triggered temper, was tough as nails and one of the best street fighters Ah ever met. The nerve of that manager callin' us trouble makers.

Then Joe said, "Let's go over there right now and clean house." Thankfully, Dominick and I managed to calm him down. We decided to get every girl that we knew to leave the club and come party with us. About six of us went to the club, pushed right past the doorman, went in and told all of the girls to come with us. They did. As you can imagine, some of the guys that were dancin' with the girls tryin' to score didn' like what was goin' on.The departure of the girls left the club with a bunch of guys and no girls. Four of those angry guys musta followed us to Cindy's. They walked right in 'n' just stood there starin' us down. Ah noticed that all of them had their hands in their pockets. Ah thought boy, This is not good. They could have guns. None of us had any weapons, the situation was tense. We were on one side of the room starin' at them, they were on the opposite side glarin' back at us. Finally Dominick said "There's knives in a kitchen drawer. Ah'll get um." Ah felt a little more comfortable with a knife in my hand, but they still had their hands in their pockets. There was complete silence. Ya could feel the tension. Suddenly, they backed out of the door without utterin' a word. Guess they didn' have guns. Whew! Dominick quickly locked the door. After settlin' down a bit Ah went back to havin' fun. The next few weekends we found other clubs that welcomed us with open arms. Our clique could liven' up any club. This brought in people and the club made money. Money talks. Every weekend about four or five of us would stand in front of the club that banned us and tell everyone to follow us to another club, promisin' more action than they could imagine. One night about fav' car loads of us were makin' our way over to a new club when all of a sudden two cars started honkin' 'n' yellin' racial slurs at us. Then they stopped in front of our car blockin' us in. Ah noticed some kerosene warnin' lamps at a nearby construction site. Ah jumped out of the car, grabbed two lamps, then ran towards the cars. Ah slammed one lamp on the ground causin a fire. Then Ah walked slowly towards the nearest antagonist car with the other lamp in my hand. Ah could see fear come across their faces. All Ah had to do was bang the lamp on top of their car 'n' they would be engulfed in flames. They lost their will to fight ‘n’ sped off.

Our old hangout was loosin’ a lot of business, so the owner fired the beady-eyed manager that banned us, then went out of his way to invite us back. We accepted the invitation. Things went back to normal, The good times were rollin’ again.

All too soon, it was time to leave. Ah really didn’ want to leave Washington. Ah coulda spent the rest of my service time there. Sayin’ goodbye was kinda hard, but Ah was startin’ to get used to it. The Army allowed me to have another brief visit with family ‘n’ friends in New Orlans, then Ah hitched a ride to Fort Dix New Jersey. This is where Ah got my shippin’ out orders for my next assignment. Ah had no idea where Ah was goin’. Ah didn’ know what country or city Ah would end up in. The only thing Ah knew for sure was that Ah was goin’ across the pond for a very long time. Ah had thirty three months starin’ me in the face.

New Jersey was the coldest place Ah’d ever been to in my life. Yeah you rite, Ah wasn’ really a world traveler yet.

At this point Ronnie and I were still together. Ah still had someone from the old neighborhood, someone who spoke the same language, someone who had my back. Ya know what Ah found out. The Army doesn’t care about how you feel. They don’t care about how many friends you have, or touchdowns you scored. And they certainly don’t care that you were homecomin’ king. Ah was in the Army now. A name and number with a job to do. Like one Sergeant in basic told us, “You’re hired killers at seventy nine dollars a month. You haven’t killed anyone lately. The Army’s paying you for nothing. You’re useless to us.

After standin’ in the cold for hours, we finally got our shippin’ out orders. Ronnie was goin’ to France and Ah was goin’ to a town in Germany that Ah never even heard of. Once again Ah felt alone. Doom and gloom came over me like a dark cloud. Ah had just left my family and friends, now Ah was leavin’ the country that Ah loved. Ah was herded into a bus that took me to my ship.

WONT’CHA LET ME TAKE YA ON A SEA CRUISE?

Getting’ onboard the ship was another tough task. After waitin’ around in the cold for hours, Ah had to lug my duffel bag up a steep ramp that led to the ship. My downtrodden mood coupled with the miserable cold caused my legs not to work right. Ah had to drag my duffle bag the last twenty yards. Have ya ever been so tired and depressed that you could hardly move?

The Army has an old saying, "There's the right way, the wrong way and the Army way." This was definitely the Army way. Once onboard we were assigned our sleepin' compartments. Mine was four decks down in the deepest bowels of the ship. Ah felt like Ah was bein' led down into the pits of hell. There were no windows, very small passageways leadin' out, and the air seemed stagnant. Na Ah know this wasn' really hell, but Ah was sure Ah could see it from here. On top of that, one of the first things they told us was that if the ship started takin' on water, a siren would blow. This meant you had thirty seconds to get out of there before the compartment was sealed off in order to protect the rest of the ship. Wha'd you say? Ah felt like askin' for a room with a view, ya know, since Ah was homecomin' king 'n' all. To this day, Ah'm still claustrophobic from my ship experience. Ah tried to make the best of it. After all, this was gonna to be my home for the next eleven days. Ya know what, there was NO best of it. Ah threw my duffel bag on the hammock and scrambled up to the top deck as fast as Ah could. The ship was startin' to move out into the harbor. We were steamin' towards the Atlantic Ocean, headin' for Europe.

Ah couldn' help thinkin' about how my Grandparents had signed on as indentured servants so they could come to America. Now Ah'm an indentured servant, goin' to Europe. My young mind couldn' quite grasp the fact that Ah was leavin' America for an unknown destination. Off in the distance behind me, the Statue of Liberty seemed to be wavin' goodbye to me. Ah felt like Ah'd been kicked in the gut. My warrior spirit was bendin'. Ah had to fight back.

Just as Ah was startin' a battle plan, the chow bell rang. Food was the last thing on my mind, but Ah started down the stairs towards the mess hall anyway. About halfway down the ship rolled, causin' the step to come up 'n' meet my foot mid-step. That was it; my stomach felt like it turned inside out. Ah thought Ah was gonna die, but was too sick. Um sure death woulda felt better. Ah made my way down towards my dungeon compartment, barely makin' it to the head. Ah rushed in to throw up. The entire bathroom was filled with others that had the same problem as me. The whole area had the worst stench Ah'd ever smelled. There were dozens of soldiers throwin' up everywhere. Once again Ah felt like death would be a welcomed blessin'. Several guys did try to kill themselves. Ah finally made it down to my compartment and remained there for the next three days. We were in the midst of an Atlantic Ocean winter storm, and it was a bad one. Our ship was tossed around like a matchbox. Even some of the sailors on board got sick.

The waves were so big officers wouldn' allow anyone up on deck. This monster storm raged on for three more days. The ship ended up with extensive damage. (My stomach felt like it had extensive damage.) Thank God the ship didn' suffer enough damage to take on water or seal off my compartment. Ya can bet Ah woulda been outta there in less than thirty seconds. When the sea finally calmed down Ah was able to eat and Ah felt my fightin' spirit comin' back. A sailor told me ah had to find my sea legs. He said, "Ya gotta bend your knees and rock with the ship." It took awhile, but when ah equated the movement to dance rhythm, Ah got it. Ah found my sea legs. What a relief. Ah started getting around more, made some friends and was even able to enjoy life a little. Every day Ah thanked God that Ah didn' join the Navy!

The Army gave us books with some common German words and phrases in them. Ah studied for hours and Ah was able to practice some of the phrases with some Hungarian soldiers that spoke pretty good German. Ah started learnin' German right off the bat. Ah was surprised to find German easy to understand. This was quite an achievement for a guy that could only speak Ninth Ward, some Cajon, 'n' a little English. By the time we landed in Bremehaven, Germany Ah'd mastered several German words 'n' common phrases.

WHERE THE HECK IS BAUMHOLDER?

Once again after hours of hurry up and wait, Ah finally got to say goodby to that stinken ol tub the Navy called a ship. After luggin' my duffel bag down this mile long ramp Ah boarded a bus that dropped me off at the train station. You can imagine how alone and lost Ah felt. Ah was in a foreign land and didn' know where Ah was goin' or what to expect when Ah got there. All Ah knew was that my orders said Ah was headed to the 293'rd Combat Engineers Battalion in Baumholder, Germany. Next thing Ah knew Ah was on a train headed south. No one seemed to know where this mysterious city, Baumholder, was. None of the other guys had orders for Baumholder. The thought of my travelin' south made me feel a little more secure. At least Ah was headed in the right direction: south. Ah was exhausted after a very long day. Finally Ah was able to relax and fell into a deep sleep. Sounds of someone speakin' a foreign language awoke me. It wasn' Yankee. Oh yeah. German Ah got it.

Due to my brief study of German phrases, Ah was able to understand that he said breakfast would be ready in a few minutes. This was music to ma ears. Ah was starvin'. Then this wise-ass Sergeant told us we would be getting' a continental breakfast. Na he knew there wasn' a one of us that knew what the hell a continental breakfast was. Ah found out soon enough. It was toast and coffee! What da? My fightin' spirit was back. Ah questioned the cooks. Where's the ham 'n' eggs, grits and all the other fixins? All Ah got was a blank stare. Then it hit me. Ah was a long long way from New Orlans. Reality began to sink in. Ah was on a train speedin' south towards Baumholder, the foreign city that no one seemed to have heard of. This mysterious city was to be my new home for the next thirty-three months.

The first big town we came to was Hannover. A bunch of guys started leavin'. Hopeful, Ah asked their sergeant, "Is this where Ah get off?"

"Naa. Stay put."

Ah never heard of Baumholder. Ah got the same answer at each stop. Baumholder? Never heard of the place. Finally, when we reached Frankfort, a sergeant answered with a smirk, "Ya I heard of Baumholder. You'll know when you're there; it's at the end of the line." He wasn' kidden'. The train came to a stop at the very end of the tracks. It had to back out of what they called a train station. Ah was the only American left on the train. There were a lot of French and German soldiers, but no Americans. Ah pleaded with the conductor. "There must be some mistake. Ah probably was supposed to get off in one of those big cities back there, right?" He replied in a stoic manner, "This is Baumholder. This is where you're supposed to be." Reluctantly, Ah got off. All Ah could see was snow and mountain tops. It was freezin'. Ah thought nooo way. This is not where Ah'm supposed to be. Ah'm supposed to be in one of dem big cities back dere.

A Sergeant pulled up in a four wheel drive jeep. "You Di Giovanni?"

"Yeah." Ah was the only one there.

"Hop in. I ain't got all day." Ah could tell right away this was no mountain retreat. We plowed through the snow and came to a stop in front of freshly painted barracks. "This is it soldier. Your new home." Yeah, there it was. That empty gut wrenchin' feelin' was back in the pit of my stomach. Ah was assigned a bunk and locker in a room that housed thirty other soldiers. Everything was clean and orderly. Ah thought, Not bad. Ah'll pretend it's a small town mountain retreat.

It was easy makin' friends with these guys. They were all anxious to hear about the world. (America). The first guy Ah met turned out to be the best friend a guy could have in this place. Ralf was a German from Hamburg. When he was a child he spent a lot of time in a bunker tryin' to escape British and American bombs. One night while tryin' to reach the bunker, Ralf suffered severe wounds to his arms and legs from sharpnel. He still had some small pieces of sharpnel in his arms, givin' him a partial disability status. Every time he received a light duty assignment someone complained because he looked healthy. Ralf would say "Why are you complaining? You guys did this to me." Somehow he managed to get to the States, 'n' ended up getting' drafted 'n' was sent right back to Germany. This was the beginnin' of my hearin' war stories from people that were on opposite sides of the war. Na this guy Ralph was a real character, my kinda guy. He knew everyone in Baumholder and the surrounding towns, includin' German soldiers. We started hangin' out together. The good times were startin' to roll. First Ah started learnin' to speak German, both proper and slang. Then along with language Ah learned all the local and national customs. It was not uncommon for Ralph to leave me 'n' a German soldier that didn' speak a word of English, alone in a gasthaus (bar-restaurant). In order to communicate Ah had to teach him English. He in turn taught me German. Within six months Ah was able to master most of the local speech 'n' customs. Not only did my German improve, My English improved as well. For example Ah found out that some people had mom's and dad's (not ma's and pops). Ah still couldn' get used to pronouncin' the last letters of words or the i's in the middle. Like, fav, ya'll say fiivee. Seems like a waste of time. Just sayn'.

Now Ah could go anywhere 'n' blend right in. The military police never asked to see my pass. Good thing, 'cause ah seldom had one. Ah had gained insight into the German society that no other officers or enlisted men in Company C had. All because Ah took the time to learn their language 'n' respect their customs. Growin' up in the segregated South coupled with Pop's love for people, gave me the tools needed for understandin' people and respectin' their culture.

On several occasions Ah actually went on the German military base. Ah saw their livin' quarters, learned about their trainin' and the foods they ate. Boy, was this an eye opener? The differences between them and us were strikin'. Some of the things that Ah found fascinating are: every soldier had their weapon in his own wall locker. They were issued and allowed to carry a switchblade knife. On top of that, every soldier had an evenin' snack right in his locker. Ah have to be honest here, Ah was a little disappointed in the way we were treated in comparison to the Germans. Our weapons were locked up in a separate buildin' from our livin' quarters. American soilders were not allowed to carry knives. However, Ah always had a knife in my pocket. Yea Ah know, but survival has always been a top priority for me.

Later Ah'll tell ya'll a story about a really cool switchblade Ah bought in France. We even walked guard duty with unloaded weapons. Na come on, think about it; the bad guys always have weapons. Jus' don't make sense. First they tell us we're hired killers 'n' then they give us rifle's without bullets! Most reasonable people would think that a U. S. fightin' man trained in the use of weapons would be trusted to use them properly. Ah still can't believe it! This kind of stuff led me to reason that there are a lot of people in powerful positions that were born with a stupid gene. Any soldier that can't be trusted with his weapon, shouldn' be in the military.

FUNNY MONEY

Another thing our government didn' trust us with was money. A short time after our occupation of Germany military personnel were not allowed to use U. S. dollars on the open market. We were paid in a special currency called scrip, often referred to as funny money. Na get this, scrip was only good on U. S. bases; ya couldn' use it in town. So on payday ya had to figure out how much scrip and deutsch marks ya needed for the entire month. What a pain. Our government didn' want to mess up the German economy. We had just bombed them into a pile of rubble, now we don't want to hurt their economy. What da? There's that gene showin' it's ugly head again.
Of course this policy didn' work. German businesses would still give us a better exchange than the military did. The black market still thrived. Items like American coffee and cigarettes were sold at inflated prices. So after several years of this failed policy our military decided to end the funny money program. It's ironic that you can't find anyone who came up with the funny money idea. They (Ah don't know who THEY are) came up with this plan that was suppose to be top secret. They determined to punish those that didn' go along with their monopoly money program. On a date known only to base commanders, scrip would be declared useless within forty eight hours. Anyone havin' scrip had to exchange it for dollars within that time period or it would be useless to them. Local businesses had to get rid of their illegal scrip or they would be stuck with worthless funny money. Military personnel had the same time frame for their exchange. Well, weeks before the scheduled money exchange German merchants refused to take scrip for their goods or services. On several occasions Ah asked taxi drivers, "Was ist los?"

They told me that pretty soon scrip would be worthless. Somehow they knew what was goin' on. See what Ah mean about that stupid gene? Pop coulda told them that ya can't control people's behavior when money is involved.

Right after revelry one mornin' Ah was called to the captain's office for a special assignment. The secret day for the scrip exchange had arrived. This 2nd lieutenant asked for me to be one of his guards. Na Ah gotta tell ya a little bit about this guy. (Let's jus' call him Henry.) It was obvious to me that Henry had led a sheltered life. He was always askin' me about street fights, gangs, 'n' stuff like dat. Ah guess he thought ah could protect him and the money. Ah was honored and thankful for the opportunity to have some excitement. After a twenty-minute briefin', Ah checked out my rifle and two clips of ammo. The lieutenant and the briefcase full of U. S. dollars he was carryin' had to stay between myself and another guard. The money had to be in our sight at all times. We went to all Company C off-base houses exchangin' scrip for dollars. Everything went according to plan. Just thought Ah'd throw in a little cold war history.

DON'T THROW THAT GRENADE!

My Company C officers were pretty good guys. All three of um were either WW l l or Korean War vets. They knew how to keep our morale up. After all we were young men servin' our country in a foreign land far from home. These officers even had a policy that allowed enlisted men to buy cars. Ah took advantage of this policy and asked for permission to purchase a car. Ya see, Ma had bought a life insurance policy on me during the war. When it matured she cashed it in and sent me the two hundred dollars. Ah partnered up with a buddy and bought a 1945 Mercedes. As it turned out, we were the very last enlisted men allowed to own a car in Baumholder. Ah felt a little more connected to the civilized world. A car provided a way to get off the mountain and check out the area. Ah became popular overnight. Everybody wanted to be my friend. Ah wasn' lookin' for new friends. Ah kept the ones Ah could trust and count on. The U. S. occupation of Germany had just ended a few years earlier. A lot of Germans were still hostile towards us. Situations can unexpectedly crop up in an environment like this. Havin' a loyal friend who will cover your back is crucial for survival. My best friend Ralph was sent back to the states, leavin' me as the only somewhat fluid German speakin' American in company C. Ah could even read German pretty good. Ah often interpreted letters for guys with German girls or wives. Not bad for a misplaced coonass. Most weeknights Ah went to downtown Baumholder. This little town had twenty-six bars in an area less than a mile. Ya think a few problems could pop up in an atmosphere like this?

Ah made friends with a bunch of New York Italian guys and started hangin' out with them, kinda like in D. C. Funny, Ah didn' consider um Yankees. Anyways, one night we're sittin' around talkin' when Ah noticed this guy bein' a complete jerk with this waitress we knew. So, Ah went over to him and very politely told him to cool it. He jus' looked at me then he left the bar. Ah put the incident behind me 'n' and went back to dancin', drinkin' beer, and havin' a good time. All of a sudden the same guy comes in the front door holdin' a concussion trainin' hand grenade. Ah knew that a concussion grenade had explosives. It just doesn' have the shrapnel. But in a bar packed with soldiers it could cause devastation. Guys started jumpin' out of windows and duckin' under things for cover. His attention was focused on me, so Ah decided not to spook him. Ah gradually came towards him talkin' in a calm soft voice. Ah was sayin' all kinds of stuff, like "Hey man, you really don't want to hurt all these people do you?" Ah didn' know what to say or do. Ah just kept walkin' and talkin'. As Ah talked, Ah noticed that he was slowly backin' up towards a smaller room, so Ah kept goin'. He held the grenade high sayin', "I'll kill all of you f***ers." Well, he finally backed up a few steps into the smaller room. Ah didn' have any idea of what to do next. I had run out of options. All Ah could think of was to just keep on talkin'. Once again, God was with me. Yes, He will come into a bar to save your dumb ass. Two big guys wearin' suits, happened to be in the small room and ended up standin' right next to the guy. Na ya know what um gettin' at. What's the odds of them bein' right at that exact spot? In the blink of an eye, one of them slammed an open palm into the guy's chest, the other guy grabbed da grenade and kept the pin in so it wouldn' explode. The bad guy hit his head on a pinball machine and was out like a light. It was over in a matter of seconds. Ah took a few deep breaths to try n' calm down so ah could look cool goin' back to my table. It didn' work, ma legs were shakin' so much Ah could hardly walk. Yea, it's kinda hard to do that tough guy strut with shakin' legs. Ah didn' feel too bad. What about the guys that jumped out of windows? How cool was their walk back to their table? Ah heard a rumor that the two big suited guys were with the CIA. Who knows? Only thing Ah know f'sure is that God placed them there. About a week later Ah saw the bad guy in a prison uniform pickin' up trash on a roadside outside of town.

THE COLD WAR

Army life is all about routines. At times it seemed downright borin'. The 293'rd Combat Engineer's were not much different from the rest of the Army. However, our location in West Germany made some of our trainin' different from stateside or Far East trainin'. The Cold War with Russia was at its highest peak. The Soviet Union controlled East Germany at this time and our Army Intelligence had informed us that the Russians had nuclear missiles aimed right at us. We knew that strategically we would have a vital role to play in the event of a nuclear attack. Ah endured hours of classes learnin' how to survive an atomic attack and then get back into action. Also, the physical trainin' was gruelin'. Our battalion could and in trainin' would build pontoon bridges sturdy enough to support troops, trucks and even tanks. We had to accomplish all of this while combatin' sniper and enemy ground attacks. Na this trainin' was f' real. Blanks were used, but the sights, sounds, and smells of battle were as realistic as trainin' could get. Blanks can cause major damage at close range.

In addition to buildin' pontoon bridges, at least once a year in mid-winter we would go up into the mountains for mock combat maneuvers. Again, this was as real as it could get without actually bein' in combat. So ya get da picture. Mid-winter in the mountains of Germany. Ah was soooo cold! Didn' the Army know ah was a Southern boy? Ah mean didn' they hear da occasional "ya'll" and maybe a few other Southern words. Ya know what? Ah don't think the Army really cared if Ah was cold or not. Ah wanted to tell them, "Ya know God don't like ugly." Of course Ah didn' cause Mama Di Giovanni didn' raise no fools!

One night Ah was walkin' guard with a full clip of blanks in my rifle and Ah was cold! My shift ended, but my relief guy didn' show up. Ah walked over to his tent 'n' quietly told him. "Yo, you're on duty." (Remember we're under mock combat conditions.) The woods were alive with enemy soldiers. Ah waited about ten minutes. The guy still didn' show up so Ah waited a little longer. Still a no show. Na Ah'll be the first to admit that patience is not one of my virtues. So Ah marched over to his tent 'n' stuck my rifle muzzle about six inches from his face, softly speakin' (with maybe a hint of conviction), "If you don't get your ass out here right now Ah'm gonna start blastin'." Ya know what? He came out. He didn' even have his boots on!

Germany played a key role in the Cold War for several reasons. Both the United States and the Soviet Union threatened to use atomic bombs knowin' that both countries and possibly the rest of the world could be wiped out.

By the time Ah got on the scene the two sides were in a stand-off. Each side was tryin' to make the other one blink. We had classes instructin' us on the situation and the role we were to play in this deadly game of cat and mouse. My outfit played a vital role in the game. Therefore, we had to be combat ready at all times. The Army devised a plan called Alerts. An alert could and would be called at any time without warnin'. They went down like this. On any day at any hour of the day or night sirens and whistles would start blowin'. This meant you had exactly one hour to put everything needed for combat into your duffle bag and go across the street to check out your rifle then board trucks and take off for a secret location known only to officers. We never knew where we were goin'; if it was a real attack or just trainin'. Every alert was treated like the real thing. We understood that the balance of world power and our way of life depended on the U. S. Military. We had to remain combat-ready until an officer informed us that the alert was over. This could take hours or even days. Na ya may be thinkin' that doesn't seem so tough to me. But what if you happened to be out really late the night before tippin' a few brews. Ya come in around 2:30 in the morning and an alert is called at 3:00 AM. Yeah, this could make ya wanna kill somebody f' sure.

The cold war is a prime example of the best way to win a fight or war. The best way to win a fight is not to fight at all. Na don't get me wrong, ya have to be ready, willin', and able to battle, and your enemy must be convinced that your fightin' spirit will not waiver. Ya can destroy a country or a person's will to fight and you win without suffering any damage at all. My part in this epic battle of wills was small but Ah'm honored to have been part of it. We didn' blink. Now Ah have li'l lagniappe for ya. Don't fight for anything you're not willin' to die for. Yeah you rite. Ah learned this the hard way.

GOOD OFFICER, BAD OFFICER

Ah could sense big-time changes comin' when my Captain retired. Then the Lieutenant under him cycled back to the States. A few months later our First Sergeant also retired. Boy was Ah right. Changes were loomin'. We got a new Captain that Ah woulda swore was a combination of Military Academy 'n' Nazi SS prison guard graduate. This guy was a combat veteran from the Korean War. Na Ah valued and highly respected his combat experience, but that was it. His idea of leadership was to break the individual's spirit then take complete control of them. He may have learned some of those techniques when he was in a North Korean prison camp. He escaped by cuttin' a guard's head off with a sickle that he was usin' to cut grass. The First Lieutenant under him agreed with the Captains prison style of control techniques. It was a toss up as to which one was the biggest control freak. Addin' to the misery, some of our Sergeants fell right in line with them. Ah wanted to say to them, "Looka here fellas. Doncha know we're on the same side?" Na Ah don't know exactly what it is inside of me that won't allow me to buckle under that type of bullyin'. All Ah know is that Ah can't. Ah won't let my spirit be broken. Maby it's in my DNA. Maybe it's my Roman heritage. Aw come on now it could be. My mind and body sensed the impendin' battle that was sure to come. Ya know what um sayin. Like right before a big game or fight.

The first skirmish was over my car. They tried to take it away! Ah had a legal team that consisted of two guys who went through ten weeks of MP trainin' 'n' a black twenty year veteran of many internal battles. Actin' on advice from them Ah contacted the battalion commander's office 'n' asked them for help. Sure enough, Ah found out that it wasn' legal for Captain Bligh to take my car away. Ya see the Battalion Commander was the one that ok'd my request for a car. My officers were not about to question his decision. Na ya gotta know this put a briar under the Captain's saddle. He went ballistic. No enlisted man had ever questioned his authority. Never in his entire career. Ah know this 'cause he told me so in the course of chewin' me out. Ah felt like tellin' him. "Ah won! Ah won! Na na na na na." Real mature response right? Of course Ah didn' '. Thinking about what he did to that North Korean guard, I realized this fight wasn' over. This was gonna be a long war. My three antagonists were holdin' all the high cards. They had the authority, power, 'n' the ability to make my life miserable. Only things Ah had were survival instincts, tenacity, 'n' a free will that would not be tamed. Why is all this so important you ask? Looka, if you lose a fight over material things like land, oil, money or somethin' immaterial like pride, you've only lost things that can be replaced or gotten over. But, if you lose the war of wills, ideology, or spirit, you've lost the essence of your bein', the core of your nature, things which make you the unique individual that you are. There would be no compromise; one of us was gonna win this battle.

The next skirmish started over hair cuts. Lieutenant Schultz (not his real name) told me Ah needed a haircut. OK. Fair enough. Right away Ah went to my legal team for advice. They checked out Army haircut regulations for enlisted men assigned to their permanent duty stations. The regulation was one and a quarter inches. So Ah went to the barber shop with a ruler and had the barber measure, then cut my hair exactly one and a quarter inches. If ya think that's extreme remember this was not about haircuts, it was about breaking my will.

Our job at this time was buildin' roads jus' a few miles outside of Baumholder. Ah was actually breakin' up large rocks with a sledgehammer. Ah'm not kiddin'. Just like ya see prisoners doin' in the movies; only thing missin' were ankle shackles. The work was hard but not a problem for me 'cause Ah always managed to have some fun. Ah was also able to stay away from the big brass for about two months. However one day my Lieutenant drove to the job site in his bran new German car 'n' he jus' happened to park near my work area. Big mistake. Ah called over a couple of friends 'n' told them to follow my lead. Then Ah proceeded to swing my sledge hammer like a golf club. This maneuver sent rock chips flyin' right into the side of the Lieutenant's new car. He heard the thumpin' sounds, 'n' turned around slowly like he was in a daze. There was this kinda sick look on his face. When he saw me he snapped back to the moment, then he bellowed, "Sergeant get that man over here now!"

Ah was called to attention as Ah approached him. First thing he said was, "Soldier, take off your hat." Then, "You need a haircut. Get one."

"Yes sir!" Ah answered.

Then he lost it again. "Soldier! Didn't you see my car? Bla bla bla, 'n' more blas."

All the while um thinkin', "Sure Ah saw your car. Ah hit it didn't I?" Starin' right into his eyes Ah answered, "Jus' tryin' to do my job, Sir!" Ah thought it would be wise to steer clear of this guy for a long time. No brainer right?

Before long the rock breakin' road buildin' project ended. Days were gettin' warmer, signalin' the onset of summer. This stirred up fond memories of Little Woods and the ice route. Ah was homesick again. Ah longed for the cool lake breeze 'n' daily adventures. Ah heard rumors that we were goin' to France for the summer.

This was music to my ears. Ah needed a change. My chain gang projects were gettin' old. Boy, did Ah get changes or what? Ya ever hear that ol sayin' "Don't wish too hard for somethin', ya just might get it? Yeah, well Ah got it all right. Seems that several veteran motor pool drivers put in for transfers to other companies or job assignments. Ya see, French road laws were very different from those in Germany. Matter of fact, everything about France was different from Germany. The French Treaty, or agreement. Ah'm not sure which, stated that military drivers involved in an accident could be held in France until their trial in court came up. This could take a year or more. Makes ya wonder what kind of negotiators we have. Ah mean who are they lookin' out for? That's not all. We also had to change our vehicle lights from white to amber, and on top of that we had to remove our mounted machine guns from all of our vehicles. Strong military stuff upsets the French. Does any of this make sense to you? Is it jus' me thinkin' that we liberated these guys usin' guns, tanks, and bombs? Now military things upsets them! We were in the middle of a Cold War that simply had to be won and leaders from the U. S. and France were wastin' our time changin' head light colors and disarming our combat trucks. Unbelieveable! Anyway, Company C needed to fill driver positions that no one wanted. Guess who they forced" into these positions? Yeah you rite. Me 'n' two of my buddies. Ah suspected that both of my commandin' officers woulda been happy if Ah was held in France forever or at least until they retired. These guys were actin' ugly again 'n' you know God don't like ugly.

In spite of their evil intentions Ah still kinda lucked out. The motor pool sergeant had seen my drivin' skills in Germany. He chose me to drive for him 'n' the head mechanic. Ah think the fact Ah didn't mind stoppin' for a brew every now 'n' then contributed to his decision. Wow, what a stroke of luck! This was great.

Movin' people, supplies, vehicles and equipment six hundred miles is an enormous task. There were months of preparation, trainin' and, of course, changin' to those friggin' amber headlights.

SUMMER IN FRANCE

The mechanic Jeep was usually the last vehicle in our section of the convoy. Whenever there was a breakdown we would see the vehicle on the roadside and make the necessary repairs. More luck, our Motor Pool Sergeant received orders for him to go down a few weeks ahead of us to prepare our new maintenance shop for the onslaught of vehicles that was sure to come. This was good news. Ah didn' even have a Sergeant to worry about. There was just a mechanic and me in my Jeep. Ya see, a convoy moves at such a slow speed it becomes maddenin', especially for type A people. The mechanic and I made a plan to avoid travelin' at the convoy's snail's pace. Ah asked my truck driver friends to have fake breakdowns. The scheme was for them to alternate breakdowns, always near a gasthaus. This way we could let the convoy pass by us while we were havin' a few brews. Afterward, we could drive sixty or so miles an hour and catch up with the convoy. (Yeah, you rite again. Shouldna' been drinkin' and drivin'. Ya'll have to remember, Ah wasn' a Christian at this time.)

When we finally arrived at our camp site near Bussac, France my heart sank. There was nothin' around but tents! Ah thought, ya gotta be kiddn', This is my new home? What a let down. There wasn' a town anywhere in sight, just tents!

Drivin' the motor pool Jeep turned out to be a pretty good job after all. It gave me a sense of freedom, an escape from the humdrum construction site and the evil lieutenant. Ah wanna tell ya, Ah kept my Jeep lookin' good. Ah washed 'n' waxed it at least once a week; even waxed under the front fenders. Ah happened to make friends with a new Hispanic kid from Texas. This guy was the best artist Ah ever saw. So one day Ah asked him if he would paint a tiger on my metal spare tire holder. Ya see one of my Uncles nicknamed me Tiger when Ah as very young. My new friend exceeded my expectations. He was an amazin' artist f' true. In his spare time, he painted the most beautiful tiger head ya can imagine. On a white background he painted a large yellow, black striped tiger head that was growlin', teeth showing 'n' all. My jeep was without a doubt the best lookin' one in the entire battalion.

Dontcha know the Lieutenant saw my tiger and ordered the Motor Pool Sergeant to take the tiger off of my Jeep and put it on his Jeep. How petty can ya get? This really took the wind out of my sails for a while, but not for long because Ah managed to find a city where the good times were rollin'. Bordeaux is a little over an hour's drive from Bussac but well worth the drive. Bordeaux had a swingin' nightlife and nearby beaches on the Atlantic Coast.

Sergeants and officers were allowed to drive their cars to Bordeaux if they wanted to. Only a few of them did cause of the crazy French drivin' laws. My padna Lyle and I were the only peons who had a car. We managed to get our car down to tent city because our Sergeant was goin' down a few days ahead of us 'n' needed a ride. Of course Ah couldn' drive him because of my mandatory drivin' assignment so my padna Lyle drove him in our car. There were no busses, 'n' taxies were too expensive. Boy did that car ever come in handy.

Ah guess ah wasn' payin' attention in the preparation classes given prior to leavin' Germany 'cause Ah was only vaguely aware of the struggle between the Algerians livin' in France and the French government. Because of our involvement with France, the Algerians hated us as well. In fact, right before we got there an American sergeant was murdered simply because he strayed into the Algerian section of town. Due to the tension between the groups, certain sections of town were off limits to us. One night we were tryin' to find this club we'd heard about. Not havin' any luck findin' it, we parked the car and hailed a cab. Unbeknownst to us, the cabbie took us to an off-limits bar, dropped us off and left. So we bopped into what we thought was an American hangout only to discover a room full of Algerian men. Immediately the room fell silent, signalin' danger. (Danger! High alert! Be vigilant!) Na it's a good thing the French barmaid was sharp and street wise. In less than a minute she came over 'n' whispered in very good English "I already called a taxi for you. Don't turn around. Just talk softly to me. When your cab gets here leave quickly through the side door, and watch your back as you leave." Ah slowly fingered the new ten-inch switchblade Ah had recently purchased here in France, but it offered little comfort 'cause Ah knew f'sure, ya can't bring a knife to a gunfight. Within minutes the cab honked. Good thing cause the natives were getting' restless. Tryin' our best to not draw attention to our movements, we slid out the door into the waitin' cab. All of us shoved a handful of bills into our courageous bar maid's apron pocket. If she hadn' called that cab as quick as she did, Ah probably wouldn' be writin' this story. Na who ya think put that barmaid in the right spot at the exact time we needed her? Come on you unbelievers, think about it.

Company C was assigned a warehouse buildin' project. Ah'm not sure, but Ah think this tent city was gonna become a military base of some sort. There was nothin' but borin' work and routine army stuff. However, nights in Bordeaux were packed with good times. There were a few assignments ya may find interestin'. No matter, um gonna tell ya about um anyway. We needed more heavy equipment so they assigned me with the task of goin' back to Germany to get it. My orders were to lead a convoy of heavy equipment from Germany back to our base in France.

We were in the mess hall eating breakfast a few hours before Ah was to when one of my friends leaned over whisperin', "DEE, the Lieutenant just came in." Ah jumped up 'n' started to leave, but it was too late. He already spotted me. There was no place to hide. This guy was determined to break my spirit. He walked directly up to me and said, "Soldier you need a haircut!" The nerve of that guy. He didn' use my name, or give a friendly greeting like wah ya at? or anything. Ah answered "Sir Ah just got a regulation haircut yesterday." His face got all red ya know kinda like a spoiled kid. So then he called a Sergeant over, stood me at attention, and said. "Sergeant you are my witness. I'm giving this man a direct order to get a haircut just like mine." (His head was shaved!) Ah couldn' let this slide, Ah answered. "Ya want me to dye my hair blonde too?" Now there was the red face face plus some veins swellin' in his neck. Yeah, and he was growlin' again. "I'm ordering you to get a haircut just like mine before you come back to France." Then he stormed out. Ah'm glad this didn' go on much longer 'cause ah probably woulda started laughin'. Ah mean with his face all red 'n' all. Ah wanted to say, "Whatsa matter boopy couldn' get your way?" Na Ah knew there was fear down in me somewhere. Ah just couldn' bring it up to the surface. The whole thing was just too funny. My friends and legal team all counseled me. The general consensus was that Ah should get the haircut. Ya see, disobeyin' a direct order is serious. Ya could end up in the brig.

Ah had a lot to think about on that long drive back to Baumholder. My choices were few. Buckle under and get a shaved head, or don't get a haircut, keep my indestructible free spirit and risk the loss of my physical freedom. What to do? Soon the sights and sounds of the open road distracted me from my plight. Ah think Ah only spent one night in Germany. Early the next morning ah was headin' back to France. This time leadin' a small convoy of heavy equipment. Ah guess my thoughts were kinda muddled because of my impendin' decision and the confrontation that was sure to follow. Somehow Ah took a wrong turn. The entire convoy followed. So now these big trucks loaded with tons of heavy equipment were on a narrow road somewhere in Germany. To top it off, there wasn' enough room on the road sides for these big trucks to turn around. There were no choices. We had to plow on straight ahead. After an hour or so we came to a wooden bridge where another unforeseen problem popped up. A German guard stopped us at the bridge. Speaking German, he explained that the bridge was not strong enough to support the weight of our big trucks. Ah tried to explain our quandary, but he kept waving his arms sayin, "Nein Nein." Then he happened to see my name tag, "Bis du Italiana?" He asked. "Das stimmt," Ah answered. That was all it took. We became bro's instantly. My new friend started tellin' me war stories about his time in Italy. This guy was an ex-German paratrooper stationed in Italy durin' the war. He told about the time he was in the town square when suddenly American planes swooped down firin' machine guns and droppin' bombs. He managed to find cover in a wine cellar. All he seemed to remember was how good the wine tasted. Meanwhile Ah was catching a lot of flack from the truck drivers. They were grumblin' about bein' stuck on the wrong road and me killin' time talkin' to comrade. Ah heard stuff like. "Yo Dee, what's going on? Stop talking to the comrade and get us out of here." For me, this was a rare opportunity to hear war stories from the other side. Ah had to take advantage of it. However we were runnin' out of daylight. So Ah reluctantly talked my comrade into lettin' us cross the bridge. He took a big chance doin' this. Maybe he was still thinkin' about the Italian wine. We had to inch the trucks across one at a time while my new friend checked the support beams. This took over an hour, but guess what? The road turned out to be a shortcut leadin' right to the highway that we needed. We had to make one last stop for gas, food, and a little break. Ah led my convoy to a nearby air force base that had everythin' we needed. Even a barbershop. Time had run out for me. Our convoy was just a few hours outside of Bussac. It was time for a gut check. Ah had to make my decision. My friends were still lookin' out for me. They kept urgin' me to get a haircut. They said, "Dee, this is your last chance. Get the haircut. Ya can't disobey a direct order!"

All along, Ah kinda knew what my decision would be, Ah just couldn' give in. After all, Ah did have a regulation haircut. Ah had to do what Ah thought Ah was morally bound to do. Ah just couldn' go along with this injustice. Ah blurted out, "Ah'm not gonna get a haircut." Ah tried to explain this to my friends in language that they understood. Ah said, "Ya see, Ah'm a warrior. The United States Army says so. They spent a lot of time and money trainin' me. Ah'm trained to resist at all times, even in captivity." So Ah considered this part of my trainin'. It was late by the time we got back to Bussac. Ah just parked my Jeep, slipped into my tent, crawled in my bunk, and tried to sleep.

Ah always got up early so Ah could avoid the shrill piercin' sound of the wake-up whistle. After Reveille Ah headed down the wooden walkway towards our outhouse-type latrine. As Ah passed the Headquarters tent Ah heard someone say, "There he goes now." Even though Ah quickened my step, Ah couldn' get away fast enough. Someone rushed out and shouted, "Stop!"

Then the Lieutenant bellowed, "Ah-tenn-chun! Get back here soldier!"

When Ah entered the tent Ah saw all of my antagonists sittin' there starin' at me. None of them looked happy. Ah felt like a mouse in a snake pit.

My Lieutenant broke the silence sayin', "Captain, I gave this man a direct order to get a haircut. The Sergeant here is my witness."

It was the captain's turn to strike. "Soldier did you get a haircut?"

"Me? No Sir."

"I wish I could bust you down a pay grade, but I can't."

Because of my previous National Guard service, Ah was awarded the permanent rank and paygrade of PFC 2nd class. It would take an act of Congress to take that away. He went on, "You will cut grass with a hand sickle" (Ah wanted to tell him don't tempt me. Remember what you did with a sickle). "And when we get back to Germany you're no longer a Jeep driver." He still wasn' done. He shouted for the on duty guard, then they force marched me to my Jeep. Ah was under the control of an armed guard, with my Lieutenant and a Sergeant backin' him up. What a sight that musta been. People probably thought Ah was some hardened criminal or somethin'. Ah was directed to drive the whole entourage to the barber shop. Na Ah had already consulted my legal team on previous occasions, so Ah knew all the military regulations concernin' haircuts. Anyways, when we arrived at the barbershop Ah was ordered out and escorted under guard into the shop. The French barbers didn' know what da heck was goin' on. They looked at the rifle first, then the guard, then me. As the barber cautiously slipped an apron over me, he asked, "Monsieur how would you like your haircut?" Before my Lieutenant could answer, Ah said, "Oh just a light trim around the sides." (Ah just couldn' resist sayin' dat. Ah tried, but Ah jus' couldn'.) Then there was that red face and bulgin' neck veins again. Strugglin' to compose himself he took off his hat while growlin', "Cut his hair just like mine." Ah had to back off cause Ah could sense that the good Lieutenant woulda' happily told the guard to shoot me if he thought he could get away with it. After my head was shaved, Ah jumped out of the chair and tried to pay for my own haircut. (Ya see, Ah knew that a soldier couldn' be forced to get a non regulation haircut and pay for it himself.) My Lieutenant was smart; he also knew this. So he pulled out money as well. It was like a Three Stooges routine. Ah would say Ah'll pay, then Schultz would push my hand away, sayin' "No, no, I'll pay." This comic scene went on for several rounds before Ah was ordered to attention. He ended up payin'. Yeah Ah know Ah lost this round, but Ah promised myself Ah'd land some powerful punches in the next round.

It took a few weeks for me to get used to my new routine. Ah had to adjust to the physical and mental aspects of workin' all day then cuttin' grass by hand with a full backpack on after work. In spite of all this, Ah still managed to sneak off to Bordeaux every now and then.

My grass cuttin' punishment continued for the rest of my stay in Bussac. Ah was happy when it was time to say goodbye to France, my grass cuttin' detail, and tent city as well. On the trip back to Germany we used the same breakdown in front of a gasthaus trick that we had used goin' down to Bussac. On our second breakdown this officer from another company pulled over to investigate. Good thing our mechanic was a wise ol' veteran. He had already disabled the vehicle. The meddlesome officer was suspicious. He poked around, asked questions, looked under the hood (ya know like guys do). He didn' know anything about trucks. Ah know this cause' he kept lookin' under the hood utterin', "hummmm." Anytime a guy does that, he doesn' know what the hell he's lookin' at. Then he gave us a wary look and asked, "How come every time there's a breakdown it's always right in front of a gasthaus?" We answered almost in unison, "Don't know sir. They break down, we fix um." Finally he left. Then it was back to soakin' up the local culture, makin' new friends, and maybe havin' a few German brews. We spent one night on an Air Force base then it was a straight shot back home to Germany. Did Ah say home? Ah was startin' to feel like Germany was my home. Memories of my home town became vague 'n' somewhat distant. It was hard for me to see and feel the sights and sounds of New Orlans. If ya ever been away from home for a long time, ya know what um sayin'. All of this was really confusin' me. First Ah was sooo homesick Ah could hardly cope. Now Ah struggled to remember what home was like. Was Ah losin' my sensitive nature? If Ah was, then who was ah becomin'? Most of you know that it takes years of yoga trainin' to live in the now. Years after my Army discharge Ah practiced yoga for over forty years tryin' to master bein' in the now. Then it came to me. Ah realized Ah had already learned to live in the here and now durin' my almost twentyeight month's tour of duty overseas. The military forced me into the now years before it became popular.

THE ATOMIC LETTERS

A short time after our arrival back in Germany my legal team went to work for me. Moon (this was his nickname 'cause he had a crescent moon shape on his gold tooth) said, "They can't force you to get a shaved head. It jus' don't seem right." So my guys hit the books. There was one last resort for me to consider. We referred to it as the nuclear option. Ah could write two letters. One to the Secretary of Defense, the other to my congressman from Louisiana, Representative Hebert (pronounced aa bhah. With a name like dat, ah knew he would help a home boy.) Moon said, "Do it. Write the letters! They can't continue treating people like dogs." The other team members were a lot more skeptical. Both of them said, "If you write those letters, all hell's gonna break loose." Ah thought it over for about ten seconds, 'n' ah wrote the letters.

Our next big buildin' project was in Wiesbaden Germany. We were sent there to help build 'n' test jump towers that were to be used for paratrooper trainin'. Wiesbaden turned out to be my favorite city in all of Europe. Ah loved the town and the people. One of my German friends told me about this pizza place that was a young person's hangout. Along with beer 'n' pizza ya could dance 'n' meet frauleins (young unmarried women). It was a great place to mingle with the locals. My ability to communicate in their native language gave me an in with the popular crowd. Ah often wonder if Ah speak German with a New Orlans accent. Whadda ya'll think? Since Ah've already deviated from my story Ah'll ask ya to bear with me a little longer so Ah can throw a little tidbit in. You won't find any detailed romance in any of my stories. My reason is simple. A real Southern Gentleman doesn't kiss and tell or even talk much about matters of the heart. Some of you may wonder if Ah'm a fighter or a lover. Allow me to clear it up for ya. Ah'm a little of both.

Even though Ma has been gone for years Ah still write thinkin' that she might read some of my stories. Who knows, she might.

Now back to my story. True to his word the Captain took my Jeep away from me. Ah was now a truck driver. Ah was assigned to drive a two-and-a-half-ton troop transport truck. Ah really didn' care that much about losin' my Jeep, Ah still had my car, and there were those fun packed nights in Wiesbaden.

Drivin' trucks on the narrow German roads was a piece of cake for me. Remember when Ah was fifteen years old Ah learned to drive an ice truck loaded with two and a half tons of ice on the narrow streets of New Orlans. The transition to drivin' on German roads was easy. However, a lot of our drivers had a hard time adaptin' to the European drivin' laws, road conditions and drivers. There were a lot of accidents causin' problems with the locals. Thank God Ah never had a single accident in my entire tour of duty. Na as Ah said before the motor pool sergeant respected my drivin' abilities. He didn' care about haircuts or the battle between the brass and me. He just wanted an end to the frequent accidents. (You have no idea of the problems that an accident with a local can cause. In some cases it became an international incident.) Remember the war was still fresh in the minds of many Germans. A lot of them lost friends, relatives, and property in the war. Most of these people weren't too crazy about Americans to begin with. Na Ah'm gonna pat myself on the back a little. Ah'm grateful that Ah was in a place and time where Ah could play a small part in their healin'. On the other hand, there were also a few instances when Ah was definitely not a good diplomat. So Ah guess it kinda evens out.

There were some people on our side that were still hostile towards the Germans. They had suffered losses and fought bitter battles with the German Army. They still considered locals the enemy. One of our sergeants still holdin' a grudge purposely ran over and killed a German motorcyclist. Some on both sides just couldn' let go of the hatred that was housed in their hearts.

We actually had two projects in Wiesbaden. One was erectin' the practice jump towers and the other was buildin' a giant dirt wall. This was needed to protect a German cemetery from the base firin' range. Somehow bullets were gettin' past the current barrier and hittin' head stones in the cemetery. Not good for public relations, f'sure.

My job was to transport troops from our base to the job sites, pick up and deliver supplies and tools and haul our work crews back to camp at the end of the day. Ah couldn' believe they gave me such an easy assignment. Ah had lot of down time so Ah built fires for the guys (warm up breaks were necessary for troop moral). Before long, German pre-teens and teenagers would gather around the fire after school. Most of them wanted to know about America. Some wanted an American friend; others were tryin' to figure out how we beat them in the war. These fireside discussions allowed me access into the hearts and minds of these post-war kids. Ah realized that these young people were Germany's future. They were going to have to rebuild their country. More importantly, this generation needed to change the entire German government and mindset. Ah had to allow them to be proud of their country, but understand that Hitler and the whole Nazi movement was wrong. Most of them had friends and relatives that were heavily involved in the war. Some had brothers and sisters that grew up in the Hitler youth programs. One kid even brought me some medals and ribbons their relatives had received for bein' good Natzis. These items were forbidden for Germans to possess. The trust that these kids put in me really tugged at my heart. Ah had no idea that these young Germans were givin' me tools Ah would use in the future. Ya see, many, many years later Ah served nine years as the youth director for a church in Western Montana. Ah worked with a lot of kids that had problems: drug problems, family issues' and a few were bein' bullied. Ah offered all of um martial arts trainin'. On Wednesday nights 'n' Sunday mornins' Ah taught Bible classes to junior 'n' senior high school youths. This was the best thing Ah ever did. Looka here, only God can take an ol coonass out of the swamps, of Louisiana send him to Germany for part of his education. Then a lifetime later place him in the mountains of Montana to help teenagers. Yeah Ah know um preachin' again, jus' couldn' help it.

Let's get back to Germany. One day the good Lieutenant saw me havin' one of my fireside chats with the German youths. He didn' like what he saw so he ordered them off of the job site. Soon after, he went to my Sergeant and insisted that he have me work with the crew whenever Ah wasn' drivin'. The kids still snuck onto the job site to say hello and talk a li'l before being run off. Sadly, my heart to heart fireside chats ended. The Lieutenant won another round. The fireside chats were over, but the fight wasn'.

Ah already told ya that Ah was trained to defend my country against any foreign or domestic enemy any time or place in the world, but defendin' myself against my own brass presented a whole other problem. Ah had to think outside of the box again. Ah had to use my street smarts. My thoughts drifted back to my ol' friend Jack. Once when asked why he fought this whole gang all by himself, his unemotional reply was "There were only fav' or six little ones." My problem was a lot different. There were fav' or six big ones. Ah had to figure out how to defeat them. Ah fell back into my routine easily. Drive the troops, build jump towers all day and slip off to Wiesbaden at night.

Gettin' off and then back on base was challengin' for me. Ya see, Ah seldom had a pass. So if Ah couldn' borrow one Ah had to find a way to leave and return without bein' seen. Not an easy task because this base had very tight security and there was a twelve foot fence with barbed wire on top surroundin' the entire area. Also, armed guards walked the perimeter. Ah don't know why this Air Force base was so security-minded, but they were. So here's what Ah did. Ah noticed a gap about a foot wide between a seldom-used locked gate and the main fence post. All fences with gates have to be built this way to allow room for the gate to open. Ah learned this from my high school fence buildin' job. First Ah had to scout the area to find the most remote spot with the widest gap between the gate post and the fence, then Ah had to note how much time there was when the guard wasn' in sight. Ah discovered that we had about three minutes to stay out of sight by hidin' in the shadows, scale the fence and disappear into the night. My two cohorts needed a little convincin'. So this is how Ah laid it out to them. Ah explained to them that we would be takin' our trainin' to another level. Then Ah asked "How can we better test our combat skills?" Na Ah was on a roll. "Trainin' is kinda like football practice. You can't know if a play will really work until you try it in a game. This is as real as it gets short of actual combat." Pretty convincin' right? You probably woulda scaled that fence right along with me. Wouldn' ya? Ah purposely left out a few minor details, like ya could get shot or end up in the brig. Yeah you right maybe Ah didn' think this one all the way through. But Ah had to see if Ah could do it.

Leavin' camp went as planned, except for one small problem. One of my guys, Tommy, caught his pant leg on the barbed wire, requirin' him to rip his pants to get free. We kept out of sight for a coupla' blocks, before hailin' a cab. After a night out on the town we headed back to camp. Gettin' back into camp tripled the risk. Wadda ya think the guards would do to three guys without a pass tryin' to get on a secure base after bed check? We managed to get back into camp without bein' seen. So much for tight security!

When the jump towers were finished Company C volunteered to do the first test jumps. Ah'm tellin' ya, this was the most fun Ah'd had since the obstacle course in basic trainin'. First there was a thirty-five foot free fall (the impact was equivalent to a parachute openin'), next about a two hundred foot zip line ride. One Saturday Ah spent the entire day jumpin'.

Our mission was complete. It was time to head back to Baumholder for winter combat maneuvers. Our outfit moved around a lot. It seemed like every time Ah started makin' new friends, we had to leave. The same thing often happened with friends in my outfit. Guys were constantly goin' back to the world (America).

Winter was comin' in like a lion. Our convoy trucks were havin' a hard time navigatin' the narrow icy roads resulting in several accidents. The most tragic one was when a tractor trailer carryin' heavy equipment slipped off the road and rolled down an embankment landin' upside down. One soldier was killed, another badly injured. Thank God Ah managed to get my troops back safely. Ah had a hard time sleepin' that night. Ah couldn' help thinkin' about my dead comrade 'n' his family. Losin' a son in a war without bullets had to be a horrifyin' nightmare.

WAR GAMES

When we got back to Baumholder we attended classes on atomic warfare for about three or four weeks. Then it was off to the mountains for war games. Once again Ah found myself on a freezin' cold mountain, except this time Ah was in the midsts of the most realistic combat you can imagine. High rankin' Officers from all over Europe were there to observe 'n' grade us. Machine guns, small arms fire, 'n' explosions were heard night and day.

The Army was serious about these games. Of course we were usin' blanks, but the whole scene felt real. If someone was shot or captured letters were written, but not sent to their parents. One night while on guard duty Ah captured two enemy soldiers. As Ah was gettin' ready to take them back to headquarters, one of them turned to me sayin' "DEE, it's me Lionel." He said, "Listen I have a smoke grenade. Let me go throw it in the Lieutenant's tent." Na ya gotta know Ah just couldn' forget about my private war with the Army. Ah remembered my shaved head and cuttin' grass after work every day. Ah thought it over for about a minute. Then Ah not only let him proceed, Ah gave him the password and pointed out the Lieutenant's tent to him. Lionel was a good and loyal friend. He managed to smoke the Lieutenant out of his tent all right, but the guards caught him. Needless to say, the good Lieutenant was way past furious. He was out of control, probably havin' flashbacks to Korea. He smashed Lionel into the ground then slapped him around. After that they started interrogatin' him. They were smart enough to know he couldna' got through the guard stations without the password. When the guards were questioned they all said he gave them the correct password and response. No matter how long they questioned him Lionel wouldn' talk. For the life of me, Ah can't remember what they did to him for punishment, but whatever it was, Ah'm sure they wished it was me.

All in all, the war games were a success. My team put a machine gun nest out of commission, killed or captured boo coo enemy troops and, to top it off, Ah got in a good shot at the Lieutenant. Ah came away from those games knowin' that Ah could inflict damage on the enemy and still survive in combat.

After we arrived back in Baumholder our atomic warfare classes resumed. The Soviet Union hadn' blinked yet we had to stay combat-ready. Most Americans don't realize how crucial the Cold War was. Our presence in Europe was the only thing stoppin' the spread of Russia's evil empire. Thank God our leaders at that time had the courage to stand firm. This is why Ah need ya to know that no nation or individual can allow their spirit or will to be broken. Russian leaders underestimated our resolve. Nikita Khrushchev said, "I will defeat you without firing a shot." He was wrong. We stood firm. Yeah you rite, um preachin' again. Ah really shoulda been a preacher.

All U. S. troops and bases were prime targets for Soviet atomic missiles. We had to be combat ready, and we were. Our survivin' an atomic attack and gettin' back into the battle was crucial for both Europe and America.

These are some of the reasons our alerts allowed us only one hour to be combat ready. And rendezvous places were kept top secret. This would be the time for all of us to put aside our petty grievances and fight as a unit. However, in the midst of a battle Ah would have to take my helmet off and show the Lieutenant that Ah could destroy the enemy without havin' a shaved head. Of course Ah would hafta add. "Yo bra. Keep your rifle pointed in the the other direction."

THE RUSSIANS ARE COMING!

About two months after our arrival back in Baumholder an alert was called. The alarms went off at about 4:30 AM. Well Ah had just gotten back from Wiesbaden about 3:15. Ah was tired and a little dizzy from a long night out on the town. No matter, not bein' combat ready for an alert was a court martial offence. By the time Ah got to the motor pool, a little dizzy had grown into a full-blown throbbin' headache. Between throbs Ah heard a calm voice say, "Young man you're gonna' be my driver today." It was the kind ol' Warrant Officer that often spoke to me when Ah was on my grass cuttin' detail in France. Ah managed to get my pain racked body into his Jeep. "Yes sir! Thank you sir." Ah was thankful for the easy assignment. Everything seemed fuzzy, but Ah had no choice. Ah had to press on. Ah managed to squeeze my Jeep into the already movin' line of vehicles. Within a short time the movement caused my stomach to churn. Na Ah was really miserable. Ah managed to drive a few more miles before my achin' body forced me to say, "Sir, Ah gotta pull over!" By the time Ah was able to drive again, the entire convoy had sped past us. It was barely daylight and Ah had already committed at least three court martial offences. Na Ah didn' know whether or not Russian missiles were on their way, but at this point Ah thought, If they are, please let one score a direct hit on my achin' head. Ah mean, it couldn' cause any more pain than Ah already had. To my surprise, Ah heard the calm voice again. "Rough night son?" Ah managed to answer, "Yes sir." He continued, "yeah Ah know how it is. Been there once or twice myself. Don't worry, Ah know where the convoy is going and ah know what you need to get ya up and running again." A short distance up the road, he said "Pull over here." Ah was never so happy to see a gasthaus in my life. Once inside, he ordered me a steak 'n' egg breakfast, coffee, and a big glass of water. Within an hour Ah was back. Ma head cleared and my stomach settled down. Ah promised myself Ah would never drink again. (Did you ever make that promise after a night of drinkin'?) Then we were able to get back on the road. As Ah sped along, my new friend spoke to me like a father. "Ah know what you're going through, son. Our brass and some Sergeants are a bunch of knuckleheads. They talk down to everyone and ah often overhear a lot of racial comments. Ah admire your courage, and ah hope ya can beat that whole bunch. Ah would like to help you, but ah just can't. Ya see ah'm about to retire with thirty-five years of service. Ah owe it to my family not to mess up now." "Ah understand Sir. You've done a lot already." Then he added, "Be careful, they're out to get you." This was the information and encouragement that Ah needed. Ah knew from the beginnin' that Ah was rite about those guys. My fightin' spirit was renewed and strengthened. We arrived at the rendezvous spot and blended in with the main body.

As the day wore on my strength returned, Ah was ready to face whatever came my way. Captains, enemy troops, atomic missiles, macht nichts (doesn't matter), to me. OK, maybe not the missiles, but Ah was ready for the rest of um. The next mornin' before breakfast Ah noticed that one of our Sergeants brought some boxin' gloves to help us cope with the tension and boredom. When Ah saw those gloves, Ah jumped up and rushed over to the group that was gatherin'. Ah dove right into the action, sparrin' with any and all willin' participants. There's somethin' about the sweet art of boxin' that relaxes ya. Slippin' punches and firin' back with quick combinations jus' makes ya feel good. After breakfast, we played a game of tackle football. This also was right up my alley. Boxin' and good ol' smash mouth football are good ways to let off steam and kill time. These activities brought back familiar warm feelings from what now seemed like the distant past. In the midst of my sparrin' sessions, my mind drifted back to Saint Mary's Italian, Ralph, Willie, and Mr. Whitey. Thinkin' about my three dollar prize money made me laugh 'n' almost cry at the same time. When all of the activities died down, Ah realized Ah was home sick again. Ah became aware of the fact that those excitin' years were gone forever. Ah was growin' up in a foreign land that at times felt like my new home. However there was a part of me that would always be Ninth Ward. Ah knew that these duelin' emotions would take a very long time to sort out. Ah also knew for certain Ah couldn' delve into my feelins' on a mountain top in Germany waitin' for a Soviet missile attack.

Ah was brought back to the now by a Sergeant tellin' me that all of the big brass were impressed by my athletic abilities. Somehow they got the impression that Ah was just some sort of trouble makin' bonehead. They didn' know me or what made me tick. They made a big mistake by not understandin' my principles and determination. We spent another tense night waitin', then after breakfast the next mornin' we got the all clear signal. Ah loaded up and headed back to Baumholder.

ALL HELL BROKE LOOSE!

A few weeks later, we received orders to modify the cemetery protection levy in Wiesbaden. Ah thought, wow this is gonna to be great! Ah couldn' wait to see my German friends and get back to the pizza hangout.

In addition to the cemetery project, we had orders to build a warehouse storage facility. Early one mornin' Ah was already in cement up to ma knees when this office boy comes runnin' to the job site yellin',"DiGiovanni! The Captain is ordering you to double time it to headquarters immediately." Na Ah knew he wasn' this excited about givin' me some sort of award or promotion.

Ah entered the room, and there they were lookin' like a pack of wolves about to devour their prey. All of my nemeses had gathered there for the kill. The Captain was so agitated that he was hittin' his leg with the swagger stick he always carried. Ah'm sure he wished he was hittin' me. The Lieutenant, and a Sergeant seemed on edge, ready to pounce. Tryin' to control his rage, the Captain growled. "I just got a letter from your Congressman!" Ah thought oh yeah, that's what all this drama is about. Ah wonder what took him so long to answer my letter (guess a lot of soldiers write their Congressmen). As he spoke—Ah mean growled—he hit his leg harder and harder. "Do you have any idea what this means to my career?" Of course Ah did. That's why Ah wrote the letter. Duh. No one has ever complained to Congress about me.

At this point, he hit his leg so hard his swagger stick broke. The guy was outta control! Ah wanted to say "get a grip," but he went on. "I wish I could do something to you. "Na what ya suppose he meant by dat? Ah looked around to see if he had a sickle nearby. Needless to say there was a lot of tension in the room. Ah could feel their wantin' to attack me, but they wouldn' dare. Ah had a pen pal in Congress and they knew Ah wouldn' hesitate to write him.

Finally Ah had all of them. My big punch had landed and it was a knockout! He went on and on, but Ah tuned him out. Ah don't remember all that he did in retaliation. No matter, Ah was on every list but the promotion list anyway! Ah can't remember the exact timeline, but eventually Lieutenant Schultz transferred to a more spit and polish outfit. The Captain put in for stateside duty and two Sergeants transferred to other outfits. Ya know what. Ah wasn' bugged about haircuts again. Ah always kept my hair at the army regulation inch and a quarter length, cause, ya know, Ah'm really a good boy and Ah listen to my Mama.

From this time on, Ah made sure that Ah kept a safe distance from those guys. They were a real piece of work. They enjoyed makin' other people's lives miserable, and could care less about ruinin' my career. My battle with that bunch of malcontents cost me a lot of money. My discharge papers (Form 214) show that Ah went in the Army as a private e2, and came out three years later still a private e2. Try explainin' that to a potential employer. Ya see, Ah was busted (demoted) twice while in Germany. Ah can't remember the exact timeline of my promotions, but Ah do remember why Ah was demoted. At some point Ah was promoted to specialist 3rd class. Ah only held that rank for about a month, 'cause one night soon after my promotion, Ah drove up to my barracks way before bed check. Before Ah could exit my car, a good friend of mine asked me to drive his visiting girlfriend home. My car padna and I were the only enlisted men with a civilian driver's licence. Ah couldn' loan my car to anyone for any reason, and Ah couldn' leave the girl there so Ah told her to hop in. Ah sped off, made a u turn and headed back to town.

Ah saw this sergeant wavin' his arms, but Ah thought he was just wavin' at me. Ah swerved around him, brought the girl home and got back before bed check. Or so Ah thought. The next day Ah was called to the Captain's Office (double time again). The Sergeant that had waived to me the night before was there and to my surprise, he claimed that Ah not only missed bed check (bed check was at midnight), but also tried to run over him. With a big grin on his face, the Captain busted me on the spot. Not only did Ah lose rank, Ah lost money as well. The second rank reduction took place some time later. Ah had carefully hidden my mattress and bunk bed behind the lockers so when they checked beds at midnight they were all there. Then Ah left for the weekend. Ah made it back in time for reveille on Monday. Once again Ah was ordered to double time it to the Captain's Office. Boy, this was gettin' old. Ah was gettin' workouts joggin' to the Captain's Office so often. This time, there were two Sergeants there. One of them was on duty the night before. It turns out, someone had ratted me out. They told the Sergeant where my bunk was hidden. He in turn called the Captain at home. He climbed out of bed and came to my barracks to witness my absence for himself. The Captain started right in sayin' "I wish I could get you for more than missing bed check. If I could prove that you were gone more than twenty four hours, I'd charge you with being A W O L and throw your ass in the brig." He was delighted to bust me again. He took my last stripe. The nerve of that guy!

There's a rule of thumb that experienced fighters use. Never let your opponent know that he hurt you. So, Ah went right outside the window, called a couple of loyal friends over, then started pointin' at the window while laughin' wholeheartedly. Some of these events occurred before the reply from my letter to Congress.

THE BATTLE AT RUSCHBERG

My Army life became routine again. There were more classes on nuclear warfare survival, construction of decontamination stations and floatin' bridge construction. A few months went by without a whole lot of excitement. Then one day a guy that Ah hardly knew said to me, "Dee I need your help. Me and two of my friends were in Ruschberg last night. We were just having a few beers when suddenly these Airborne guys jumped us and beat the crap out of us. Look at my face!" Yeah, Ah could see. This guy's face had been used for a punchin' bag. Bear with me as Ah lay this out for ya. These Airborne guys were new arrivals to Baumholder. Our trainin', jobs, and mission were polar opposites. Their trainin' centered around physical fitness exercises, parachute techniques, and mock battles. They used the jump towers that we built in Wiesbaden for reality-type trainin'. They spent a lot of time shinin' boots and starchin' their uniforms. We, on the other hand, were combat engineers. We built bridges, buildin's, missile launch pads, and roads. Our trainin' gave us the tools to complete these tasks while under enemy attack. It's not feasible to do construction work with starched uniforms and shined boots on. Our outfit was not prone to spit and polish. Now that Ah think about it our brass didn' even understand this. All of them came from spit and polish outfits. My officers were tryin' to put round pegs in square holes. We certainly didn' need any additional exercise. Ah'm here to tell ya breakin' rocks with a sledge hammer is a pretty good workout! Vast differences between Airborne and Engineer troops were bound to cause conflicts between the two groups. Na Ah gotta take another shot at our brass. Good leaders could have prevented a lot of hostilities by simply teachin' both sides to respect each other.

Ruschberg was a very small town located a short distance from our base. There were only two gasthauses in the whole town. One was frequented almost entirely by blacks, and the other by whites. Another interestin' phenomenon was although all waitresses and female patrons were German, some would only work in the self segregated black establishment while others would only work in white ones.

OK, let's get back to my story; it's a good one. So this guy that got beat up (Ah'll call him Joe) asked me if Ah could get some guys to help him even the score with the Airborne guys. Joe claimed that he was attacked simply because he was an engineer. After work that day, as people were gettin' ready for an evening out, Ah told um about Joe's problem with the Airborne guys. Then Ah added, "Anyone who wants can meet up at the gasthaus in Ruschberg around seven thirty tonight." Ah was surprised by the response Ah got. At least fifteen people said they would be there. Isn' that amazin'? Guys will risk life and limb for pride. We have some kind of primal instinct that makes us think that fightin' impresses the ladies. It impresses them all right; they think you're stupid for fightin'! A smart person will avoid a pride fight whenever possible. Ah learned this the hard way. Please remember this. NEVER fight for anything you're not willin' to die for.

As my car padna approached me, Ah noticed a troubled look on his face. "What's up, Lyle?" Ah asked. He paused, then asked, "Dee would you think that I'm a coward if I didn't go tonight?" "Of course not," Ah answered. Looka, ya think Ah'm not uneasy about tonight. If someone is not tense before a fight, Ah would be concerned about their mental stability. You do what's best for you—whatever you choose—Ah got your back." A slight smile of relief crossed Lyle's face, then he said, "I'll drive a carload of ya'll over then come back in a couple of hours and pick ya up." We hung out a couple of hours, then fav of us piled into my car. Lyle drove. It was go time. We entered the bar, waited for a few others to arrive; then we developed a spur of the moment battle plan. There was only one visible door for enterin' and leavin' the buildin'. There was a very large typical bar that streached from one end of the room to the other. Ya know the scene. Juke box near the entrance, full length mirrors behind the bar, and glasses lined up on the bar for speedy service. The back section of this room led to a double door size entrance to the dinin' area. Our battle strategy was for myself and another guy to position ourselves just outside on either side of the doorway and to have all of our other people sit at tables in the dinin' room. Once the Airborne guys were in the room, the two of us would seal off the exit then we'd battle it out.

There was only one guy at the bar when we entered. He didn' even seem to notice us. Joe started mouthin' off, tellin' the barmaid that we were lookin' for paratroopers. Suddenly, Ah got a bad feelin' about this whole situation. Joe was breakin' every street rule there was. Loud boastin' in a bar is just plain stupid. Then the guy at the bar looks right at Joe and asked, "Are you guys (musta been a yankee) lookin' for a fight with us?" Joe answered "Yeah, we're gonna kick your asses." Na Ah knew f' sure Joe was a jerk, but it was too late. The battle lines were drawn. The guy says, "Wait here, I'll be right back," then he left. Na um really edgy, Ah ordered a beer and waited. Ya ever hafta sit and wait for somethin' bad to happen? Kinda like waitin' for the dentist to work on ya. That's how Ah felt. The rest of our group were in the back room drinkin' beer and startin' to have a good time. They were unaware of what just took place. About fifteen minutes went by before Ah heard a whole Platoon of Paratroopers chantin' as they jogged, "Hup, two, three, four. Airborne all the way. Airborne all the way."

The chantin' got louder and louder as they approached. They kicked the door off its hinges. Ah knew we were in trouble f'sure. Instantly there was a whole platoon of troopers inside the bar area demandin' to know where the Company C Engineers were. The barmaid nodded her head, "Back there." Within seconds they stormed into the room yellin' and tauntin' our guys. While this monkey dance was goin' on we just sat still tryin' to figure out the next move. We didn' have to wait long. One of the troopers punched a seated engineer behind the ear. That was the spark we needed. Ya hafta understand the Airborne Troopers were bigger, combat trained, tough, full of pride, and eager to punch it out with us. We, on the other hand, were basically construction workers trained to defend our projects in a combat situation. We always had to think outside of the box. Not so with the Troopers. Their trainin' was rigid. They expected a fist fight. They didn' get one. An Engineer hit the attacker with a beer bottle. Blood and glass went flyin'! Before the Troopers could process what was happenin' all the Engineers stood up and started peltin' um with beer bottles. They didn' have anything to throw back cause they hadn' ordered yet. The whole place erupted into a battlefield. Chairs, bottles, ashtrays, anything that could be thrown was thrown. The Troopers were shocked. They didn' expect this kind of fight. They had to retreat cause beer bottles were findin' their targets. Now, everything was comin' right at me. Troopers, bottles, 'n' chairs were all comin' straight at me. Ah used my chair like a lion tamer fendin' off punches and flyin' objects as well. Battle sights and sounds are confusin'. Ya can't panic. Ya need to adjust to whatever comes your way. The bar manager wasted no time callin' the MP's. He also told them that Company C Combat Engineers were one of the participants in a riot and his gasthaus was bein' destroyed.

The MPs then called our Captain at his off base home. As the Troopers were battlin' their way out, Engineers continued their bombardment. Bottles shattered the mirrors. Then before the last trooper could get out Ah threw my chair at him. Ah missed 'n' hit the jukebox reducin' it to a pile of broken glass. A half dozen or so MPs were tryin' to round up people. Ah slipped into the wooded area that separated Ruschberg from our base. Ah had to make my way through about a mile of woods in the dark with MP's in hot pursuit. Somehow Ah got into my barracks before they could catch me. Ah just barely got my shoes off when Ah heard them comin'. Ah had to jump under my blanket with all of my clothes on. Ah could hear a lot of vehicles parking and people shoutin'. "Check every building in Company C." Ah managed to slip my pants off and pretended to be asleep.

Shrill whistle sounds startled me. Lights were turned on. Then Ah heard my Captain shoutin',(jus' my luck, he hadn' left yet), "ahh---tenn---shun, fall in." Ah thought, "How did this guy get here so quick? Does he stay awake waitin' for someone to mess up?" So there we were standin' at attention in our skivvies. A lot of people came pilin' into my barracks. MP's, lieutenants, 'n' Sergeants. The night duty corporal trailed behind my Captain. He slowly removed his cigar from his mouth, tapped his leg with a swagger stick while lookin' us over. All at once he tore into us with a sorta controlled growl that Ah was very familiar with. "I don't like getting woke up in the middle of the got damn night. My wife doesn't like getting woke up, neither does my dog. This puts me in a bad mood, makes me angry, and when I get angry everyone around me is going to suffer. "Ah wanted to say, "Amen to that Sir! Ah know it f' true!"

He continued, "Do you people know how much trouble you're in? Four Airborne personnel ended up in the hospital getting stitches. The bar in Ruschberg was completely destroyed, and an MP was injured trying to apprehend someone. Do you have any idea of what's going to happen when this reaches the base commander?" Then there was the wary look up and down the line. When he saw me, he fixed his gaze on my face for at least thirty seconds. Ah could feel it. Ah didn' even twitch a muscle. He slowly walked over to me, stuck his face real close to mine and hissed through tight jaws. "I might of known that you had to be involved. You better have a good explanation or I'm gonna throw your ass in the brig tonight." Ah didn' think he could do that cause almost all of Company C was involved in the fight, but Ah wasn' sure. Ah had to think fast. Imagine havin' gone through a big brawl, escapin' capture by runnin' through the woods and standin' at attention in your underwear with an angry captain hissin' threats in your face. Ya think ya could think fast under those conditions? Ah had to do it. Ah had a lot of experience thinkin' fast in front of this man. Without hesitatin' Ah started explainin'. "Sir! We were fightin' for our colors. They beat up two of our guys just because they were Engineers. They claimed that Engineers were not even soldiers and couldn' fight their way out of a wet paper bag."

As Ah told the story Ah almost believed it myself. It sounded pretty good to me. Ah could sense the Captain softening a little. He went up and down the line askin' others if this was true. Everyone confirmed my story. Some even added to it. Ah was shocked when our Captain did an about face and stormed out.

Na before ya think too ill of me, remember we went to Ruschberg thinkin' our comrades had been unjustly beaten. Afterward Ah learned that Joe had started the whole thing over some fraulen.

A few days later we were informed of our share of the gasthaus repair costs and we would have to pay for them. The total cost to us was $350 American dollars. Ah knew they had given us an inflated estimate, but didn' complain. Sure beats the hell out of jail time right? Ah also knew we had touched a chord with all Company C personnel includin' most of our Officers. So, here's what we did, on payday we put a big jar next to the paymaster with a sign that read, DONATIONS FOR THE BATTLE OF RUSCHBERG. A lot of people donated. We ended up only payin' about $10.00 dollars each. Ah learned some valuable life lessons that night in Ruschberg. Mainly, never get into a pride fight. Don't get sucked into a dangerous situation by some jerk. Avoid the pre-fight monkey dance and there won't be a fight. Finally above all, THINK before ya act. These rules are relevant in an actual physical encounter, workplace, or even in social situations.

VIETNAM, NEVER HEARD OF IT

One night Ah was in Wiesbaden with a coupla of friends enjoyin' some bockwurst and beer. Ah struck up a conversation with some guys who turned out to be French Soldiers havin' a night out on the town. After a few beers some captivatin' war stories came pourin' out. They told us about their involvement in a shootin' war that was goin' on as we spoke. They gave us details about some of the fierce battles they were in and they told emotional stories about comrades they had lost. Ah was a little skeptical, so Ah asked, "Where is this war takin' place, what country are ya'll fightin'?"

They said they were fighting in Southeast Asia: Vietnam. Ah thought Vietnam? Never heard of the place. Ah encouraged them to continue talkin' cause Ah enjoyed their stories and wanted to learn everything Ah could about combat. Some of them became angry when they told us about the inhuman conditions they were subjected to, but Ah could tell it was seein' their friends die that hurt the most. These fellow soldiers were on leave get-ting' a little rest before returnin' to the battlefield. Ah couldn' help thinkin' this could happen to me at any time. What if the next alert was f' real? Ah couldn' imagine watchin' a friend die. We showed them around town hopin' so they could forget about the war for awhile. Ah looked at them thinkin', *These guys don't look like hardened combat soldiers; they're just young men hopin' for a bright future just like me.*

Years later, while doin' research on the Vietnam War Ah learned that whole platoons of French soldiers were massacred in Vietnam before the U. S. entered the war. My thoughts drifted back to my brief friendship with those French soldiers in Wiesbaden wonderin' if they got back to France in one piece. Army life doesn't foster an atmosphere for long-term friend-ships. Few Army friendships are lastin'. This lifestyle was hard for a guy used to makin' friends that lasted a lifetime.

QUICK AND BOLD

Ah was startin' to enjoy attendin' atomic warfare classes; they kinda re-minded me of high school. In addition to classes, there was several bridge buildin' projects under combat conditions. In our spare time there were al-ways various construction projects around our area. For some reason these projects always seemed to have a lot diggin' involved. One assignment that really got to me involved Companies A, B, and C. We were ordered to dig connectin' trenches three feet deep, two feet wide and about a quarter mile or so long. To this day, Ah still don't know what those trenches were to be used for. Na get this, the ground was just beginnin' to thaw out and it was full of rocks. On top of that we were on a mountain side and it was freezin'! This was pick and shovel hard grub work under miserable conditions. We worked on this project for about two months. Afterwards our non-commis-sioned officers—bless there little hearts—stopped us from diggin'. They decided to order in heavy equipment to re-dig the trenches. Things like this bring to light the ol' Army sayin' Ah told you about before. There's the right way, the wrong way, and then there's the Army way. Yeah and sometimes the Army way makes ya wanna' hurt somebody! A short time later they sent us to bridge buildin' field trainin'. Ya see why Ah didn' need any additional exercise!

Even though Ah was no longer in the motor pool, necessity forced my superiors to give me special drivin' assignments. There wern't enough certified drivers willin' to navigate the narrow roads or were able to read the German signs, much less understand the German driver's mindset. Road accidents and a lack of drivers was a fact of life that motor pool sergeants and officers had to deal with. This is where Ah came in. Ah had a clean drivin' record, could read the road signs and Ah could drive anything except tractor trailors. Occasionally Ah was assigned to deliver a vehicle needin' major repairs to the larger shop in Kaiserslautern. Repairs such as replacing a motor, body work, paintin'; virtually anything too big for our shop to handle went to Kaiserslautern. So Ah would drive one vehicle down, drop it off then bring a refurbished vehicle back to Baumholder. Pretty simple task right? Kaiserslautern was about forty miles south of Baumholder and at least seventy miles from Wiesbaden.

One day Ah drove a truck down from Wiesbaden, had lunch then headed back with a two and a half ton truck that just had the engine replaced. Ah was glidin' around the mountain roads at a pretty good clip (maybe a little over the speed limit) thinkin' about getting' back to Wiesbaden in time to have a night out in town. As Ah rounded a curve Ah saw a makeshift roadblock. There a stern lookin' comrade (We called all Germans comrads). As usual, he was wavin' a red flag. Ah stopped. Comrade came over and informed me that the road was closed until they smoothed out the gravel and poured the blacktop. The road was goin' to remain closed for the rest of the day. He informed me that there was an alternate road about twenty-five miles behind me. Then he went off to one side and started talkin' to the German driver behind me. Ah sat for a few seconds, slipped my truck into gear, gunned the motor and sped around the barricade onto the freshly smoothed gravel.

Ah went barrelin' down the unfinished road, gravel and dirt was flyin' everywhere. Several workers started chasin' me swingin' and throein' shovels 'n' rakes at me. Ah swerved around the other barrier back onto the main road headin' towards Wiesbaden at breakneck speed. Without even realizin' it Ah had used their own blitzkrieg attack on them. Swing into action quickly without hesitation, 'n' be bold enough to surprise everyone. The Germans used that same tactic on the French when they invaded France in the beginnin' of World War ll. It's called blitzkrieg, (lightning war). No one could think or act fast enough to stop me or even get my truck number. Now that Ah'm a lot older Ah understand my actions were self servin', dangerous, 'n' certainly didn' help restore German-American relations at all. Ah wasn' tryin' to start a war, all Ah wanted to do was get to Wiesbaden 'n' have a li'l fun.

Ah was drivin' on a regular basis once again. Ah even had several Sergeants that put in special requests for me to drive for them whenever they had long trips to make. Ya see, Ah knew the roads, could speak pretty good German, and most important, Ah would stop at gasthauses and get a brew every now 'n' then. The Sergeants could have a couple of brews and still get back to their destination on time. Ah became the most popular Jeep driver in Company C. One day our Captain, Bligh (Ah'm usin' a fake name to protect myself. Ah get a kick outta writers who say they're usin' false names to protect the innocent. Ya know that's a crock. They're just protectin' their own butts.) Anyways ol' Bligh comes to the motor pool 'n' says to the Sergeant. "I don't know what's going on around here, but Di Giovanni must be the best got damn driver in the motor pool." Everybody is requesting him to drive for them." Without pausing he told my Sergeant to assign me back into the motor pool. He went on. "We're going back to France in a few of months. We're going to need drivers. Assign him to the motor pool again." Ah think he was beginnin' to like me, don't you? So then my Sergeant said to me "I don't know what's going on either, but whatever you're doing, don't get caught, or your ass is grass and I'm the lawnmower."

EVERYONE HAS A DARK SIDE

A few days later Lieutenant Schultz, (he hadn' left yet), said to me, "I want to see why everyone's requesting you to drive for them. You're gonna be my driver today." Yeah, a fun day! True to form, ol' Schultz decided to take a short cut. Ah tried to tell him that the road was very steep, windy, and it cut right through the back side of the German camp. His reply was, "Don't argue with me soldier. Do as you're told." So without another word Ah drove on. Sure enough, we came to a back entrance to the German camp. There was a gate with a German soldier guardin' it. As usual, Lieutenant Schultz tried bullyin' to get his way. He snapped at the guard, "Listen, I'm an American Officer! Open that gate!"

The guard just kept sayin, "Nein nein sie dokument brauchen!"

Ah told Schultz, "He's sayin' you need a pass."

He came unglued, face all red 'n' all. He began cursin, "I don't give a s*** about a pass!" 'n' then chewed the guy out. (Ah guess Ah gave him a lot of practice with chewin' out stuff.) Of course, the guard didn' understand a word he was sayin'. He just stood there with this puzzled look on his face.

Ah was embarrassed for our Lieutenant. He'd been around long enough to know that a German soldier was gonna follow his orders. As Ah started to back up, he bellowed, "Stop! "Go back over there and chew that guy out. Tell him exactly what I said. Make him understand every word." Then tell that got d*** krout that he needs a haircut!"

Ah started to reply, "But sir, Ah can't -"

He cut me off mid-sentence. "I'm ordering you to do what I said now!"

Ah had no choice. Ah walked over to the guard and smiled while sayin', "This guy is crazy. Ah'll talk, you look surprised, say somethin' back, then Ah'll get him out of here."

It worked. We left without further incident. So now, just like Ah warned we were forced onto a steeper narrower road with hairpin turns. At times Ah had to drop into four wheel drive.

Mountain air is thin, sounds are magnified and my strainin' jeep motor sounded like a big truck. We were both a little tense. Neither of us spoke. As we spun along my front wheels kept gettin' closer and closer to the edge on every sharp turn. For a moment my mind drifted deep into its dark side. Ah felt the Lieutenant tense up as we rounded each curve. Ah'm sure he was feelin' my thoughts. All Ah had to do was jerk my wheels hard to the right, roll out of my door, and the good Lieutenant would be on a 3,000 ft. free fall straight to hell. Na if ya know me ya know Ah could never do that. However, Ah have to say, those thoughts felt good. Maybe my front wheels did come real close to the edge a coupla' times, and maybe Ah was teachin' Lieutenant Schultz a lesson on humility. Ah'll let ya'll decide. All Ah know is Ah could hardly keep a straight face when Schultz started makin' nice. He spoke in a soft voice, tryin' to divert my thoughts. Ah didn' say a word, Ah just let da sucka' squirm. Ah could hear my mother saying, "Michael how could you even think such a thing? Ya know Ah raised you better than that." Schultz 'n' I were both happy when we arrived at our destination. On the way back Ah stuck to the main roads. Ah didn' get any objections from Schultz. What a fun day!

DEATH OF AN OL' FRIEND

So na Ah was back in the motorpool travelin' around Germany, Luxembourg, the cities and towns fascinated me. The ancient City of Trier on my circuit. Ah was lovin' it. Trier was always an added treat. As Ah looked at the buildin's Ah couldn' help wonderin' about the thousands of people that lived and died in those interestin' old houses. Yeah and the wine was pretty good too.

Ah had worked myself into a pretty good position. Ya see, Ah could go on special details that other drivers couldn' or wouldn' do. For example, let's say our motor pool needed some special tool or piece of equipment like a trailer or somethin'. My Sergeant, (let's call him Mack) would tell me what he needed 'n' say, "See if you can find one." Ah knew exactly what he meant. In a lot of ways military procedures are really cumbersome; it could take weeks or even months to get somethin' ya needed. Sometimes we didn' have time to mess around with all the paperwork. That's where Ah came in handy. Ah would scout around other areas, find what was needed, and try to make a trade. But one way or another Ah got what we needed. Before long, we had accumulated a lot of unauthorized stuff. Once Ah even saw a bran' new jeep trailer buried because of a surprise inventory inspection. When we knew an inspection was comin' Mack would have the mechanics load all of the unauthorized tools and stuff into my jeep trailer. Then he would give me a trip ticket to an Air Force base located about 100 miles away. All Ah had to do was leave before the inspection, drive up there, eat some fantastic airforce meals, spend the night, then return the next day. Ah loved it. Alone on the open road, stoppin' when Ah wanted, makin' new friends, and enjoyin' the freedom. Can't beat dat wid a stick.

This is just an example of a reason why ya should NEVER vote for any tax increases. Ah mean, a person like my Pop with very little education could figure it out. He would say, "if ya give um money they're gonna spend it. If ya give um power, they're gonna abuse it."

Ah got a letter from Ma one day. Eager for news from home Ah ripped it open. My excitement turned to sorrow as Ah read, "Michael Ah'm sorry Ah have to tell you that your dog Tiny has died." My heart sank. Tears welled up in my eyes. A feelin'of dread came over me like a dark cloud. Tiny had been with me since about the fourth grade. It was hard to imagine that Ah would never see him again. Goin' home wouldn' be like Ah visualized without Tiny there to greet me. Ah thought Ah would have a little more time with him, but it wasn' gonna happen. Some of my friends noticed my heavy-hearted mood. One of them asked "What's wrong Dee?" Holdin' back tears Ah told him, "My dog died." Ah was disheartened when Ah didn' get the compassion Ah expected from my friends. They started tellin' me Ah had to suck it up. They said let's go to town. Ah didn' want to go to town. Ah just wanted to sit around and pine for my friend. One friend advised, "Ya gotta get your mind off of it. You're in the Army thousands of miles from home. This is our life until we get back to the world." Ah went, but still coudln' get Tiny out of my head. However Ah did welcome the diversion. Later, that night, alone in the dark, Ah gave my ol' friend the tears and memories a loyal partner deserves. To this day Ah have never loved another dog like Ah loved Tiny.

Army life is all about changes, new assignments, new trainin', new work projects and even new people. This doesn' give ya time to dwell on your personal problems. Ah had to put Tiny in the back of my mind for now, but Ah knew that fond memories of him would remain deep inside me forever.

BACK TO TENT CITY

We were already preparin' for another trip to Busack, France. Fortunately Ah had a lot of leave time on the books so Ah decided to put in for a fourteen day leave to Barcelona, Spain. Busac was only about three hundred or so miles from Barcelona. Ah thought it would be a perfect road trip. Remember, Ah still had my car. Ah thought it would be wise to put in for my leave while still in Germany. Ah submitted my leave request about three months ahead of time. Ya see, the Battalion Commander had to OK all leaves to Spain, because durin' the 50's, Spain was still under the dictatorship of General Franco and ya had to have a special passport that was hard to get. Three of us, managed to get permission and passports, so yay! Road trip! But first, we had to change our friggin headlights back to those amber lights and take the machine guns off of our trucks. Once again, Lyle was gonna drive our car down, but this time Ah was gonna drive it back. A good friend of mine, Marcus, wanted his wife and son to ride back to Germany in my car with me. He couldn' afford to pay for train tickets and didn' want his family to travel alone in a foreign country.

Marcus and I became really good friends back in Wiesbaden. Ah found out that he'd been a professional boxer before enterin' the Army. Ya shoulda seen this guy. His arms were like tree stumps. He musta' scared his opponents to death! After we became friends, he spent a lot of time sharin' his boxin' expertise with me. One night Marcus and a few of his friends (all of them were huge) invited me to have a few drinks with them. Without thinkin' about racial differences (Marcus and his friends were black), Ah went along. We ended up in the all- black gasthaus in Ruschberg. Except for some local German girls, Ah was the only white person in the place. The music was a lot like back home. Ah couldn' help tappin' ma feet and hands in time with the music. Marcus knew Ah liked to dance, so he says, "If ya wanna dance, go on over to that table an ax one of dem girls ta dance." Ah said "really," Marcus?"

"Yea go on over."

So Ah bopped on over. When Ah got to the table, the guys and girls looked bewildered, kinda like, are you kiddin', stupid, or suicidal? Ah wasn't kidden'. You can decide about the other two. Then Ah asked in German "Fraulein, tanzen wir?" This pissed off the guys, but they still looked confused. When they glanced over at my table, Marcus and his friends just smiled at them. They got the message. Ah danced a coupla times, brought the girl back, looked at the guys, and strode back to my table. Na ya see why Ah didn' mind doin' a favor for a guy like dat.

Our convoy made it back to Busac, havin' only one notable incident. We had to post a guard at major intersections for traffic control. This procedure worked fine in Germany, but for some reason French motorists were impatient and seemed annoyed by our presence. In one town our guard was harassed by a bunch of Algerian teens. They even spit on his boots! He didn' have any way to defend himself. When Ah found out about this incident Ah was furious. First, at the Army's absurd gun policies in France; second, at French attitudes towards our military; finally, at those Algerians. Ya see why Ah value loyal friends? Ah have no use for fair weather-friends.

Life in tent city was the same as it was last time: miserable. We had to hang our clothes on a rope cause' tents don't have closets. Na the Army doesn' cut ya any slack. We still had big inspections. On one of these inspections the brass noticed that my civilian clothes took up more space than my Army uniforms. Ah had some really cool clothes. They ordered me to take all of my civilian clothes to the supply area. Those f****ers took my civilian clothes away! Ya think they were still holdin' a grudge 'r what? Ah don't think these guys were ever taught to play nice. Yeah, and they also tore my made-up bunk apart almost every day. Macht nichts, Ah just borrowed clothes and rolled with the punches. Maybe Ah could teach these guys to be more personable before Ah left the Army. Ya think?

Company C was given another construction project just outside of tent city. We had to erect prefabricated steel buildin's. These types of structures were fairly new at this time so we had to learn the construction techniques on the job. All of the buildin' pieces were delivered to the job site in enormous bundles. First we had to pour the cement footings, and cement floorin'. After the cement dried the buildin' could get started. Ya get da picture. There was a lot of diggin' and cement work involved. Na who ya think they assigned those back breakin' task to? Yeah u' rite. Me 'n' ma friends. No matter, Ah always managed to have some fun. And besides, they still had to learn a lot about how to treat people. Ah was determined to teach um. In fact, Ah considered it my duty to teach um. My job was to feed the cement mixer with sand, gravel, cement, and water. After that, we had to fill wheelbarrows with cement and muscle the mix to the finishers. So, how do ya make a job like that fun and teach at the same time? Well, first Ah wouldn' put enough sand in the mix. Then when the Sergeant yelled, "We need more sand," Ah would put in a lot more sand and leave out some gravel. After a few fun filled days of this, they would assign me to another project, usually far away from them.

Ah was transferred to another buildin' where the cement work was finished. All of my new jobs had a lot of climbin' involved. Hummm, ya think they were hopin' for a slip and fall? Not a chance. Na Ah'm not braggin' when Ah say no one in our division could even come close to my climbin' skills. Remember Ah grew up swingin' on ropes and climbin' in trees every day. Na um not sure if it was my climbin' skills that prompted them to assign me high-up jobs or if they were just hopin' for a slip and fall. Wadda ya think?

After all the fun and games a night out in Bordeaux was always a welcome diversion. One night Ah was ready to head back to base when this Puerto Rican Sergeant asked for a ride. Ah already had a full car load, but Ah managed to squeeze him in anyway. On the way back he says "There's a really cool bar nearby, and I'd like to see a girl that works there." Ah was a little hesitant cause my car wouldn' start at times. Ah had to either get a push, or park on a hill so Ah could pop the clutch. You young people can google clutch to see what it is. We went to the bar anyway. Before we could even order this guy looks at us 'n' says, "What are you white boys doin' in here?" One word led to another, then he starts yellin', "hay, y'all get down here, dere's a bunch of white m****ers from Germany in here." Ah never saw anything like it. Guys started comin' out of rooms, upstairs, downstairs, everywhere. There musta been at least a dozen of um. Our Sergeant (Ah'll call him Carlos) hit the closest one then grabbed beer bottles off of tables. Once again, we started throwin' beer bottles as we made a "tactical retreat (just a face-savin' way of sayin' we got the hell out of there). Thank God we made it to my car. Some of us jumped in. Two guys pushed the car then hopped in as it started down a hill. Carlos opened the sun hatch, stuck his head 'n' shoulders out and continued his beer bottle barrage. The guy musta ben' a baseball pitcher or sumthn' because he held them off. This is why Ah still teach bottle throwin' in my street fightin' classes. And for all of you potential teachers, ya gotta' remember whatever ya teach is only a theory unless you've tried it. Ah popped the clutch and the car started on the very first try. Once again God saved ma bar hoppin' butt. Boy Ah'm sure glad. He never tires.

We built several buildin's in record time. Ah thought that we were helpin' America and our Allies win the Cold War, however, none of us were aware of the increasin' hostilities between France and the United States. General de Gaulle wanted NATO to get more involved in France's conflict with Algeria, so in March, 1966, de Gaulle told the United States to leave France. Ah guess this was de Gaulle's way of protestin' against NATO members. This was six years after Ah left the military, but Ah still became so angry Ah could hardly see straight. Ah mean, didn' they see all the crosses on Normandy's beaches? The engravin's on some of those crosses tell some heartrendin' stories. We lost a lot of people liberatin' France from German occupation. Then de Gaulle, had the audacity to confiscate our buildins' and tell us to leave the country. Hard to believe.

Ah don't know if our brass smelled a rat, but in the summer of 1959 we started movin' some of our equipment out of France. Ah was leadin' a convoy of tools and equipment from France back to Germany. Na ya already know that most French roads are very narrow. There's not much space between northbound and southbound traffic. Sure enough, we met a large NATO convoy goin' south. As Ah rounded a long sweepin' curve Ah looked in my rearview mirror to check on my vehicles. Ah witnessed one of our trailer's sideswipe a NATO troop carrier. Both vehicles rolled over several times. Injured NATO soldiers were on one side of the road and injured Americans on the other side. There were at least ten injured NATO Soldiers, and four Americans needed medical attention.

Our very own Lieutenant Schultz was the highest rankin' officer in our convoy. The NATO convoy was led by a Colonel. The NATO Colonel reasoned that since he was the highest rankin' officer he should be in charge of the entire accident. This would place American troops under his command. Schultz walked right up to the NATO Colonel, looked him eyeball to eyeball and informed him that American troops would never be placed under the command of a foreign power. Ah coulda hugged him. The NATO Colonel replied, "But you must. We both belong to NATO and I am the ranking officer." Schultz stood his ground, "These Americans will remain under my command." Ah thought, Adda Boy Schultz, hang in there. This was becomin' an international incident. Ah was proud of our Lieutenant and very proud to be an American. Despite our differences, Ah always respected Schultz's warrior spirit. Things were gettin' out of control. NATO soldiers were linin' up behind their Colonel, we were linin' up along side of our Lieutenant. Then one of our Sergeants came up with a possible solution. He called Schultz over to one side and whispered to him, "Let them take care of their own, we take care of ours. Let the higher-ups on both sides decide who pays for what. If they agree, we can keep our drivers out of NATO control and French courts." Schultz didn' ask for a compromise. He told the NATO commander what we were gonna do. In the meantime, first aid was given to the injured personnel. We still had a problem. Some of the injured NATO soldiers needed to be hospitalized. They sent me and a Sergeant to find help. We jumped in my Jeep 'n' sped up the road lookin' for the nearest town. Ah found a small town less than ten minutes away, bolted into the police station seeking help. No one spoke a word of English! After several attempts at tryin' to explain our plight, Ah jus' threw out, "Spricht hier jemand deutsch?" (Does anyone speak German?) One officer turned around saying, "Ja ich spreche deutsch." Ah was then able to explain about the accident, that a lot of people were injured and we needed their help. They swung into action tout de suite. Ah led them to the accident scene. My Sergeant went over to Schultz 'n' told him that Ah had saved the day.

Schultz said "What? Di Giovanni a hero? He still needs a haircut."

Ya gotta' love the guy, right? We got the help that was needed. All of the injured NATO soldiers went to French hospitals. Our guys chose to get their treatment in Germany (a wise decision). We administered first aid, made them comfortable 'n' got out of there before anything else could happen.

Our convoy made it back to Baumholder without further incident. After all of that, Ah still managed to get a night out in Wiesbaden. After that it was back to tent city. By the time Ah got back to France it was almost time for my leave to Spain. However, there was one detail that had to be resolved before Ah could enter Spain. First Ah gotta' give ya a li'l history so you'll understand what was goin' on in Spain at this time. Ya see, Francisco Franco took control of Spain after winnin' a civil war. He intended to turn Spain into a totalitarian state like Nazi Germany, but after the defeat of the Axis Powers in World War II, he decided on a more autocratic kind of dictatorship. Franco was tryin' to show the the United States the world that he was powerful. Spain didn' allow foreign military personnel to wear their uniforms in Spain. Na remember Ah had all of my civilian clothes taken away from me. Big problem f'sure. So, here's what Ah did. Ah took my leave papers, signed by the battalion commander, to supply 'n' told them Ah needed my civilian clothes for my trip to Spain. Of course supply had to call our company commander, who happened to be Lieutenant Schultz (Capn' was in Baumholder at the time). At first he said, "No way!"

Ah showed him my leave papers, 'n' said, "Looka here. This leave was approved months ago. Um sure our battalion commander knows about Spanish policies, Sir."

Schultz was silent for a long time. He knew Ah would complain all the way to Washington if Ah had to. Schultz would in effect have to override a battalion commander and imply that he didn' know what he was doin'. Needless to say, Ah got my clothes! Ah gotta admit it always felt good when Ah outwitted ol' Schultz. There's that dark side raisin' its ugly head again. Sorry Ma.

ROAD TRIP

Early the next morning we loaded up the car. Ah took all of my civilian clothes (hangers 'n' all) and stacked um from floor to ceilin' in the car. Tommy and Lyle copied my speedy packin' procedure. We ate breakfast 'n' hit the highway. Road trip. Yay! Ah couldn' believe Ah was on my way to Spain. This was one of the reasons Ah joined the Army. Ah knew there was a great big world out there and Ah wanted to see it. Ah wanted to meet the people, eat the foods, see the sights, 'n' hear the sounds. Now was my time to do it and it felt good. We were headed for Barcelona, Spain, but since Bordeaux was on the way we decided to stop there for a visit with some locals we knew. Ah had to park about two blocks away from a ?????? restaurant/bar where our friends worked. We ate a little, had a nice visit, and headed back towards the car. As Ah rounded a corner, Ah noticed a very nervous Algerian lookin' all around. I kept an eye on him while waitin' to cross the street. When Ah glanced over at my car Ah saw a guy in it! Ah whispered to my friends, "Act like tourists, there's someone in our car. "Ya'll walk ahead of me. Don't even look at the car. Just keep walkin'." When Ah got even with the open car door Ah acted like Ah was going past it. Then Ah spun around quickly, dove in, grabbed the guy's collar, and put my opened switchblade right up to his throat! (One of the best moves Ah ever made.) He dropped our things. With eyes big as saucers, he started babblin' in French. Um guessin' he was pleadin' for his life. So, na Ah got this guy, and Ah don't know what to do with him. Somehow Ah had to resolve the situation. Ah jerked him out of the car with my knife still real close to his throat. He was still babblin'. Ah noticed that a crowd was starten' to gather. My friend Tommy kept sayin' stick him Dee, come on stick um and let's get outta here. Ah saw a policeman a short distance away, but it became apparent that he wasn' gonna help us. Tommy was right; a lot of Algerians were watchin' us. Ah heard um sayin', "Americans" as they pointed at us. We were in a tight spot, Ah had to make a quick decision, and it had to be the right one. Think about it. What would you do? Here's what Ah did. Ah pulled him away from the car then pushed him as hard as Ah could. He stumbled a bit, then ran. Ah'm guessin' that he probably had a long talk with his lookout that night. We jumped in our car 'n' and sped away from what was now a large, hostile crowd. Ah'd had enough excitement for the mornin' and was glad to get back to our road trip.

Ah wound my way through the city, found the highway then headed south towards Spain. There's somethin' about the open road that jus' makes ya feel good. Ah felt free, free from Army life, free of commitments; just the three of us and the road ahead. Ah was anticipatin' excitement as we rounded each curve. Ah didn' have to wait long. We came upon a three-car accident, and of course, Ah stopped to help. All three cars appeared to have been totaled, but thank God no one was seriously injured. This thirty-something French couple spoke pretty good English. The guy shocked me when he asked us to drive his wife to their home thirty-five miles away. Come on na, how many of you would put your wife in a car with three foreign men? She hopped right in 'n' started chattin' like nothin' had happened. This charmin' lady managed to make drivin' the extra thirty-five miles a pleasant experience. C'est la vie, (such is life). Ah drove on.

A coupla' hours later we were in the Pyrenees Mountains waitin' for a shepard to get his goats across the road. We saw Basque herdsmen tendin' their flocks, horses runnin' free, and breathtakin' mountain scenery.

Na Ah have to admit, Ah was not very well informed on Spanish politics. At that time, Ah didn' even know who General Franco was, or that he was a dictator. Before long, Ah saw the Spanish border loomin' in the distance. Ah was about ta get a quick lesson on Spanish politics. Lyle was drivin' cautiously as we approached the submachine gun totin' border guards. These guys looked stern, Ah wanted to say, "Lighten up podna. Smile a little. Did ya'll hear the one about the border guard that walks into this bar….." Yeah, u'rite, Ah kept those thoughts to myself. They ordered us out of our car, searched us and the car (my knife was hidden in a winter coat pocket). Lyle thought they were finished 'n' started to drive across the border. Three guards aimed their weapons at us while yellin' "Halt! Halt!" Ah joined in screamin,' "STOP!" Ah knew those boys warn't messin' around. They came over 'n' said a lot of stuff in Spanish and finally let us go. Whoa!

My first experience with an authoritarian government. Makes ya realize how blessed we Americans are.

Ah was relieved 'n' felt free once back on the road again. We were windin' down the other side of the Pyrenees headed towards Barcelona. The scenery goin' down was just as magnificent as it was goin' up. Ah couldn' help noticin' the people didn' smile; they had this oppressed look about them. Livin' under a totalitarian government showed on their faces. When ya experience these things first hand, ya know f' sure that America has the best form of government on earth. Na Ah gotta' caution ya. Never allow any smooth talkin' politician or whinin' group tell ya how bad America is or get ya to give the government more power. Ah know Ah'm preachin' again, but that's what Ah do.

As darkness set in, we could see the lights from Barcelona shinin' in the distance. Ah hoped the atmosphere would be different down there. We drove into town, checked into the cheapest hotel we could find 'n' made our way downtown. Ah thought, Wow! "This is what Ah came to see 'n' experience. The place was jumpin'. Barcelona was a lot different from the mountain towns. Ah never saw anything like it. There was music everywhere, 'n' when the guys saw a pretty girl they would clap their hands 'n' stomp their feet in time with the mariachi music that seemed to be floatin' around in the air. Ah joined right in. Ah was havin' so much fun Ah didn' notice that my limited cash had dwindled a lot faster than expected. Fortunately, meals were included in the price of our hotel room. Meals were served family style at designated times. That was it. No room service. This routine turned out to be one of the highlights of my vacation. Ah got to break bread with hotel personnel, along with their families and visitors from all over the world. Topics of conversation were generally surface and light, but Ah managed to dig a little deeper into their everyday lives. After Ah gained their trust. They whispered about what life was really like under Franco's totalitarian rule. Wow! Ah felt privileged 'n' honored that these families allowed me into their lives. Ah was able to get a glimpse into where they were at.

Ah was still havin' a lot of fun 'n' didn' want to slow down, but my lack of cash forced me to. Ah went to my favorite bar one night 'n' ordered my usual glass of wine. Ah noticed that the price had nearly doubled. Of course, Ah asked the bartender about it. His unemotional reply was, "The fleets in. Sailors will take over this town tonight. Any time that happens, prices go up." Ah thought great. This is gonna put a bigger dent in my wallet. Ah even arm wrestled some locals for drinks 'n' and won a coupla rounds. Still it wasn't enough to keep us there.

Sure enough, that night Navy guys took over the whole area. (For some reason they were allowed to wear their uniforms.) Ah guess money talks, even to a dictator. There was a sea of white uniforms everywhere. This atmosphere kinda took the wind out of our sails (pun intended). After a night of high prices and loud, drunken sailors, we decided to head back to France. Good thing, cause when we checked on our finances all three of us were almost broke. Ah bid a fond farewell to my new friends at the hotel 'n' left. After fillin' up with gas, we pooled the rest of our money, bought three loaves of bread and three bottles of wine. On the way out of town Ah somehow took a wrong turn and got lost somewhere in the Pyrenees Mountains. Here's the dire situation we were in: we were lost, had only bread 'n' wine for food, didn' speak Spanish, and had only enough gas money for two more fill ups. Experience had taught me to remain calm and think when faced with an emergency situation. Ah reasoned we had to go north, over the Pyrenees into France. The problem was Ah didn' know which way north was. We were at a fork in the road. One road to our right, the other to our left. We couldn' afford to make a mistake. The situation was serious. We had to make the right choice or we would be wonderin' around in the Pyrenees mountains til we ran out of gas. Ah didn' know what Ah'd do if that happened. Ah got out of the car 'n' looked around. By the grace of God Ah noticed a stream flowin' near the road on our right. "That's it" Ah shouted! "Let's see which way that streams flowin'." My friends looked puzzled, but it was clear to me. The stream had to be flowin' downhill. If we went the opposite way, we would eventually get up and over the mountain into France. Ya ever have that little voice tell you, this is right; you're gonna be OK. Na Ah gotta tell ya again. Ah wasn' a Christian at this time, but now Ah know, God had a plan for this worthless ol' coonass. Sure enough, the stream did lead us north, right to the border.

It was dark by the time we got down the mountain into France. Ah ate some bread, drank some wine then went to sleep in my car. The next day was pretty uneventful. Ah sustained myself on bread 'n' wine. We drove open road all the way back to tent city. Ah was the first one in line for chow that evenin'. Ah gotta tell ya, Army food never tasted so good. What a great road trip! Ah experienced life under totalitarian rule, met some wonderful people, learned that all people want the same things: life, liberty, and the pursuit of happiness. Sound familiar? To top it off, Ah got to keep my civilian clothes. Even if Ah have to say so myself, Ah had some pretty cool clothes.

Ah also fancied myself as kind of a trend setter. For example, on our Army Base in Baumholder ya had to wear a tie whenever you were in civilian clothes. In my opinion, this was jus' another annoyin' Army regulation that didn' accomplish anything. Ah mean, a drunken soldier, tie on or off, is not a pretty sight. Anyways, the regulation stated that ya had to have a tie on. It didn' say it had to be tied. So, Ah started just puttin' my tie on without tyin' it. The untied tie offered a kinda' casual look. My relaxed casual style caught on. Within three months everyone was walkin' around with untied ties. Ah know the Army musta' appreciated my fashion statement and my makin' life easier for the troops. They probably jus' forgot to thank me.

Ah cut my leave a few days short 'n' went back to work. My jobs were kinda borin', but by now ya know Ah always pursued that happiness our forefathers talked about in the Declaration of Independence. Ya know, Ah had this sneakin' suspicion that the Army really didn' care whether or not Ah was happy. Matter of fact, Ah don't think they even wanted me to pursue it.

FOREST FIRE, C'EST LA VIE

One day just as Ah was gettin' into my work routine, this Sergent comes flyin' up to my jobsite shoutin, "There's a big forest fire threatening some houses! The French fire department needs our help!" From my rooftop position, (yeah, they still had me up high but Ah hadn' slipped yet), Ah saw the smoke billowin' on the skyline. He continued, "I need a bulldozer, some men, trucks and drivers, on the double! Di Giovanni, get down here. You're gonna drive me and the dozer operator to the fire." When we arrived we found the dozer on a flat-bed ready to go. Without hesitation our operator hopped on, drove a short distance 'n' started clearin' brush away. Our troops were using rakes 'n' shovels, doin' what they could. This was a big fire that was ragin' out of control. Meanwhile, the French firefighters hung around awhile then they cracked open some wine and took a break. Ah was shocked beyond belief. We were riskin' lives and equipment protectin' their houses while they were takin' a break! Ya gotta love their c'est la vie attitude right? Ah was runnin' around gettin' food and water for our guys. They were eatin' on the go and givin' everything they had.

On one of my trips to the fire line, Ah realized that the flames were getting' bigger and a lot closer. Ah parked my Jeep a safe distance away then started luggin' food and water to our troops. Suddenly some soldiers and the dozer operator came runnin' towards me shoutin', "Drop everything!

Get us out of here!" We all ran for my jeep and one other truck that was in the area. Ah couldn' help thinkin' this was the ultimate race. There was no medal to be won, no one cheerin' you on. The prize was savin' your butt. Na that'l put a little zip in your step f'sure. Everyone piled in 'n' we raced ahead of the flames to safety. Our outfit ended up losin' a bulldozer, two trucks and a lot of other equipment. Finally, the fire burned to an area that we had cleared of trees and brush 'n' burned out. Ah'm not 100% sure, but Ah think we saved all of the houses.

THE ODD COUPLE

After things settled down a bit, we started wrappin' up our construction projects because it was about time to head back to Baumholder. On the day before we were to leave Ah found out that Ah was assigned to drive a Jeep in the convoy. My Sergeant was nearby so Ah went over n said "Sarg'., Ah can't drive my Jeep in the convoy. Ah already have permission to drive Marcus wife 'n' chil' back to Baumholder." He replied "Oh yeah, Ah remember now. Ya better go straighten this out with the Lieutenant. He's in charge of the convoy now." Ah thought, Great. This guy could care less about Marcus, his wife, chil', or me. Ah went to see him anyway. After ah told him about my promise to Marcus, he replied just about the way ah thought he would. "Tough ----t." Ah wanted to remind him about God not likin' ugly, but simply replied. "Sir, Ah still have four days leave time that's already been approved by our Captain and the Battalion Commander. Ah'd like to use it." He reluctantly agreed, but first called Marcus in 'n' asked him why he wanted me to drive his family back to Germany. Marcus answered, "Cause Di Giovanni's the only one Ah trus' wid' ma son. My boy's gonna be a champion someday." When Marcus was out of earshot, ol' Schultz gave me a look of disapproval then uttered a slur 'n' stormed out.
The next day, Marcus introduced me to his charmin' wife. They had a son about ten months old. Before Ah left, Marcus made a very emotional request. He had tears in his eyes when he said, "Take care of the future champ. He means the world to me." Ah gave him a firm handshake 'n' said, "Ya know Ah will." Marcus's wife, Ella, was engagin' 'n' easy to talk to. Ah could tell that we would get along and have a relaxin' trip. At this point, navigatin' European roads had become second nature for me. Ah knew my way around 'n' drove like a native. When lunch time rolled around, Ah took a little detour and headed for a nearby Air Force base. At first Ah didn' notice all of the attention we were gettin, but Ella did. She said, "These people

think we're a couple. Let's give them something to talk about and maybe broaden their minds a little." All through lunch we talked, chuckled, and tended to little Marcus like any married couple would. Ah really didn' think that a mixed race couple would draw so much attention in France. Boy was Ah wrong. The most disapprovin' looks came from the black males.

We continued with our guise. Ella held my hands and looked into my eyes as we spoke. Then we walked out arm in arm. Ah thought the whole thing was fun.

When we got to the on-base housin' in Baumholder, Ella asked me to come in and meet some of her friends. What an experience that turned out to be. Ah was caught completely off guard. When Ah walked in all these women started checkin' me out 'n' makin' comments to Ella. Ah heard um sayin' "Uuuum, um, looka here! Ella done got herself one of dem cute li'l white boys, what ya'll been doin' all dis time. Dat boy can drive me back to France any time." Ah could feel my face gettin' all flushed 'n' red. Ah hadn' been this self-conscious 'n' embarrassed since grammar school. 'N' Ah guess Ah was actin' like it. Ah was wrigglin' and stutterin' like a school boy. After a while, Ah managed to get over my shyness and all of us had a good ol' knee slappin' fun time.

Army life was always hard for me. Ah jus' couldn' get used to how they did things. Army logic jus' didn' make sense to me. They always—and Ah mean always—did things the hard way. Yet, there were a few things that Ah liked about military life. Ya always had a lot of friends around to do things with, there were places to go and there were plenty things to do and see. Ah saw new places and made friends with people from all walks of life. Ah experienced life under different forms of government and came away with a greater appreciation for America.

Ah still had a lotta time left before Ah could start thinkin' about what life would be like after my tour of duty was over. It seemed like Ah'd experienced a lot in a relatively short span of time. Someone once said, "Ah wouldn't take a million dollars for all the experiences I've had. But Ah wouldn' give a penny to do them over again." Ah couldna' said it better.

THE GOOD LIFE

A short time after we got back there was another alert, then a pontoon bridge buildin' test. We had to build a pontoon bridge in a certain amount of time while under attack from enemy troops. They were usin' blanks and concussion grenades. These tests were good trainin'; they made us feel like we were in a combate zone.

After this we went back to Wiesbaden for a short, temporary duty assignment. As usual, Ah ended up in cement up to my knees.

Ah found out from friends that we were goin' out in the field for another week of combat trainin'. Ah was beginnin' to get fed up with all the trainin' and not gettin' to play in the big game (combat). Besides, it was startin' to get cold again. We were on an Air Force base that served really good food 'n' Ah didn' relish the thought of sleepin' in a cold tent. On top of that, Ah was out dancin' 'n' havin' fun every night. Besides Ah had a German girlfriend that lived in Wiesbaden 'n' didn' want any changes.

One day, while on a lunch break, Ah felt a little pain in my ankle. Na this was not unusual, cause my ankles were pretty beat up from my football playin' days. Ah can't count the number of ankle sprains Ah suffered durin' my football career. Anyways, Ah took my boot off 'n' noticed that there was a li'l swellin' in the ankle area. All of a sudden light bulbs went off in my head. When lunch was over Ah jumped right into the wet cement. As Ah was rakin' it around Ah purposely twisted my ankle a little bit at a time until Ah could feel some pain. Ah continued twistin' until Ah could tolerate more and more pain. Pretty soon Ah could feel my ankle swellin' and pushin' against my boot. Ah didn' say anything for awhile, then Ah made my way out of the cement, sat down and took my boot off. It didn' take long before a Sergeant came over wantin' to know why Ah wasn' workin'. Ah calmly replied, "Ah feel a li'l pain in my ankle 'n' thought Ah'd look at it." Well, just as planned, my ankle had swollen up like a balloon 'n' was all black and blue.The Sergeant's eyes got real big. He said, "Get in my Jeep. I'll take you to sick bay right now."

The doctor took one look at my swollen ankle and said, "You have a sprained ankle. I'm putting you on sick leave until further notice."

He gave me a pair of crutches and ordered daily whirlpool treatments. Everythin' was goin' accordin' to plan except there was another week before field maneuvers. Ah couldn' get a pass to go to town. Ah had to borrow someone else's pass and slip off the base unnoticed. Marcus would always lend me his pass cause he seldom used it (him bein' married 'n' all). Ah would hobble to the mess hall on my crutches then hobble back to my barracks, wait until dark, slip out to my car and head for town. Dealin' with a li'l pain seemed like a small price to pay for the good times.

Ah would twist my ankle with both hands while sittin' in the whirlpool so when the doctor checked my ankle, it was still swollen. The doctor couldn' figure it out. He would scratch his head and say, "Your ankle is not healing the way I thought it would. This swelling should have gone down by now. That sprain musta been worse than I thought." Ah replied, "Ah was hopin' it would be better. Ya see, we're goin' out in the field in a coupla' days and Ah really want to go." Ah was lyin' like a dog. The ol' doc said exactly what Ah wanted to hear. "You're not going anywhere. I'm putting you on two weeks sick leave starting today." Ah was so happy Ah coulda' jumped up 'n' down with joy, but under the circumstances Ah thought ah better not. Na don't sit there and tell me that you wouldna done the same thing. Let's see, go out in the field, sleep in a freezin' cold tent, work your butt off, and eat lousy food. By the way, on field maneuvers we were eatin' 'C' rations that were left over from World War II! Ma woulda had them arrested if she knew they were feedin' her son canned spaghetti and meatballs made from mystery meat. Or would you rather stay in a nice city, sleep in a warm barracks, go out on the town every night, and eat delicious Air Force meals. Na Ah don't know about you, but for me it was a no brainer. Marcus stayed back 'cause he had guard duty at the base. We would practice some boxin' moves, play music and dance around, then Ah was off for a night out in Wiesbaden. Ah gotta tell ya. This was one of the best temporary duty assignments Ah ever had.

ELVIS WAS HERE

When Ah got back to Baumholder, Ah heard that Elvis Presley had been in Germany since October 1st, 1958. Ah guess Ah wasn' payin' much attention to American celebrities at this time. Elvis' time in Germany made me think about how long Ah'd been in Europe. Ah was there when Elvis came and Ah was still there when he left. It seemed like Ah'd been in Europe my whole life. Ah couldn' even remember the names of all my friends that had already gone home. Once again, Ah was tryin' to figure out where Ah fit in: Germany or America. Sometimes Ah had a hard time distinguishin' whether people were speakin' German or English.

After chow one mornin', my First Sergeant sent word that he wanted to see me. At first Ah was a little nervous, but when Ah thought about it Ah couldn' think of anything Ah'd done wrong lately. When Ah got there, he informed me that there was a new Army regulation for overseas military personnel. An overseas tour of duty could no longer exceed twenty-four months. Since Ah was already there twenty seven months, the new regulation required them to take three months off of my remainin' time. This meant that Ah only had about three weeks left in Europe. Finally, Ah was a short timer! Ah couldn' grasp this information. Ah had a lot to think about. My brother Paul was married and had three children. My younger brother Gerard was about four years old when Ah left, now he was in third grade. My friends were married and mostly all of them were workin'. Life in the States had passed by me. Ah had a stable life in Germany with military and civilian friends. Ah was even offered a job as an apprentice in a German cabinet shop. What to do? Ah could file for a three-month extension in Germany, get discharged there and stay in Europe a few more years, or go home early. After a lot of thought Ah decided to stay a li'l longer. Ah filled out the paperwork and submitted it to my first sergeant. He studied my paperwork a few minutes, then looked up at me and said, "I'm going to give you a bit of fatherly advice son. If you decide to stay here, you will fulfill your full time in service. That means no early out. You will be here close to four more months. You don't have any stripes left. If you mess up, you'll end up in jail, 'n' I'm telling ya they're out to get you. Three months is a long time. You won't make it. You've been here a very long time, longer than anyone else in the company. Go on home to your family. Think it over for a few days and then decide."

My mind raced back to my family and the sights 'n' sounds of New Orlans. Ma's cookin', Pop's warmth and wisdom, my brother Paul and my little brother Gerard whom Ah didn' even get a chance to know. Yes! Ah would go home. Sayin' goodby to all of my German friends wasn' easy. Ah tried to explain how the Army did things, but the goodby's were still hard. Then there were my Army friends, my comrades that had shared good times and bad, guys that had my back in some really tight spots. Wow, Ah still get emotional thinkin' about those times and the guys who shared them with me. But, Ah had to face it; this part of my life was over.

My military service enabled me to understand the big picture a little better. Ah reasoned that civilian and Army life are like a series of temporary duty assignments. Think about it. You go through grammar school, high school; after that, it's either college or a job. Next comes marriage and raisin' children. Ya see, all temporary assignments. Really makes ya think about your final permanent designation doesn't it.

BACK TO THE WORLD

Someone drove me to the bahnhof (train station) in Frankfurt where Ah got on a train headin' north to Bremerhaven, the last German city Ah would ever see. Once again Ah was alone on a train, but this time Ah knew exactly where Ah was and where Ah was goin'. Ah was headed to some of the towns Ah'd visited while on leave. What a difference from my first train ride; and Ah now knew what a continental breakfast was! Ah was a veteran world traveler, but Ah still couldn' sort out my muddled feelin's. Ah was leavin' people and places that were familiar to me, goin' towards people and places that should be familiar but weren't. After Ah arrived in Bremerhaven a military bus drove me to my ship. Reality began to sink in. Ah was homeward bound.

Once again Ah found myself walkin' up a gangplank towards a strange ship, but this time it was a lot easier. As Ah walked memories and emotions came floodin' into my mind and body. There were just too many things for my young mind to digest. A young New Orlans boy really shouldn' be away from home that long; it could mess up his head.

Ah couldn' believe that in a very short time, Ah would be out of Germany, out of the Army, 'n' back in the States. There were a lot of unanswered questions. How would Ah connect with family and friends after bein' out of touch for so long? Where would Ah go for good times? And what kind of job would Ah end up with? Let's see, Ah knew a lot about guns, combat techniques and how to survive an atomic attack, but not much else. Na those qualifications should get me a really good job f' sure.

Ah maintained my Army mentality and determined to make this boat ride a pleasant one. Ah resolved to stay in the now. Here's somethin' else the Army taught me. Happiness is a choice. Na Ah know from experience that this is easier said than done, but if ya bear with me Ah'll try to explain how Ah came to this conclusion. For example, if ya have some annoyin' task to do like breakin' rocks with a sledge hammer or diggin' a trench for no reason you can be all downcast 'n' miserable, or you can make it fun. And if ya have an opportunity to take a shot at the cause of your misery, ya might even enjoy your job a li'l.

My voyage back was indeed a pleasant one. The seas were calm and Ah made a lot of friends. Ah got my sea legs right away and didn' even get seasick. There was a fantastic talent show after a few days out. As it turned out, our ship was loaded with talent. One of the singers became very famous a short time later. Sorry, Ah can't remember his name f'sure, but Ah think he may have been Smokey Robinson. After eight days at sea Ah saw the most beautiful sight Ah'd ever seen: the Statue of Liberty, invitin' me back home. Ah'm not ashamed to tell you Ah cried. The joy was so overwhelmin' Ah couldn' overcome my emotions. Hours seemed like days before we were finally allowed to come ashore. Ah was home! Yeah Ah know, Ah was way up in Yankee territory, but it was still home to me. Ah was loaded into a bus and driven to Fort Hamilton, an Army base in Brooklyn. Ah was still in the Army!

First thing Ah did was call home. When Ah got the operator Ah realized she was speakin' English. She understood every word Ah said. Well, almost every word (some German stuff was added to my Ninth Ward, Cajon Southern accent). When she asked, "What number are you calling?" Ah said, "Please Miss can you just talk to me?" Ya see, except for Marcus wife, Ah'd only heard a coupla females speak good English in over twenty-seven months. Ah'll never forget that kind operator. She laughed and asked me questions about myself. She told me that she had a son about my age and couldn't even imagine him being gone so long.

After Ah spoke to my family, Ah called one of my really close Army friends that lived in New York. Matter of fact, this guy had been on my legal team back in Baumholder. He got a hold of another friend of ours and together they drove out to Fort Hamilton, picked me up, and showed me around New York. What a city! The lights were spellbindin' and the streets seemed wide compared to European roads. Everything appeared to be so big. It was overwhelmin'. We had a lot of fun, but it couldn' come close to a night out in New Orlans. Ah mean, we spent most of the night drivin' from one borough to another. In New Orlans the good times are rollin' everywhere, twenty-four seven. New York people seemed to be a li'l up tight. Brooklyn felt kinda like home cause the folks there sounded more or less like me. In Europe, Ah could go up to anyone, young, old, male, or female and talk to them. Ah found out ya can't do that in New York. When Ah tried to talk to some girls they looked at me like Ah was gonna mug um or somethin'.

After an agonizin' week, Ah got my honorable discharge from the Army. Finally, after eight months, twenty-six days in the Army National Guard, two years three months sixteen days foreign and sea service, a total of three years, six months, fourteen days of service to my Country, it was almost over. Ah still had a two-year Standby Reserve obligation! Macht nichts, Ah refused to dwell on the past or the future. Ah was on an airplane going south, back to my family, back to New Orlans, back to the Ninth Ward, places where Ah could speak ma native tongue and be understood.

Ah'm honored to have had the opportunity to pay my debt to America for allowin' my Grandparents to come here. Now Ah gotta preach a li'l more before my plane lands. All of us have to remember that freedom is not free; it costs a lot. Every American has a duty to fight for it.

My plane landed at the New Orlans airport in Kenner, Louisiana, located about sixteen miles west of New Orlans. The airport lobby was packed with people, most of whom were my friends and relatives. Ah was treated like a rock star! There were a lot of long overdue hugs 'n' kisses. Paul drove me straight to Pop's fillin' station. A lot of things had changed while Ah was gone. Pop had to give up his ice route because refrigerators were in almost every home, even in East New Orlans. Pop still had to work seven days a week at his Mobil gas station. He worked longer hours, but didn' have to walk or lift as much. His only time off was on Sunday afternoons. Workin' all those hours was not a choice; it was a necessity for him to keep his business afloat. In my book that's what courage is all about. He had a duty to his family and he did it ignorin' his personal sacrifices. Get this!, He even tried to pull his own tooth out with a pair of plyers 'cause he didn' have time to go to a dentist. (Of course it didn' work, the tooth broke in half. He still had to have a dentist pull the other half out.)

Ah was still in my uniform when Pop saw me. He just stood there lookin' at me, tears started rollin' down his face. He hugged me 'n' said, "Son ya been gone too long. You were just a boy when ya left. Na look at ya. You're a man all grown up. Ah missed ya Son!"

Ah knew exactly how he felt. Ah've felt the pain of missin' people, places and things too many times to count. Some things ya just neva' get used to. My emotions combined with the heat and humidity caused my knees to buckle a li'l. Pop took me to a cool spot and got some water for me. Ah realized that even the Army couldn' toughen me up enough for just an ordinary day in East New Orlans.

There were a couple weeks of celebrity treatment. Friends took me to restaurants so Ah could eat some of the foods Ah'd missed. Ah'd forgotten how good boiled crabs, crawfish and raw oysters tasted. After a'while, Ah needed some alone time to feel the pulse of New Orlans. You know what Ah mean, kinda like gettin' ya' sea legs. So, Ah went down to the View Carre' 'n', just hung out, absorbin' the sights 'n' sounds of downtown New Orlans. Once Ah got my sea legs, Ah hit the streets. Ah mean Ah really hit the streets. Night 'n' day; grabbin' a coupla hours sleep when Ah could, then right back out. Ah guess Ah was tryin' to make up for lost time. Ya know what Ah found out? Ya can't!

Here Ah am, an 18-year-old kid straight out of high school, in 1957 in the United States Army at Basic Training at Fort Chaffee, Arkansas.

That's me in the postion of Port Arms with my M1 Garand rifle. Ya can see the barracks behind me where Ah lived for a couple of months.

Here are my barracks at Baumholder, Germany. This U.S. Army Garrison was affectionately known as "the Rock" by us soldiers.

This is my German friend Ralph standing in front of his childhood house in Hamburg, which was destroyed during World War II.

Ralph had suffered serious injuries trying to reach this Hamburg bomb shelter during a bombing raid when the war was taking place.

That's me taking a break from breaking rocks for a road construction project in Baumholder. There's my Sword of Freedom patch.

And here are some of my fellow soldiers with me, Ah'm the one in the middle, working on the same road construction project for the army.

Here in Baumholder Ah'm posing next to my Mercedes 170, which was the late 1940s S-Class. My friend and Ah paid $350 for it.

That's me, in the middle, during War Games in the mountains. Can ya tell that it's real cold? To the left is a 1 ton water buffalo trailer.

That's me under the .50 Caliber M2 Machine Gun, mounted to the top of the 2 1/2-Ton 6x6 Cargo Truck, during the War Games.

Typical U.S. Army! Digging a ditch to nowhere! That's me on the left with a pick in my hands. *A little hard work never hurt anyone.*

Uta, Silva, and me in front of our hangout in Wiesbaden, Germany. Uta is wearing her Fasching (a German celebration) hat.

Yet another one of my homes while serving in the U.S. Army. It's in Bussac, France. It's a tent city located 136 kilometers east of Bordeaux.

And, this is that same tent city the following year in 1959. Ah guess the U.S. Army didn't think Ah had got enough camping experience.

That's me and Tommy heading into the very small French town of Bussac-Forêt. Ya can see all the jealous soldiers behind us.

Me, on the left, back in Germany on alert for a possible Russian attack. Don't forget that this was the Cold War with the Soviets.

Even though we were on alert, and tensions were high, we managed to find time to play a little football. That's me running on the right.

The Russians decided not to invade West Germany, so after the alert Ah (second from the left), and my buddies, go on leave for a few days.

Chapter 5

STATESIDE LIFE

BECOMING A STREET RAT

Na Ma was never one to mince words. Ah came home one mornin' after an all night outing 'n' tried to slip quietly into bed, but Ma was waitin' for me. She looked right at me and said, "Michael you're becomin' a street rat!" Ah gave my usual answer, "Ah Ma um just havin' a li'l fun." Later when ah had more time to think about it, ah realized she was right. She always was. But bein' a street rat was fun!

One of my older friends had opened up a nightclub right in my old neighborhood. Na ya talk about good times; this place was really jumpin'. Everyone ah knew hung out there. Single people and married couples were always around. Bosco's was the place to be. Good times were rollin' every night of the week 'n' twice as much on weekends. Na you know by now that um not braggen' when Ah say my street smarts were light years ahead of the locals. Experience had taught me to observe my surroundings and the people around me. Ah could spot hustlers and troublemakers in a second. Ah watched this one barmaid hustlin' drinks from these guys, left and right. She was very attractive, personable, and had an allurin' smile that captivated every guy in the place. Ah kinda smiled to myself, none of these boobs had a shot at takin' her home.

One night she broke away from the usual crowd surroundin' her, walked over to me and asked me to buy her a drink. She was shocked when ah told her no. Ah said, "Listen, when ah wanna buy someone a drink, ah'll ask them if ah can. So ya can stop wastin' your time 'n' get back to your hustlin' drinks." She was mad and surprised that ah was aware of her scheme. She turned her back to me 'n' asked, "Who wants to buy me a drink?" No less than fav' guys waved and replied come on down here and talk to me; i'll buy you all the drinks ya want.

Now if you're wondering how bartenders can drink all night long and never get drunk, ah'll let you in on their secret. They always order a straight shot of whiskey with a cola chaser on the side. They put the whiskey in their mouth ‘n’ hold it there, then they pretend to drink some cola, but instead, they spit the whiskey into the like colored cola glass. Ah continued talkin’ to my friends, dancin’, ‘n’ drinkin’ a glass of wine every now and then. After a coupla hours that same barmaid came over to me ‘n’ said, “Ah got a break coming in a few minutes. Take me over to Martin Bros. and I’ll buy you a sandwich. Ah’d like to know more about you.” When ah walked out with her there were a lot of guys glarin’ at me. Ah knew ah’d hafta watch my back from then on.

A short time later ah started hangin’ out with and datin’ Brook, the barmaid. One night ah left the club a little early. As ah started to unlock my car ah noticed that two of my tires were flat. A closer look revealed they had been slashed! Ah was furious. Now ah knew f’ sure somebody was givin’ me a warnin’, or more likely, a threat. My antenna went up. Ah don’t take threats too kindly. Ah was gonna be ready. So, ah casually mentioned to Brook that ah would like to have a gun. Well, about three days later ah entered the club, made my way to the far end of the bar so Ah could see everyone ‘n’ pulled up a barstool. As Ah sized up the room, Brook came over to me ‘n’ said “Ah got somethin’ for ya.” Before Ah could even ask what it was, she placed a fav’ shot 32 caliber pistol on the bar, better known as a Saturday Night Special. She said, “Take it, it’s your’s.” Ah slipped it into my waistband, pulled my shirt tail over the handle, ordered a glass of wine then mingled into the crowd. Ah felt about ten feet tall. Ah was ready for the tire slasher, knife ‘n’ all.

THE BAR SCENE

The good times were rollin’, but so was my money right out of my pocket. Seems ya can’t even be a street rat without money. Ah managed to pick up a few odd jobs here ‘n’ there, maybe even a hustle or two, but. It still wasn’ enough. Ah needed a job. Brook knew everyone. Ya know how it is; everyone wants to be friends with the barmaid, especially the pretty ones. Anyways, she introduced me to this rich guy that owned two or three restaurants and a coupla motels. He also owned a closed down bar/nightclub further out on Chef Highway, right in my ol’ East New Orlans neighborhood. Sam, the rich guy, told me that he decided to close his bar because there were too many fights. His bar was gettin’ damaged. He couldn’ keep a bartender, and his reputation was gettin’ ruined. He told me this gang of trouble makers ran off all of the good payin’ customers. Ah asked, “Why didn’t ya have them arrested?” Sam replied, “Ah did, but there friends just came back 'n' tore up the place, causin' the bartender to quit. So there you have it, that's the situation you'd be faced with." In the course of our conversation Sam had mentioned the names of some of his tormentors. Ah knew every one of them. Ah'd gone to school with them. Ah knew some of these guys since grade school and played sandlot football with um. At times we hung out. All of um were longtime friends of mine. When Sam offered me the job of managin' his bar, ah jumped on it. After all, Ah'd spent a lot of time in bars all over Europe. Ah thought ah knew a lot about the bar business. Wrong! The customer side of a bar is a whole lot different from the bartender side. First thing Ah did was try to spruce da' place up a bit. It took three days of patchin' holes and paintin' to get the place lookin' good enough to open for business. Boy, those guys sure did a number on the walls. One afternoon ah ran into some of the guys that Sam had told me about. Before they could get off their motorcycles, Ah walked over 'n' greeted them sayin' "Wah ya at?" Ah was pleased and relieved when they replied with, "Mike! Wha' ya been? Haven' seen ya around." Ah answered, "Ah was in the Army. Went across da' pond for a while, but Ah'm back now." Then like street guys do, they started braggin' about how bad their friends were. Normal people brag about their friend's achievements. Street guys brag about their friend's wrongdoin's. First thing they asked was, "Did ya hear about Jawn 'n' Henry? They're in jail for murder! They killed a guy in the French Quarter."

"Yeah Ah heard." Then after a li'l more street news, they got to what was really on their mind.

"Whatcha doin' here? Sam banned us from his bar, and the next thing we know the place is closed." Ah capitalized on this opportunity. "Ah'm the new manager. Ah'm gonna open up this weekend. Ya'll can come on in and have a good time, but ya need to help me out a little and not cause any trouble." Ah got the reply ah was hoping for, "You got it. We don't want no trouble we were just havin' a li'l fun."

Ah had learned a long time ago that it was always wise to hedge my bet, so Ah asked my brother, Paul, to work the door and double as bouncer on the first few weekends. Ah also asked some cops ah'd grown up with to stop by 'n' have a few drinks, on the house of course. Remember, this was New Orlans. It wasn' uncommon for cops to drink in uniform while on duty. With jus' word of mouth advertisin', 'n' Brook bringin' over her regulars (Brook was now my barmaid), my grand openin' was a big success.

Business was good, but Ah had a lot to learn. Mixin' drinks is an art. Ah had to learn how not to bruise a martini. Ah thought, How the hell do ya bruise a martini?) And a lot of other things. Pretty soon personnel from the French Quarter started comin' to my place on their days off. Especially strippers and barmaids. They didn' want their regular customers to get too friendly with them. So they kinda hid out clear across town where no one knew them. When they saw what a greenhorn Ah was, they began teachin' me tricks of the trade. What a break for me. (Ah started to say what a blessin', but Ah don't think the Good Lord is into blessin' the bar business.) Anyways, Ah learned how to mix drinks 'n' keep um flowin'. Ah also learned how to keep the music goin'. Every time it died down, Ah would ask some customers to roll my poker dice. The losin' hand had to put a coupla' bucks of quarters in the jukebox. My Bourbon Street friends showed me how to hedge my bet. Ya see, Ah was the one that picked up the dice, placed them in their container 'n' rolled um out. Best poker hand won. Aces were always wild, so ah would palm an ace with my little finger, place the other dice in the container, shake um up 'n' roll um out slidin' the ace face up. This way, Ah always had at least a pair to start with every time. Ah seldom lost. Another common practice was switchin' expensive popular brand name whiskey with a cheaper one. Let's say you have an empty expensive bourbon bottle and a full bottle of a cheaper bourbon with the exact same ingredients. All ya gotta do is pour the cheap whiskey into the expensive bottle and you've increased your profit about 50%. Ah never had one customer notice the difference. Of course, this is against the law. You're supposed to break all whiskey bottles as soon as they're empty. Na ya got all the information ya need to be a first class street rat. But, Ah gotta warn ya, once ya start dancin' with the devil, you're on a downhill path to destruction.

One of the biker guys stopped by with his young cousin. He told me his cousin was in a teen band that had just won the New Orlans Battle of the Bands contest. He said they were tryin' to get some exposure so he asked if they could have an audition. When Ah heard them play, Ah was completely blown away. They were great! Ah wanted to hire them, but first Ah had to figure out how to pay them. Brook came up with the answer; add a cover charge and up the price of drinks while the band is playin'. Ah hired them for Friday and Saturday nights. None of the other clubs in East New Orlans had a live band. Ah had a good feelin' about my decision. Ah knew that a live band would be a money maker. Once again, Ah'd hedged my bet. Street rule number one: always—"Ah mean always—hedge your bet. If your opponent is big, have a knife. If he has a knife, you have a gun. If he has a gun, get the hell out of there! My competitors didn' have live music, therefore, my club havin' a band made perfect sense to me. Unfortunately, Sam didn' see it that way. Sam was a typical kinda young, rich guy with a very big ego. He wasn' happy about me makin' decisions without checkin' with him first, and some of his older customers had complained to him about the cover charge. He wasn' used to not havin' complete control over everything. Na ya know that wasn' gonna work with me. Ah knew that the band was a good idea, and a money makin' venture. Ah was right, we were so crowded on weekends Paul had to turn people away. Ah was makin' money hand over fist, and except for a few old grouches, everyone liked havin' live music. One group that really wasn' happy were my competitors. Word spread all around East New Orlans that Sam's was the place to be on weekends. Paul's friends, my friends, and Brook's crowd all stopped by. Ah heard that the other bars were dead on weekends. You know what? Ah really didn' care. Ah don't think any of those owners were happy about my success. Go figure.

Livin' life in the fast lane had a lot of perks. Ah knew everyone in the area, there was always a table available at restaurants, and ah always had money. This afforded me with the opportunity to buy and sell things. Ah bought and sold televisions, guns, rings, and a lot of other stuff. Pop always said it takes money to make money. On the other hand, Ah was workin' long hours, had to put up with drunks, hustlers, weirdos, 'n' troublemakers. Ah was so busy Ah had to hire another barmaid for the day shift. However, most days Ah ended up workin' from two in the afternoon until two-thirty or three o'clock the next mornin'. Ah had a back room equipped with a cot and intercom so Ah could rest and still listen for trouble in the bar. Sometimes Ah would lay on my cot 'n' think about a quote from one of my favorite books, On the Road. "Live fast, die young, and have a good looking corpse." Was this happenin' to me?

My entire band was made up of teenagers, so naturally they attracted a younga' crowd. This wasn' necessarily good, cause young people usually don't have a lot of money, but on the other hand, they'll spend what they have without thinkin'. Business continued to grow at my place and decline in neighboring bars causin' hate and discontent among the owners. Ah could feel tension in the air, but was too busy to give it a lot of thought. Ah probably shoulda listened to my instincts.

My favorite part of the bar scene was meetin' all the interestin' characters. There were so many of um, Ah'll just mention a couple. There was this cook who worked in a greasy spoon diner across the highway. He would come in 'n' talk to me after his shift. There was somethin' about Jim's smile that made me think that he was hidin' somethin'. Ah suspected that he was concealin' a dark side. He told me, when he was drivin' into New Orlans his car broke down right in front of this sleazy mechanic/junkyard. You know, jus' like the ones ya see in the movies. Well, when Jim came to get his car, the mechanic said he wouldn' release the car until Jim paid for a bunch of added charges. Jim calmly told him, "I'll be right back." He came back all right, but this time he had a double barrel, sawed off shotgun with him. He told the sleazeball mechanic, "I'm taking my car. If you try to stop me, I'll blow your f****** head off, and if you try to call the cops I'll get to you before they get to me!" Jim got his car without any further trouble.

Ah was right, this guy could be dangerous. Another time about one-thirty in the mornin', Ah kept hearin' these kinda muffled gunshots but couldn' locate where they were comin' from. A little later Jim came in 'n' Ah asked if he had heard any gunshots. He started laughin', "Yeah it was me. Ah was shooting rats with my boss' pistol!" Makes ya wanna eat in that diner, right? Ah got the idea that maybe ol Jim wasn' dealin' from a full deck. You could feel the unpredictable vibes surroundin' this guy. Ah knew he could go off at any time. Ah was friends with him but kept him at a safe distance. A short time later he just disappeared. Ah hafta admit Ah was pleased when he didn' show up for our late night talks.

Another interestin' character came into the bar fresh out of prison for writin' bad checks. Ah knew this guy, he was known all over town for writin' rubber checks. Anyways, Ah had a TV for sale. He says he wants to buy it. Ah say "OK. That'l be forty dollars." He says "OK. Ah'll just write you a check!" Ah laughed 'n' threw his ass out.

One Saturday night Ah was workin' the door, greetin' people, 'n' checkin' IDs. A group of about six cute young girls came up to the door gigglin' 'n' laughin', like young girls do. Three of um presented drivers licenses that showed they were eighteen. The other three or four girls said they forgot their wallets at home. They started pleadin' "Please, please, please let us in. We just want to listen to the music. We know 'dose guys in da ban'." Na Ah have to admit, Ah was still learnin' the bar business 'n' Ah didn' know all of the laws. Ah was still young 'n' kinda naive. Long story short they charmed me into lettin' um in, but Ah was firm when it came to drinks. The girls without I D would be served soft drinks only; no hard liquor at all. Ah seated them at a table 'n' went back to work. About an hour later Ah noticed some guys gatherin' around out in the pawkin' lot. They were jokin' with each other 'n' foolin' around like a bunch of high school kids. Some of um had top coats on 'n' started doin' James Cagney routines, you know the line,

"OK Louie, drop the gun." Stuff like that.

Ah didn' think anything of it 'n' went on about my business. All of a sudden those same guys came bustin' in yellin', "This is a police raid! Stop the music, everyone stay where you are!" It took about a minute to sink in. Then Ah realized oh s***! Ah've been set up. My competitors had set me up, those rottin f***ers set me up! The young girls were part of a sting. The cops went right to their table 'n' asked them how old they were. They chirped out their ages in chorus. Na Ah knew it was a setup f'sure. Right away, Ah tried to befriend one of the cops, but Brook, not bein' from New Orlans, tried to argue with them. Big mistake. The lead cop (probably the one bein' paid off) got right in my face 'n' said "If you don't get her under control, you're goin' to jail, she's goin' to jail, and Ah'll go get the owner and put his ass in jail too. Do you realize that you have sixteen and fifteen-year-old girls, in here."

Ah said, "But officer, Ah only served um soft drinks."

He replied, "Ah don't give a f***! They're not even suppose to be in here at all!"

My instincts kicked in. Ah had to act fast to avoid jail. Ah pushed Brook out of the way 'n' told her in no uncertain terms to be quiet. Then Ah told the cops Ah was closin' down right away. Ah could swear the cop had a smile on his face when he fined the owner, told me the band members were also under age 'n' couldn' ever be in there again. Before leavin' they warned (threatened) me one more time. Then they left takin' the girls with him. New Orlans cops are pretty bold. They didn' even try to hide their obvious set up.

Ah had put up a pretty good fight against the Army, even got in a few pretty good blows, but New Orlans cops were a different breed. Ya can't beat um 'n' Ah knew it.

Ah decided the nightclub business jus' wasn' my forte. Besides, Ah'd been at this job about four months. It was time for another adventure. Ah couldn' seem to find my niche in life. At this point Ah wasn' sure if Ah wanted to find it. Or if Ah even had a niche. Ah had a lot of livin' to do before ah settled into my role in the business world. The only job that appealed to me was President of the United States, 'n' that job was already taken. Ah hung around another week then left the bar scene for good. Sam's turned back into jus' another roadside bar.

LOVE YOUR NEIGHBOR

Pop started givin' me part time shifts at his fillin' station. The work was easy but the hours long. It was durin' those long hours that Ah learned the true meanin' of the Bible phrase, "love your neighbor." Pop's station was a magnet for a variety of people from all walks of life. Winos, schizophrenics, lonely people, and businessmen all passed by (pass by = stop by in New Orlans speak) to talk and socialize. Pop didn' just sell gas, his fillin' station was a gatherin' place that provided comfort to people no matter what their social status was. Pop gave everyone respect. He understood their condition and did what he could to ease their pain. Someone once asked Pop why he gave this wino money when he knew he would jus' buy wine with it. Pop said, "Looka here. That man is not gonna stop drinkin' whether or not Ah give him money. He needs that wine in the mornin' just like you need your coffee." Now that's lovin' your neighbor without judgin' him. Ah told ya Pop could teach psychology.

TARZAN

Right off the bat, Ah could tell Tarzan was gonna' be one of the most interestin' people A'd ever know. If you saw him you'd know why. He had long blond hair 'n' ripplin' muscles that made him look like a bodybuilder. Tarzan was a combat-hardened Korean War vet. Highly trained in some sort of Special Operations outfit, he'd seen a lot of action and suffered from what we now call post traumatic stress. (There wasn' a term for this condition back then; we called it shell shocked 'cause loud noises could set um off.) Like most war vets, Tarzan wouldn' talk much about his combat experiences. It was obvious he'd seen some pretty horrible stuff. His combat experience intrigued me, and at the same time made me leery of him. On slow nights he would show me some of his real combat tested hand-to-hand combat techniques. Ah had some hand-to-hand and bayonet trainin' in the Army, nothin' compared to what Special Ops guys get though. Tarzan was tryin' to show me that boxin' 'n' sport oriented stuff wouldn' work in a deadly life or death situation. Ah understood what he was sayin, but Ah really didn' want to kill anyone. Ah disregarded Tarzan's techniques that ended in death to the adversary (which was pretty much all of his techniques). It scared me when he'd get this far off look in his eyes like he was back in Korea. Ah didn' want his killer instincts to kick in and have him mistake me for a North Korean!

As a side note, about twenty years later Ah trained with Jim Wagner, the first person to come up with a comprehensive modern reality based system.

His system can be used in any situation. Ah trained with Jim for several years and studied his methods. Eventually, Ah incorporated some of the methods in my knife 'n' street fightin' classes.

But, back to Tarzan. Sometimes Tarzan and I would just talk. Ah think he needed those talks more than Ah needed the trainin'. Ah noticed that our conversations always drifted to his estranged wife. From what little information he was willin' to share, Ah found out that she had left him for a New Orlans cop. This big highly-skilled, ex-military combat survivor was taken down by someone he loved and trusted. The pain that was buried down deep inside of him showed in his wide-eyed stare. Ah saw somethin' else in those eyes: instability. Ah tried to give him some advice but soon realized it wouldn' help. All Ah could do was try to change the subject. It was hard seein' this highly-respected combat veteran mortally wounded by his closest companion. Every time Ah tried to divert his attention, his mind went right back to his ex and what she did. It was obvious to me that if he didn' get his mind under control somethin' bad was gonna happen. Na Ah hafta admit, Ah was kinda relieved when Tarzan stopped comin' around; he had become a powder keg about to explode.

Ah went on with my life. One day a friend of mine stopped by 'n' asked, "you know Tarzan don' cha?"

Ah said, "Yeah Ah know him pretty good; he's a friend of mine."

The guy went on, "Tarzan was speedin' one night when this cop stops him 'n' asks for his driver's license. When the cop shined his flashlight on the license, Tarzan was able to see his face. It was the cop that was datin' his ex.! Somehow Tarzan managed to get the cops gun away from him and killed him with it. The problem was when they found the cop he still had Tarzan's driver's license in his hand. Tarzan's gonna be in for a long time; he might even get the death penalty."

Ah felt sick, Ah remembered that look—that wounded animal look. All of his pent up pain and fury musta came pourin' out. That poor cop didn' have a chance. Ah thought, Here's a guy that could whip a bear with a switch, fought gallantly for his country, feared no man, was always respectful of others; but couldn' handle his broken heart! Stuff like this hasta make ya think about life 'n' what's it all about. Where do you put your trust? In a person? In government? Ya gotta be kidden'. What then? After a lot of years Ah found the answer. There's only one person that you can put all of your love and trust in. That person is Jesus Christ! He'll never let you down.

Sometimes you think you know someone. Ya might think they're shy and kind of a nerd, then ya find out they've been stealin' money from the church Christmas fund.

HENRY

Ah got another true story that'll blow you away. Ah promise, it's a good one. This young seventeen-year-old kid used to come by Pop's station. This kid, Henry, was tall, skinny, and always neat as a pin. Henry looked kinda out of place around his Ninth Ward peers. He just didn' seem to fit in. Ah got to know him pretty good; or so Ah thought. He usually came around on weekends with his li'l fourteen year old girlfriend. Anita was cute as can be. She had long wavy brown hair and big eyes as dark as black diamonds. Her parents were a li'l old-fashioned. They were Cajon's from Laplace, Louisiana. Anita looked and acted like a little angel. Ah thought she was. Sometimes when we didn' have any cars to wash Ah'd let Henry wash his own car 'n' only charge him half price. After he washed his car he'd hang around until it was time to pick up Anita. Well, one Sunday afternoon Henry was talkin' to me about Anita's Mom not wantin' them to get too serious. She told um they were seein' too much of each other and Anita was too young for a serious relationship. Henry looked troubled 'n' uptight, so Ah gave him my unprofessional ex-bartender advice. Ah said, Tell her how ya'll feel about each other and stuff like dat." He listened for awhile then left the station at about two o'clock in the afternoon. Ah finished my shift and soon forgot about the young lovers' problems. The next day, when Ah got to the station, one of Pop's customers showed me the headlines 'n' asked, "Didn' Ah see this kid hangin' around here?"

Ah looked at the picture. It was Henry! Ah couldn' believe the headlines under his picture. They stated that Henry and Anita had both taken part in murderin' Anita's Mother. Ah'm tellin' ya, it's still very difficult for me to think 'n' write about this. My mind jus' can't grasp it. Those kids couldna done that. And the way they killed her was was even more unbelievable. They savagely beat her to death with a hammer!

Ah kept thinkin', that skinny kid, that angelic li'l girl, they jus' couldna'. If Ah hadn' seen it in the paper, if someone was tellin' me this story, Ah woulda called um a liar. When my mind cleared, Ah read the rest of the article 'n' was shocked even further. They killed her Mother because she wouldn' let Anita go to the movies that night! The murder took place on Sunday afternoon at 3:15 PM. About an hour after Henry left the station. Ah said out loud, "Ah was jus' talkin' to that kid right before the murder." Could Ah have said or done somethin' to prevent this tragedy from happenin'? That thought still haunts me.

LOUIS

Na um gonna tell ya about one more character, then Ah'm gonna have to lighten up a bit 'cause Ah still get emotional after all these years. Louis was another character that passed by Pop's station. He was about my age. Na Ah couldn' tell if Louis was a little slow, took too much drugs, or jus' couldn' talk rite. Yeah Ah know how could anyone tell? Some people have a hard time understandin' the natives. One visitor wrote about her visit to New Orlans 'n' said the language is like Brooklynese on quaaludes. Ah'm a native 'n' Ah could hardly understand Louis. Na he wasn' a bad guy, he jus' hung around with the wrong people. One day he came by with two baby alligators and gave them to me. They were real cute but when Ah tried to pet one, the little sucker bit me. Louis explained the situation to me. His cousin and some friends had hijacked a truck, broke the lock and made off with a bunch of crates. When they opened them there were all of these baby alligators. They had stolen a bunch of illegal alligators. These guys warn' all bad either, they sold and gave them away so the gators wouldn' die. Na Ah had two pet alligators.

As time went on, Ah noticed that Louis was gettin' deeper into drugs 'n' committin' crimes to support his habit. He probably felt his life spinnin' out of control. One day he rigged his rifle up so when someone opened the door to his room it would fire. Then he sat in front of it and yelled for someone to come in. When his cousin opened the door, the gun went off and killed Louis. After Louis's death his cousin became more messed up than he already was. On top of that, the police didn' believe it was a suicide and tried to pin a murder rap on Louis's cousin. It took several months before the charges were finally dropped. When Ah thought about it, Ah became a li'l skeptical about the whole thing myself 'cause there were drugs involved. But it was what it was. Louis was gone.

MY GIRLFRIEND BROOK

Na Ah'll lighten it up a li'l. Every evenin' when it was about time for my shift to end, Pop would start clearin' things and people away from the door and driveway, cause Brook would come flyin' into the station—tires screechin'—as she slid to a stop. Ah would dive through the open window, then she peeled out. We usually went to clubs around town. Sometimes we

ened up in the French Quarter.

WHITE MEN CAN'T DIG

Workin' at Pop's station was interestin', but Ah wasn' makin' enough money. Ah needed more money, some new friends, 'n' jus' a change in general. Pop introduced me to this young guy that ran a construction company for his father. This guy wasn' exactly like a typical rich kid; but close. He had ta put in long hours. He bossed several labor crews 'n' the crane/dredgin' crew. Anyways, he says, "Ah herd ya binlookin' fa a job, so Ah'll tell you what, (In New Orleanese, the Ah'll do is understood. So there's no need to waste time sayin' it). You can work as a laborer, the job pays union wages, a $1.95 an hour. (That was big bucks in those days). But there's one drawback, You'll have to work on an all black crew and hide from the union rep when he comes around." Remember segregation was still in full swing at this time, and it worked both ways. The black union leaders wouldn' allow whites in their union. Ah jumped at the opportunity to make some big bucks. "Ah'll take it. When do Ah start?"

My first day on the job was an eye opener for me. The whole crew looked like da Green Bay Packers offensive line; they were huge. When Ah got to the job site, they all stopped workin' 'n' just stared at me for a full minute. They were probably wonderin' what this li'l 140lb. white boy was doin' on dere job site. There were no introductions, the foreman simply said, "Jump in 'n' start shovelin'." There Ah was back in a trench diggin' again. The only difference between here 'n' Germany was the heat and humidity

At first the all black crew didn' trust me. They thought Ah was a spy for "the man," but after a while, afta' Ah dug my way halfway to China, they began to trust me. Ah made some good friends 'n' experienced life in a way that few, if any, white men ever did. Ah was even invited to have a few brews with them after work. Of course Ah never did, 'cause it would have put them in an awkward situation. They would've had to protect me from their friends 'n' neighbors.

There was no way Ah could shovel as much or as fast as those guys, so they gave me a different job. My new job was hod carrier for a bricklayer. Hod is a cement mix that holds bricks together. My job was to stack bricks at arms length for the bricklayer, mix the hod by hand, then deliver it to the bricklayer. Na a good bricklayer can lay about 2,000 bricks a day. The hod carrier had to keep him supplied with bricks 'n' hod without slowin' him down. The job was challengin', but before long, Ah found my rhythm. In about a week Ah was able to keep the bricks 'n' hod flowin'. Ya talk about hard work. Ah guess Ah was burnin' up boo cue calories, 'cause Ah would eat fav' sandwiches, two moon pies, some bananas, chips, and drink several soft drinks. Ah could eat all dat stuff for lunch, then eat a big supper 'n' still not gain or lose weight.

Workin' shirtless in the hot sun made me almost as dark as my co-workers, 'n' at some point Ah musta blended right in with um 'cause the union rep never did ask to see my union card. Anyways, almost every day when Ah was mixin' my hod, these three girls would come by 'n' talk to me. It wasn' long before the owner's son noticed them. He was married but that didn' seem to matter to him. He was still a hound dog. Ah guess Ah betta tell ya'll about the moral code in this area. Basically, there was none; but everyone would say they were God fearin' people. If ya axed um if they drank they'd say no, only on special occasions. Upon further inquiry ya find out they drink on the followin' occasions: his and his wife's family's birthdays, includin' nieces, nephews, cousins, and their families, all holidays, and of course, Mardi Gras. They were drinkin' almost every day. Na Ah'll try to explain the Ninth Ward religious philosophy. From Monday 'til Saturday ya live it up, drinkin', dancin', doin' whatever. Then ya go to confession and receive communion on Sunday. When Monday rolls around ya start partyin' again. Ya just hafta hope ya don't die before ya get back to confession that week! Ask any Ninth Ward street rat what they think about their relationship with God 'n' they'll tell you, "Me 'n' God are good. Ah just went to confession last week." Does any of this make sense to you? If it does, you should move to the Ninth Ward.

When lunchtime rolled around, the boss's hounddog son called me over 'n' asked me to set up a water skiin' day with the girls. He said, "Ah got a boat, skis—everything we need. Ah'll also pay you for the day. Na let's see, mixin' hod by hand, 'n' stackin' bricks in the hot sun or, water skiin' on a nice cool lake with some pretty girls 'n' gettin' paid for it."

Is that a no brainer 'r what? But ya know what? Ah didn' feel good about it. Somethin' inside of me didn' feel rite. Ah didn' know what what it was. Maybe the Tarzan disaster had somethin' to do with it, or maybe because if Brook found out about it she'd kill me. Then Ah thought oh well, guess Ah'll just hafta live in the moment.

We were on the boat gettin' ready to water ski. Ah was talkin'to the girls 'n' said somethin' about my boss bein' married. The girl he was with looked at him and exclaimed, "you're married? Take me home right now!" That ended what started out to be a pretty good day. My boss was mad, the girl was mad, and Ah was confused. Only thing Ah could think of was that those girls couldna been from New Orlans. Turns out Ah was right; they were'nt. Ah ended up datin' one of um for awhile but it didn' work out. She couldn' get used to the New Orlans lifestyle.

Ah continued doin' construction work a few more months, then wanderlust set in. The Army had kindled a fire that had been buried deep down inside of me. Ah felt a compellin' need to travel. My tour with the Army was for the most part in Europe. Ah wanted to see more of this wonderful country. Ah had to see those purple mountains and fruited plains. Ah wanted to meet people 'n' learn about their lives. Ah still had a lot of livin' to do before Ah settled down. Too many of my friends were either in jail or dead. It was time for new friends. Ah'd learned to speak German; maybe in time Ah could learn to speak Yankee. Besides, Ah had a Grandfather Ah'd never seen. Grandpa Di Giovanni had moved to California before Ah was born. Ah'd heard stories about him all my life, but hadn' had a chance to meet him. Ah thought, yeah California. That's where um goin'. Besides my life in New Orlans didn' seem to be goin' anywhere.

Brook was gettin' too serious, my job became routine 'n' Ah needed adventure. So, after an argument with Brook one night, Ah decided to leave. On my way to work the next mornin' Ah made up my mind to do it. Ah said out loud, "Ah'm goin' to California."

Ah slammed on my brakes, made a screechin' u-turn, went back to my motel room, packed my ol' Army duffel bag 'n' started out. First Ah had to say goodby to Ma. She was surprised to see me so early in the mornin' 'n' naturally thought somethin' was wrong. Ah tried to comfort her right away, so Ah blurted out, "There's nothin' wrong Ma. Ah'm goin' to California!"

She was sad 'n' happy at the same time. Ma didn' like the street life Ah was livin'. She didn' like my friends, the girls Ah was datin' (especially Brook), the places Ah hung out, or anything about my street rat lifestyle.

She asked, "When did you decide to leave?"

Ah answered, "This mornin'. Please tell Pop, my brothers, 'n' everyone Ah said goodby, 'n' Ah'll see um soon."

My next stop was my job site. Ah told my boss, "Ah quit, Ah'm headed for California. Where can Ah get my paycheck?"

Ah picked up my check, cashed it, then pointed my old 1951 Studebaker West. Ah didn' even have a road map. Ah just followed the signs that directed me towards Baton Rouge. The sights and sounds of the city faded from my rearview mirror. Once again Ah was alone with my thoughts on the road, headed for an unknown destination.

Ah was almost to Baton Rouge before Ah realized Ah didn' even tell Brooke Ah was leavin'! Ah thought boy is she gonna be mad. Ah had a feelin' Ah'd find out soon enough. Ah looked up at the sign that was hangin' from my mirror, LIVE FAST, DIE YOUNG, 'n' Ah pressed on the gas pedal.

Chapter 6

CALIFORNIA ADVENTURE

CALIFORNIA HERE I COME

Soon after Ah crossed the state line into Texas, my ol' car started smokin' like a chimney, about every 100 miles or so, Ah had to put in four quarts of oil. No matter, oil and gas were cheap. Gas averaged about thirty-cents a gallon and Ah could get four quarts of bulk oil for two dollars. My mind was made up, Ah was goin' to California 'n' nothin' was gonna stop me.

The landscape in East Texas is much like Louisiana: flat and swampy. There wasn' any noticeable change in scenery until Ah got outside of Houston. As Ah rolled into the central Texas hill country Ah began to feel the loneliness of the open road; Ah felt like a grain of sand in this vast, sparsely populated region of the world. After what seemed like endless miles of nothin' but road and open space Ah began to wonder if Ah'd driven into another dimension. Everything was so big 'n' beautiful; maybe this was the land of Oz or somethin'. Ah had to get a grip. Ah coulda been seein' things, cause by now my whole car was filled with smoke. Ah had to tie a handkerchief over my nose so ah could breath. What a sight that musta ben? Picture this: a masked guy drivin' a car with a cloud of smoke belowin' out behind it.

As Ah entered New Mexico (The Land of Enchantment), Ah could see what inspired Katharine Bates to write, "America the Beautiful." Snow covered mountains seemed to roll right into cactus filled deserts. The high dry air combined with exhaust fumes made this land seem captivatin' and somewhat magical. My ol' car limped across New Mexico to the Arizona border. On my north side way off in the distance Ah could see mountain ranges with towerin' peaks, grassy plains with elevated mesas stretched out in front of me. Wow! What a variety of beauty and grandeur. That evenin' Ah was treated to one of the most spectacular sights Ah'd ever seen. On the horizon in front of me Ah saw this majestic saguaro cactus sunset, a sight that is forever burned into my mind.

Finally, Ah crossed the border into California. Ah started yellin' 'n' singin', "Ah made it! Ah made it! Ah'm in California! Cal- ah- forn- ya here Ah come, Cal- ah- forn-ya, Ah'm here!"

Yeah, Ah didn' have a radio and Ah'd been alone on the road for seven days. Ah had to entertain myself. Did ya ever do that? Ya know, sing really loud while alone in a car? Makes ya feel good, don't it? Ah knew Ah was way off key, but it didn' thwart my excitement. Ah had fulfilled a lifelong dream. Ah was in California. There were stories back home that California didn' have roaches or mosquitos. Could that be true? Was this really the land of milk and honey?

STUCK IN THE MIDDLE OF NOWHERE

After Ah passed through Yuma, a fillin' station attendant told me about a shortcut. Ah decided to try it. Ah found myself on a seldom-used highway that skirted the Mexican border. My only distraction from the flat open road was some mountains way off in the distance, a few desert shrubs, and white sand dunes. Ah was about 165 miles south of San Diego, somewhere in the middle of a desert. Suddenly my ol' car jus' up and died. My light- hearted mood took a dive, There wasn' a house, car, or person anywhere in sight. What to do? Ah couldn' start walkin' cause Ah had too much stuff. Everything Ah owned was in my car. Ah had a goatskin wine flask (from Spain), full of water, enough to last about a day.

Ah never felt so alone 'n' helpless in my life. Then Ah realized that God was always there to save my worthless butt. I started to pray, (Ah wonder what unbelievers do). Ah prayed, Lord Jesus, if ya get me outta' this one Ah'll make better decisions 'n' try not to bother you next time. Yeah, Ah know. Pretty lame, but Ah really didn' know how to pray back then. He heard me anyway. When Ah looked down the highway behind me—way off on the horizon—there was a black speck barely visible through the dust devils that were dancin' in the road. Ah squinted 'n' took a closer look.

Could it be? Yes! It was a car! Ah looked up 'n' said, "Thank You."

Seconds later, the car came to a screamin' stop inches from my back bumper, three sailors hopped out 'n' asked, "What's the problem kid?"

They were older men, probably in their mid thirties. Ah could tell they'd been drinkin'. They reeked of alcohol 'n' kinda slurred their words. All of us gave my car the usual once over and concluded it just wasn' gonna start. One of the sailors noticed my Army duffel bag, 'n' asked if Ah was in the military. Ah told um about my land and sea service, (Ah left out the part about how much Ah hated that stinkin' ol' tub Ah sailed across the pond on). That was all it took; we became instant bro's. They said, "Hop in your car. We'll push you to the nearest mechanic."

Good thing there wasn' another car in sight, cause within a coupla minutes we were flyin' down da road at eighty-five miles per hour. They pushed me right on through Calexico, then we started a gradual climb up the Cuyamaca mountains. The narrow two-lane road soon became steep and windin', but the sailors didn' even slow down! They kept pushin' me at breakneck speed. Ah hung on to the steerin' wheel with both hands. Ah couldn' hit my brakes cause they were right up against my bumper.

We came skiddin' around a turn and came upon a slow movin' haytruck about 200 yds in front of me They sped up to about 75 mph then backed off, affordin' me the opportunity to coast around the truck. Problem was, Ah couldn' see if there were any cars comin' around the blind curve ahead of me.

As Ah coasted around the curve, my live fast die young sign seemed to start flashin'. Die young! Die young! Die young! You're goin' too fast; you're gonna die young!

This same scenario happened two more times before we finally reached a fillin' station. When we stopped, the sailors (Ah never did get their names) came over and each of them shook my hand. One of them said, "Kid, you can really drive."

Another one chimed in, Ah, never saw anything like it." (Ah knew they musta had booze in their car cause they were drunker now than before.)

After a mechanic checked out my car, the station manager told me that it would cost too much to fix. He said the engine was shot and the timin' chain was broken. He offered me $15.00 cash for my car. All three sailors got in the guys face 'n' started yellin', "You're not gonna take advantage of this kid. His car is worth a lot more than $15.00 dollars. We'll push him clear to San Diego!"

The thought of them pushin' me all the way to San Diego brought two words to mind, *Nuh uh.*

Ah got between the station manager and the sailors, stuck out my hand n said, "Ah'll take the fifteen dollars."

One of the sailors said, "Okay kid. If that's the way you want it. You drive. Just make sure you don't pass up any places that sell beer."

We loaded my stuff into their car and hit the road again. Ah was drivin' at a pretty good clip, but they kept yellin', "Come on kid! Drive the car! We'll never get to San Diego at."

Good thing Ah was used to bein' around drunks. At this point in my young life, Ah'd been around the block a coupla times. Back in New Orlans we used to say, "It's not the age, it's the mileage that counts." Usin' that formula, Ah had to be at least ninety! Anyways, Ah didn' argue or let them get under my skin. (Some advice: neva'—Ah mean neva' argue with a drunk.) Ah jus' kept drivin'. By the grace of God, we finally got to the Navy base in San Diego in time for supper. These guys were well known on the base. They musta held some kind of Navy rank. They knew where Escondido was and how to get there.

After we ate one of the sailors says, "Let's get you to Escondido, kid. You're still drivin'. Head North on Highway 18 and stop at the first liquor store you see."

Boy, these guys jus' wouldn' quit. They were determined to get in all the drinkin' they could before their leave was up. Ah stopped for their liquor then headed north towards Escondido.

HEY PODNA, DO YOU KNOW MY UNCLE JIMMY?

We were almost to Escondido before Ah discovered that Ah'd left my family's phone numbers 'n' addresses in my car. As Ah entered town Ah slowed down to a crawl lookin' for a phone booth. (Aren't ya glad you have a cell phone?). Don'cha' know there wasn' a phone booth in sight. Then Ah thought, Uncle Jimmy was always a man about town. Someone around here is bound to know him. Sure enough, Ah saw a guy comin' out of a bar, pulled up along side of him 'n' asked, "Hey podna do you by any chance know a guy named Jimmy Di Giovanni?"

The guy says, "I sure do. He was in here drinking with me about a half hour ago. My car is just across the street. Follow me I'll lead you to his house." (My uncle's house was about three minutes away. Was that luck r' what?)

Uncle Jimmy gave me the traditional Italian greetin': hugs, kisses, and sayin' my name in Italian, "Michele, (Mee-keh-leh), Michele, it's so good to see you! How's your Papa 'n' Mama? Come on in."

The sailors introduced themselves, my uncle introduced us to his girlfriend (that ol scoundrel. Ah told ya he was a man about town). He had a wife back in New Orlans). It was time to say goodby to the sailors because they were staggerin' around like, you know, drunkin' sailors. My uncle and I both offered them money, but they wouldn' take it. Ah still don't know how they got back to their base.

SOMETHING STINKS AROUND HERE

The very next day Ah was introduced to the fertilizer business. Boy, ya talk about hard stinky work! We went to dairies in and around Escondido, used a tractor to rake the cow pens and made fertilizer hills high as telephone poles, then we used a front loader to dig into that pile of ****, loaded it in my Uncle's truck. Finally we delivered our scented load to orange or avocado groves (we call avocados alligator pears in New Orlans). Next we used a tractor to pull a fertilizer spreader to spread the sweet smellin' stuff. Na Ah already had a really dark tan, but the California sun made me even darker. Once again Ah experienced prejudice because of the way Ah looked. Ah thought people outside of the South were not supposed to be prejudice. Boy was Ah wrong. Ah found out that people are pretty much the same no matter where they live. There's always one group that looks down on another group. Have ya ever searched deep down into your own soul to see what your prejudice is? Ya notice how Ah slip in a li'l preachin' every now 'n' then, Ah can't help it; it's what Ah do.

Most people thought Ah was my Uncle's Mexican helper. Some of them even made rude remarks like, "Hey Jimmy. What are you doing bringing your wetback help in here for lunch?" They would laugh and joke about it when he told them Ah was his nephew. Ah didn' think it was so funny, but Ah kept my mouth shut, cause of my Uncle.

Ah worked about three weeks for room and board, until it became clear, that at this rate Ah would never be able to get a car or better myself (besides my Uncle was not on speakin' terms with the rest of my family). Ah desperately wanted to see my Grandpa and hang out with my other uncle and cousins. Things worked out. One day my Uncle Jimmy took me to a motel paid a few days rent 'n' said, "Ah'll see you later."

GRANDPA DI GIOVANNI

My other uncle, Uncle Joe, heard about this, 'n' came 'n' got me. He offered me room, board, 'n' wages for helpin' him with his fertilizer business. Now Ah could finally see my Grandpa. Grandpa Di Giovanni was an amazing man. He looked 'n' spoke like he'd just gotten off the boat from Italy. He would say some words in English and some in Italian. Ah could understand him pretty good, 'cause in New Orlans people often don't complete sentences. Ya hafta figure out the endin'. We hit it off right away. He told me wonderful stories about Italy and making his way in this country.

He went from cuttin' sugar cane in White Castle Louisiana to a prominent business owner in Escondido California. His stories were fascinaten'. Ah'll try to remember some that you might find interestin'. He explained how the Di in our name came about. It indicates it's a title of respect. This is exactly what my Grandpa told me. "Many years ago, the Di Giovanni's ruled a certain province in Italy. It was probably located in or around Santa margherita de Belice 'cause that's wehere Grandpa was born. When the Di Giovanni's were defeated in one of the many struggles for power in that area, they were put on a reservation. You need to understand, Di Giovanni was not just a family name; it was a whole group of people, kinda like an American Indian tribe. To insure that they would never regain power all of their weapons—'n' most tools—were taken away from them. (They didn't have 2nd amendment rights.) And on top of that they were denied any type of education. Ah don't know how far back this policy goes, but Ah do know none of the Di Giovanni's that came over from Sicily could read or write. Grandpa was a young man when he was forced to work in the sugarcane fields to help pay off his family's boat passage debt. One day he got fed up with the whole cane cuttin' thing and jus' walked away. He made his way to New Orlans, got married 'n' had four kids in a short time. He became an iceman to support his growin' family.

This was in the early 1920's when prohibition was in effect. Well, Grandpa decided to augment his income by buildin' a whisky still. In a very short time, He made more money sellin' whisky than ice. Doncha' know, the Feds came bustin' in, chopped up his still with axes 'n' threw my Grandpa in jail! My Pop was a young boy, about Seven years old. Pop told us that on Sundays he would bring Grandpa's spaghetti 'n' meatballs to the jail. The guards would search through the dish for weapons and say things like, "Ya can't trust these spaghetti bendin' WOP's. Can you imagine how this made Pop feel?

Grandpa lost his ice business 'n' almost everything he had. When he got out, he converted his ice truck into a produce carrier and 'n' started buyin' produce from farms in nearby small towns, He would take the produce to New Orlans 'n' sell it at the French Market. On the way back from one of those small towns his truck turned over as he was roundin' a curve comin' off of the Huey Long Bridge. When he woke up Grandpa found himself trapped in the truck with blood runnin' down onto his face from the head wound he'd suffered. Instead of people helpin' him, they stole his produce 'n' and left him trapped in his truck bleedin'. The Highway Patrol finally arrived and gave him the help he needed. His truck was damaged beyond repair so after he recovered from the accident he tried his hand at runnin' a dairy farm. Grandpa had some friends that knew the dairy business and desperately needed jobs, so he leased a dairy farm just outside of New Orlans. He hired some milkers to help him with his new business venture. Grandpa's whiskey business didn' work out too good. Na he hoped to achieve success in the milk business. This was about the time of the big stock market crash in 1929. Grandpa's dairy business failed along with thousands of other businesses across the country. Grandpa worked at various jobs for about eleven years. Na Ah don't know how he did it but Grandpa managed to buy another truck. (Ah'm pretty sure Pop co-signed for for the truck 'n' ended up payin' for it). Grandpa put a canvas cover over the back, loaded up his family, possessions, 'n' one young man that had no family,'n' took off. Grandpa started the Di Giovanni families' gradual migration to California.

When they got to the Arizona-California border they found lines of cars on both sides of the road. Families were livin' in makeshift shelters. Grandpa's English wasn' very good (Ah know you're probably thinkin' neither is yours), 'n' he was always wary of government officials, so he sent his young ward to find out what was goin' on. He found out that California had established quotas for migrants. Southern Europeans, Jews, Mexicans 'n' some other ethnic groups were targeted. Others had to have some sort of job skills or a potential employer.

Ya see, the U.S. economy had tanked due to the depression and dust bowl conditions in the mid-west. People were flockin' to California in droves. Long story short, Grandpa didn' have the necessary documents to enter California. They were stuck there at the border. So they decided to go back to a fillin' station a few miles away to regroup. While fillin' his truck with gas, Grandpa met an Italian family that were goin' back to the East Coast. They told their paesano's about a seldom-used dirt road that skirted around the checkpoint. Their new friends cautioned them about a section of the road that was washed out due to recent rain storms. For lagniappe, (lan yappe) their paesans told them that there were fruit pickin' jobs in the Escondido area. So my family went around the checkpoint 'n' headed for Escondido (Hidden Valley in English).

About ten miles up the dirt road they rolled up to the washed out section of road. It was deeper and wider than they thought it would be. Grandpa's truck was big and set up higher than cars but without knowin' the water's depth, they couldn' chance tryin' to cross. The young man that was with them found a long stick. He waded into the water, placed the stick on the road bed at the waters deepest point, 'n' marked the waterline. Then he compared the water height to the engine's vital parts 'n' found out that they could make it. Next they tied a long piece of rope to the truck's front bumper, waded across the road 'n' tied the other end to a tree. Everyone pulled on the rope while Grandpa inched the truck across. Life's lesson here. Ya gotta think, *If the good Lord didn' want you to use your head he woulda given you two asses!*

In those days people had to do whatever it took to survive. From this point on it was clear sailin' all the way to Escondido. Ah don't remember exactly how long they had to use the truck for shelter. They found jobs pickin' oranges 'n' grapes in 'n' around Escondido.

From these poor, undistinguished circumstances, my Grandpa managed to purchase three-and-a-half acres of land in the heart of Escondido, plant a grape vineyard, make legendary wine, and own a combination liquor grocery store. So now ya can understand why these stories were so captivatin' 'n' inspirational for me.

Ah learned the fertilizer business, worked hard, 'n' finally saved up enough money to buy a nice li'l 1954 Chevy. Things were goin' along pretty good, but soon boredom set in. Escondido was a very small town. The biggest hangout 'n' most excitin' place was the bowlin' alley. Ah even ran into a guy that Ah'd known in Baumholder in this popular gatherin' place. Aside from a few trips to Tijuana, Mexico with Uncle Jimmy's Mexican helper, there wasn' any other excitement around. It wasn' long before Ah realized Ah needed more. A lot more. Ah mean, they rolled up the banquettes (oh, sorry, it's sidewalks in English) at nine o'clock. Yeah, Ah needed a lot more excitement.

Ah got in touch with an ol' army buddy that lived in San Francisco. This guy was a really good friend. When he first got to Germany Ah showed him around 'n' taught him the ropes. After Ah left Germany, my friend Darrell fell in love with one of the German girls that we hung around with. He married her and brought her back to the states. They had a baby boy 'n' gave him Dee for a middle name. This touched me deeply cause he did this to honor me. Ya see, Dee is my nickname. So, my ol' Army pal, (by the way, Darrell is the guy that threw the smoke grenade in our good Lieutenant's tent), offered me a job plus room and board. Ah said my goodbye's to everyone in Escondido 'n' took off for San Francisco. Darrell lived in a kinda industrial area with high density apartments mixed in. San Francisco is nothin' like Southern California. It seemed jus' like the East Coast to me. Everyone was in a hurry and up-tight. Parkin' was a nightmare, and homeless people were as abundant as the litter. My first impression was not a good one. Darrell had two businesses goin' for him. One was refurbishin' old furniture, the other was goin' around to houses pickin' up unwanted items and haulin' them to the dump. Ah was the helper on both jobs. Things were goin' along pretty good until Ah made a phone call home and spoke to Pop. He was so emotional 'n' so choked up that he could hardly speak. My heart melted when he said, "Son you were gone a long time in the Army. Na ya gone again. You shouldn' be way out der'; you need to be home with us."

Ah said, "U'right Pop. Ah'll be home for Thanksgivin".

Ah worked and saw the sights in and around San Francisco for about two months then that compellin' urge to hit the road began wellin' up inside of me again. Ah thanked Darrell and his wife, said goodby to my little namesake and headed for the open road.

GET YOUR KICKS ON ROUTE 66

There's somethin' about the open road that's addictin'. It's like floatin' through space. Time stands still. There's nothin' but the sky above 'n' endless road ahead. Ah wound my way through the city 'n' headed south searchin' for that now familiar feelin' of freedom 'n' excitement that comes from anticipatin' what's around the next curve. When Ah entered Needles, Nevada, Ah saw a road sign directin' me to the most famous highway in America, Route 66. This highway was the subject of books, movies, 'n' a very popular TV series. Ah felt a connection to the thousands of people that had experienced what Ah was now experiencin'. Once alone on the road, that euphoric feelin' of bein' suspended in time and space engulfed me.

Ah spent the night in Flagstaff Arizona, woke up 'n' found myself in a winter wonderland. Ah hadn' seen snow and ice since Ah left Germany. Ah also found out that my heater didn' work. Macht nichts, (doesn't matter), Ah put my nice warm German top coat on. The weather warmed up as Ah rolled through Albuquerque, New Mexico. Ah veered off Route 66 in Amarillo, Texas 'n' headed south, then east towards New Orlans. Ah decided to spend a night in Baton Rouge, Louisiana, to kinda get my sea legs 'n' savor the anticipated joy of seein' my family again. Ah made it back to my family just in time for Ma's fabulous Thanksgivin' dinner.

Chapter 7

LIVING BACK IN NEW ORLANS

BACK TO MY OL' HAUNTS

Ah started hangin' out in my old haunts, but once again things had changed. Some of the old crowd had moved on, some settled down, others hung out in different clubs. Ah was only gone about ten months, but it seemed like Ah came back to a different city. Most of the dance styles had changed. The new craze was the limbo.

One more thing happened while Ah was gone. Brook had a gun 'n' vowed that she was gonna shoot me on sight.

Yeah, Ah probably shoulda told her Ah was goin' to California. But "shoot" me! Ah had to really watch my step.

Ah mastered the limbo, 'n' in a short time became the limbo champion at Bosco's. One evenin', Ah was havin' a blast doin' the limbo and drinkin' a glass or two of wine when Ah ran right into Brook. She was hopin' mad, but thank God she had left the gun in her car. Ah managed to calm her down. We talked 'n' even dated a few times. But after awhile, we agreed to go our separate ways.

HOUSE OF BEAUTY

Pop wanted me to stick around for awhile so he asked me to look into enrollin' in a barber school. The thought of goin' back to school—any school—sounded good to me. Ah started askin' around to find out if any of my friends knew where a good barber school was. Fortunately, one of the girls Ah knew suggested that Ah check out Marinellos Beauty School located in the downtown area. Ah thought it over. Let's see, barber school with a bunch of hairy guys or beauty school with a whole group of beautiful girls. Ah hopped in my car 'n' headed downtown to Marinello's. As soon as Ah got there, Ah knew Ah made the right decision. The place was packed with pretty young ladies. Ah was about to enter into a society most men never have the opportunity to be a part of. Ah signed a contract agreein' to pay ten dollars a week until Ah obtained the 1,500 hours of hair stylin' trainin' required by the state for a cosmetology license. Ah had a feelin' it would be worth the time and money for the scenery alone. Everything else would be lagniappe. My trainin' in stylin', cuttin', 'n' colorin' hair was nothin' compared to the education Ah acquired about women. Some of my classmates used language that would make a sailor blush. Where Ah came from men always treated women with utmost respect. In my new environment, the women reversed everything. They were the ones that told the off-color jokes 'n' came on to the men. Ah thought, oh-well Ah'll jus' have to roll with the punches. School was nothin' but fun. Ah received facials, hair treatments, 'n' neck massages, all part of the trainin'. Ah really had to tough it out; ya know what Ah mean. On top of that, Ah went to lunch in the French Quarter with no less than two or three girls everyday. This was like bein' in an amusement park with a gift card.

Bosco's was still the best place to be at night. Ah usually knew everyone in there, but one night Ah saw this distinguished young woman sittin' at a table with some of her friends. She had jet black hair that reached down to her waist 'n' her sky-blue eyes sparkled in the dark. There was an aura around her that said, "If you come over here you better bring your A game."

Ah felt up to the challenge 'n' made my way over to her table with a confident self-assertin' strut 'n' asked her to dance. She accepted. In the course of one dance Ah found out her name was Sylvia, she was a divorcee, 'n' she was born 'n' raised in the Irish Channel. This information explained a lot. The Irish Channel was a haven for gangs and hoodlums from several ethnic groups. Outsiders were not welcomed, especially young males datin' local channel girls. To top it off, Sylvia lived in a project in one of the worst parts of the channel. Growin' up there made her streetwise 'n' tough as nails. We had a lot in common, so durin' the course of the very next dance, Ah asked, "Are you busy next Saturday? If not, let's get married!"

She laughed. "Sure, let's do it."

We started a whirlwind courtship for about two months then we got married. Our weddin' reception was typical New Orlans, complete with several heated arguments and a fist fight. What is it about weddin's 'n' funerals that makes people act like this?

We were off to a rough start. The only money Ah had was about two hundred dollars from weddin' gifts. Ah was jus' out of beauty school, strugglin' to make a few bucks in a two chair shop. Sylvia had a low payin' receptionist job near the French Quarter. Ya may wonder why anyone would get married under those conditions. The answer is simple. Why not? We don't know what the future holds for us, besides in New Orlans, ya gotta live one day at a time; it could all end in a second. Sylvia's Mother died of cancer when she was forty-four years old, her Father died of a heart attack at fifty-five. We experienced as much life as we could whenever we had an opportunity to do so. That's the way life was.

Ah soon found out that the hair stylin' business wasn' nearly as much fun or excitin' as the classroom. For example, oftentimes a women that really didn' have much to work with (ya know what Ah mean), would come in with a magazine picture of a beautiful young model 'n' say, "Make me look like that."

Ah had to bite my tongue to keep from sayin', "That ain't gonna happen dawlin."

Ah tried my hand at runnin' my own beauty business, but it didn' work out. At this point Ah knew three things f'sure. Neither the bar business, fertilizer or beauty businesses were a good fit for me. (Ah was only twenty-four-years-old at this time, but with all the milage Ah had racked up Ah felt a lot older.) My beauty salon wasn' even makin' enough money to pay the rent, so when one of my friends asked if he could use the back of my shop for a gamblin' den, Ah was tempted to do it. However, after Ah thought it over, Ah decided to do what Ah knew Pop would do. Ah would dig my way out of this financial situation with hard work and perseverance.

My first attempt at makin' more money was workin' on the Mississippi River shippin' docs as a longshoremen. What an experience that was! The only way you could get work was if you knew somebody or bribed a union official. Fortunately, my wife's Uncle Joe was the guy that hired people at one of the docs. It's not easy for a longshoreman to get a few days of work. You have to be hired each day for that day only. The person that does the hirin' has a list of names of people that get the first jobs. He points his finger at them and says, "You, you, and you, go to work. The rest of you can try again tomorrow."

My job was way down in the belly of the ship shovelin' corn kernels into one hundred pound sacks. Ah didn' like bein' down in the hole, Ah didn' like shovelin' corn, 'n' Ah didn' like the daily hirin' process. So Ah only worked a few days 'n' quit. Ah needed a job. Ah was havin' a hard time payin' the rent (fifty-five dollars a month) on a little one-bedroom shack. Ah began to understand how Pop musta felt. Ah was doin' the best Ah could, but with my limited education 'n' work experience it wasn' enough. Ah even went to an employment agency where Ah received the same reply Ah always got. "You don't have enough work experience."

Ah didn' want to be rude, but Ah had to ask the lady, "How do you expect me to have work experience when Ah was in the Army protectin' your butt, while you were gettin' big bucks 'n' livin' the good life."

My cousin Mary Jane's husband Eddie (Ah call him "Cuz") informed me that the Southern Railroad was hirin' switchmen. He was workin' for them 'n' managed to arrange an interview for me. Ah had a three day on-the-job-trial (no pay). Ah got the job, but had to be accepted into the Brotherhood of Railroad Trainmen Union before Ah could start workin'. The union acceptance ritual is a by-gone historical practice. Union meetings were held in a dilapidated old buildin' on the second floor above a sleazy bar. Ah had to go to a meetin', stand before the union members, tell them about myself 'n' answer their questions. Each of the members held a white ball and a black ball (they were actually marbles) in their hand. Then the group was asked if anyone had anything to say on my behalf, or against me. Next, they voted by placin' either a white or black ball in a box. Finally the union boss opened the box and examined the contents. If a person got two black balls they were denied union membership, cancelin' all job opportunities. Ah didn' get any black balls 'n' was finally able to work at a job that paid decent wages.

AH BEEN WORKIN ON DA RAILROAD

Railroad work is all about timin' distance and speed. A good switchman had to master all three. The work was challengin' 'n' dangerous. Ah had to be aware of ma surroundings at all times. My athletic background 'n' natural instincts afforded me the tools Ah needed. Within about four months Ah became a pretty good switchman. After all, Ah'd spent a large portion of my youth playin' on trains.

The social aspects of the job were another story. All of the old-timers called me kid. They never used my name. It was always "Hey kid, throw dat switch over dere, hop on, or stand where Ah can see ya signals."

It wasn' a big deal 'cause when Ah hired on they made it perfectly clear, that seniority ruled in every aspect of the job.

First um gonna tell ya a li'l about what a switchman did back in the sixties. Then Ah'll tell ya about some of my on the job experiences that you may find interestin'. When Ah worked a yard job we would breakdown incomin' freight car trains that usually came in from Meridian, Mississippi. Our job was to sort the inbound cars, place them on various designated tracks, then make up a train with them. The most coveted jobs were the ones that transported the made-up trains to either Kenner or Chalmette. The other jobs gathered cars from the yard then transferred them to various industries where they were spotted at the customer's business or warehouse. Ah worked the ten-thirty PM to six-thirty AM industrial job pretty often but didn' spot the cars. Ah passed signals from the spotter to the engineer. There were no verbal communications. Just hand signals in daylight hours 'n' switchman lamps at night. The foreman, Carlos, always looked out for me. Ya see, railroad work in the dark is especially dangerous. We had to rely on each other for safety 'n' efficiency.

IS THAT YOU CARLOS?

About a year went by, 'n' Ah still hadn' spotted cars on this job. In the meantime, Carlos had a heart attack and died. One night my foreman decided it was about time that Ah spot the cars. Mind you, Ah had never been on any of these loadin' docks. It was a pitch dark night. You couldn' see your hand in front of your face. Our engine's bright lights stirred up the bats that were nestin' in the warehouse eve's causin' them to swarm all around us. The whole atmosphere was eerie. The engine was pushin' the cars, Ah was hangin' on the side tryin' to locate the loadin' dock. When Ah got about fifteen feet from the dock Ah heard a voice say, "Jump kid! Jump!"

Ah hopped off the car just in time. There wasn' enough room between the loadin' platform 'n' the boxcar for a person. Ah undoubtedly woulda' been crushed. Ah flagged the engine down 'cause Ah was totally shaken up.

When my crew members asked, "What's wrong?" Ah said "Carlos just told me to jump off of that boxcar!"

They looked at me like Ah'd lost it or was smokin' funny cigarettes or somethin'. However, my story gained credence in the weeks and months that followed 'cause several other guys told about hearin' or feelin' Carlos's presence on that job.

A COONASS NAMED NICK

One of the most interestin' characters that Ah worked with was this coonass named Nick. Ah knew Nick was gonna be a fun guy to work with when Ah overheard a coworker ask him how many kids he had. Nick answered, "Six."

The guy says, "Man that's a lotta kids."

Nick replied, "Yeah Ah had fav of um and one on the way before Ah knew what was causin' it. When Ah found out, Ah quit doin' dat."

Neither of us had a lot of seniority so we had to work off of the extra board or take night jobs with week days off. Nick was the kinda guy that some people didn' like to work with cause he liked to fool around, have fun, and didn' always follow the rigid railroad rules. For example, it was not uncommon for the senior foreman to push and hound the new hires all night. Well, this loud mouth foreman was on Nick's case all night long so when the shift was over, Nick challenged him to a fight. The foreman said, "We can't fight here; we'll get fired."

Nick replied, "We're gonna fight, either in here or we can go out in the street off of railroad property. It's your choice. Ah don't care, but we're gonna fight."

So the foreman followed Nick out into the street, but he grabbed a piece of two by four 'n' threatened Nick with it. Nick took it away from him and proceeded to kick his butt. From that point on, the seniors laid off of the new hires. Nick and I became friends 'n' we often worked the same jobs.

WHO LET THE DOGS OUT?

One of my favorite jobs was the ten-thirty pm to six-thirty am sugar refinery job in Chalmette. The evenin' job weighed the raw sugar cars then placed them in designated tracks. Our job was to weigh any remainin' loaded cars, make up a train, 'n' take it to the New Orlans yard in the mornin'. Most nights we could get our train made up and still have an hour or so before it was time to leave Chalmette 'n' head back to the yard. Nick would disappear into the swamps. Ace, our foreman, would sleep cause he had two jobs. He worked his railroad job all night then worked a day job with the city. Ah used the time to explore my surroundings. Nick always came back with two or three giant bull frogs 'n' say "These are for tonight's supper."

One night Ah was walkin' around shinin' my light into the swamp. All of a sudden, my light landed on a pair of eyes scarin' the hell out of me. (Ah probably had a li'l hell left in me.) Ah froze, keepin' my light on the eyes. Then Ah saw another pair of eyes. Ah moved my light around a bit and discovered a whole bunch of eyes, all starin' at me. At first Ah thought they were nutrias, but closer examination revealed a pack of wild dogs huntin' for their evenin' meal. Ah didn' want it to be me! Ya see, for years people had abandoned unwanted dogs in the area. Some survived, formed packs and roamed around lookin' for food. Ah kept my light in the lead dog's eyes. Ah knew that bright light made most animals freeze in place. Ah also knew ah couldn' keep um there all night. Sure enough, they charged. Ah began shoutin' and swingin' my lamp at them. Thankfully my bluff worked, they veered off and disappeared into the swamp. As soon as Ah caught my breath Ah made my way back to the engine and stayed put.

THAT SURE IS A NICE GOLD WATCH

All employees connected with the operation of our trains had to have accurate watches. New hires had to purchase an approved gold railroad pocket watch before they worked their first shift. Railroad watches have always been coveted items that sometimes attracted the wrong people. After a couple of our switchmen were robbed, some of us started puttin' pistols in our lunch bags. Of course this was against the rules, but Ah always believed that protectin' yourself is a natural right that trumps rules written by some guy sittin' in a nice safe office.

About twelve-thirty one mornin' Ah was on my way to the Southern Pacific yard in Kenner with a cut of railroad cars that stretched out a good mile or so behind us. We had to stop in the clear of our main line to let a road freight train headin' for Texas, cross in front of us. (ya see why accurate watches are so important). We didn' have a caboose so Ah had to walk all the way back to the end of our cars and light warnin' flares to warn any trains that might come up behind us. It was a hot, humid night and the air was still, causin' perspiration to sting my eyes. The clickety clack sound of the passin' trains wheels was pleasant 'n' it kinda relaxed me. Light 'n' music comin' from an open bar door caught my attention. At first Ah wasn' very concerned cause the bar was some distance away, 'n' a huge drainage canal between the bar 'n' our railroad tracks separated us. However, there was a foot bridge that allowed pedestrians to cross over the canal.

Drainage canals 'n' pumpin' stations were installed throughout the city because New Orlans is surrounded by water 'n' most of the city is at or below sea level. The drainage canals 'n' pumpin' stations are designed to pump excess rain or storm waters out of the city, into the lake, river, or swamps. Ah noticed two guys standin' in front of the bar lookin' 'n' pointin' at me. My fight or flight instincts kicked in. A chill ran up my spine when Ah realized that this was the area where the two switchmen were robbed.

Instinctively Ah felt my waistband 'n' searched my pockets hopin' to find my gun. It wasn't there! My equalizer was over a mile away on the engine. Ah quickly assessed my situation. There were two of them 'n' they probably had weapons. You know as well as Ah do that the bad guys always seem to have weapons no matter what laws they break. If they obeyed the laws ‘n’ followed the rules, they wouldn’ be bad guys.

Ah watched as these two characters made their way across the foot bridge. When they reached the tracks they turned ‘n’ slowly walked towards me. Na Ah knew these two malcontents had bad intentions in mind f’sure. Ah had to take my only other option: flight. Ah lit another warnin’ flair thinkin’ the bright light would attract my stalkers attention. Then Ah turned off my switchman lamp, set the flair on a flat car, ‘n’ hopped onto the movin’ train. It worked, My pursuers couldn’ see me ‘cause my waitin’ train separated us. They musta thought Ah vanished into thin air.

Ah could feel an increase in speed when the road train Ah was hangin’ onto accelerated as it’s powerful engines reached the main line. Neither my crew nor the road crew were aware of the predicament Ah was in. Ah had to get away from my pursuers then jump off the boxcar Ah was on before the road train picked up more speed. In the midst of my dilemma Ah thought if only Ah were allowed to carry my gun, Ah coulda solved my problem ’n’ Ah wouldn’ be hangin’ on the side of a boxcar headin’ for Texas. Ah don’t understand the logic lawmakers use when they take away law abidin’ citizens constitutional right to defend themselves. Ah mean, where’s the cops when ya need um, ‘n’ what about women or old people? How are they supposed to defend themselves when Cain’s descendants break into their house?

The risk of serious injury increased with every moment of hesitation. Here’s the situation Ah was faced with: Ah had to jump off the side of a speedin’ train onto an unstable surface with about a three-foot distance between trains, keep my balance while runnin’ on loose track ballast, duck down quickly to avoid gettin’ hit by a wide load, door handle, or a broken metal tie down strap. Then Ah had to scramble through my train hopin’ Ah was far enough away from the bad guys so ah could put my light back on. Somehow, Ah managed to do all of the above without any physical damage. Ah could see the potential robbers some distance away; they were still lookin’ all around. They probably couldn’ figure out what happened to me. Finally the engineer gave three short blasts with the whistle signalin’ me to return to the engine. Ah was standin’ near a partially loaded flat car so Ah gave the engineer a highball signal givin’ him the OK to leave without waitin’ for me to walk back to the engine. Then Ah hopped on the flatcar, found a comfortable spot ‘n’ tried to relax.

NUTRIAS, SHRIMP BOATS, AND CRAB NETS

Ah'm gonna assume that most of ya'll don't know what a nutria is, so Ah'll tell ya a li'l about them. A nutria is a large semiaquatic rodent that looks kinda like a beaver. (They're native to South America.) Nutria fur is used in the fashion industry. Nutria meat (it taste like chicken), is eaten throughout Southeast, Louisiana.You can find nutria on the menu in many restaurants in the area.

Most of the swamp areas in and around East New Orlans are overrun with nutrias. They're destroyin' wetlands, and eatin' everything in sight, includin' rice and sugarcane crops. The li'l suckers are unpredictable and are able to inflict serious injury to humans by bitin' or clawin'. Nutrias are generally nocturnal, so on night jobs around swampy areas Ah really had to watch my step. Ah was workin' the Kaiser Aluminum job in Chalmette one night makin' up a train of cars loaded with aluminum ore. Loaded ore cars are heavy so one of our guys walked ahead of the engine linin' up switches allowin' us to keep a slow steady speed. A nutria was right in front of the switch that Joe had to throw, 'n' the li'l sucka wouldn' move. So Joe lit a flare 'n' flicked hot sulfur at the nutria tryin' to make him move. He moved all right, the ill tempered li'l varmint made a full on attack! Joe tried holdin' him off with his flare, but had to retreat. Ah was on the front engine step, when we got close enough, Ah lit a flare 'n' flicked more hot sulphur at him. Then Ah threw my flare at the li'l bugger. Joe hopped on the engine before throwin' his flare as well. Finally the nutria scampered off into the swamp. You see what Ah mean about nutrias causin' a lot of trouble. That one little nutria took on two switchmen armed with flares, 'n' made a whole train stop for him, causin' a thirty minute delay.

On our way back to the New Orlans yard we had to pass by a nutria-infested swamp. Because of their voracious appetites this swamp was dyin'. Native animals can't compete with nutrias so they either die or move on. Most of the vegetation was gone 'n' many of the moss covered Cyprus trees were dead. We decided to take it upon ourselves to lessen the nutria population, so we started shootin' at um right out of our train engines windows. Na Ah'm not a bettin' man, but Ah'd be willin' to wager that you don't know anyone or have even heard of anyone that shot nutrias from a movin' train window.

SHRIMPIN' AND CRABBIN'

Ah wanted to learn more about shrimpin' and crabbin' so Ah contacted

Johnny Thorne a commercial fisherman 'n' one of my longtime friends. Johnny's whole family were fishermen for generations. He knew more about fishin' than anyone so Ah asked him to teach me a few things. Ah knew Ah could learn everything Ah needed to know about fishin' from him. New Orlans' tight-knit fishin' communities usually didn' welcome outsiders into their fold, but Johnny treated me like family.

Johnny was sixteen years old when he married his fourteen-year-old sweetheart. Johnny's young bride Joyce was my wife Sylvia's best friend, aother Irish Channel girl. After they got married they moved to a camp at the Rigolets where they remained the whole time Ah knew them. (The Rigolets is a twelve mile strait that connects Lake Pontchartrain 'n' Lake Catherine to Lake Borgne, and then to the Gulf of Mexico). Johnny was already a commercial fishermen 'n' continued on after he married Joyce. Johnny supported his wife 'n' fav, kids from what he caught in 'n' around the lakes. Yeah, Ah could learn a li'l about crab fishin' from this guy f'sure. First Ah helped Johnny on his shrimp boat whenever Ah could; boy, what an education. He patiently taught me how to work his forty-foot trawl by hand. Trawlin' is hard dangerous work; ya gotta know what you're doin'. Ah didn' have a clue about anything. Johnny went about his tasks with the precision of a watchmaker. I on the other hand, felt clumsy 'n' confused. When we muscled the heavy net over the side Johnny had to yell, "Let go of the rope and get your foot away from it!"

Good thing Ah had quick reflexes or Ah woulda' been fish food. After the net was in the water, Johnny steared the boat in about a two mile circle. He continued makin, smaller 'n' circles until we got back to where we started. Next, we muscled the net in 'n' dumped the catch on-board. At the end of each day, Johnny always gave me as many of what he called trash fish as Ah wanted. We ate baked flounder 'n' fried catfish steaks almost every day. Ah also helped him run his crab traps. In return, he taught me how to crab with nets like they did before crab traps were around. Johnny used to knit his own crab nets. He could knit a perfect net in less than fifteen minutes. He patiently tried to teach me this part of the trade, but after Ah tried it a coupla times Ah told him Ah'd betta' buy my nets. He laughed 'n' whipped out another net as we spoke.

Crab fishin' with nets is a bygone art. It took a lot of practice, but after awhile Ah managed to become a weekend fisherman. Crabbin' soon became my favorite passtime.

First Ah had to find out what tools Ah needed, then Ah had to learn how to use um. Ah needed nets, strong twine, large corks, 'n' a long pole with a forked prong attached to it. Ah also needed some help so Ah recruited my old friend Johnny Bajon. You remember Johnny; the guy from the burnin' at the stake incident. Ah'll call him Jawn to avoid confusion. (As Ah was writin' this story, Ah found out that Jawn had died. Needless to say, his death makes this story more meaningful to me.) Johnny showed us how to run crab nets a cupola times, then we had to practice on our own. When my next off days rolled around, Jawn and I headed for the nearest boat rental place. We rented a fifteen foot skiff, motor, gas 'n' all for fifteen dollars, what a deal.

Finally, the fun began. We baited, our nets and threw them out every twenty feet in a two mile circle. Ah stood in the bow of our skiff with the forked pole as Jawn steered the boat in at the first net. Ah snagged the cork, lifted the net 'n' swung it around to Jawn. He dumped the crabs onto the boat deck, then Ah swung the net over my other shoulder and placed it back in the water. Jawn steered the boat out towards the next net. Johnny Thorne did all of this by himself. He steered the boat with his legs, speared the cork, swung the net over one shoulder 'n' dumped the crabs. Then he swung the net over his other shoulder, placed the net back in the water; weavin' in 'n' out around his three mile circle of nets. Of course Jawn and I were a lot slower, but we didn' care. We were catchin' crabs. We lumbered all the way around the entire circle of nets enjoyin' every minute of it. On the final run we brought both nets and crabs into the boat. It only took us about an hour or so to harvest two hampers of crabs (about fourteen dozen). As we became more experienced, we managed to cut our time in half. When we got our catch home, we invited friends, family, 'n' neighbors to pass by our house for a good ol' New Orlans style crab boil. Na Ah probably shoulda' spent more time with my wife and kids, but Ah was workin' so much, Ah needed a distraction on my days off.

GANDY DANCERS

Gandy dancer is a term we used for the section crews who laid 'n' maintained our railroad tracks. Crews in our area were all black, with a white foreman. The foreman would position himself a distance away, squat down to check the rails alignment and give hand signals to the crew designatin' places where the rails were out of alignment. An assigned caller started the chants, the crew responded. Rhythm was necessary to synchronize the work 'n' to keep the crew's morale up. A typical chant went like this: "If Ah could Ah surely would, stand on the rock where Moses stood."

"If Ah could (rap it, rap it), Ah surely would stand on the rock where Moses stood. Come on na move it! Huha!...."

Legend is that some of these songs were so sweet birds stopped to listen. Ah was always tryin' to make as much money as Ah could so Ah worked the extra board whenever there was a lot of work. At times Ah worked every other eight hours; eight hours on, eight hours off, then right back to work again. After a few days, it was hard to figure out what day it was.

One evenin' while Ah was workin', a sudden squall came up creatin' near hurricane winds 'n' torrential rain. Ah had to tough it out 'til my shift ended. It was almost midnight by the time Ah drove my tired, wet, miserable body home. It seemed like Ah'd just crawled into bed when Ah heard the phone ringin'. Ah glanced at the clock as Ah reached for the receiver. It was four thirty AM. My mind couldn' focus on the Yardmasters words so Ah hung up. Seconds later my phone rang again. This time Henry (the yardmaster) yelled into the phone as soon as Ah picked it up, "Don't hang up, this is an emergency call! We have an engine with the whole crew on board stuck out on the lakefront (Lake Pontchartrain). Ah need you to be here by six-thirty."

Ah had to drag myself out of bed. When Ah finally got to my feet everything seemed fuzzy, kinda like a hard punch had landed on my jaw. (Have you ever been so tired that your mind and body were numb?) After two cups of strong coffee with chicory, Ah was ready to face the emergency.

When Ah arrived at the yard, my crew foreman briefed me on the situation. In the early mornin' hours, gale force winds blew several boxcars of an inbound train off the tracks (three of them were in the lake). A crane fastened to a flatbed was sent out to recover them; however; while they were workin', waves 'n' a rainstorm washed out the track ballast in front of the engine causin' railroad ties and tracks to sink into a deep pit. The tracks behind them were out of alignment. They were trapped! They couldn' move forward or backward.

Our job was to supply the section crew (Gandy dancers) with track ballast, crossties 'n' rails necessary for the repairs. We had to push the cars from our yard in order to keep our engine away from the work area. Ah hung on the side of the lead car lightin' flares at major crossin's.

The sky was dark 'n' threatenin', but the wind 'n' rain had stopped by the time we got to our destination.

Ah was amazed by the speed, 'n' productive work that the Gandy Dancers performed. My job was signalin' the engineer to move ahead 'n' slowly dumpin' the track ballast while the Gandy Dancers smoothed 'n' leveled it.

After the first car dumped it's load, we backed up to the nearest side track, placed the empty car in it, backed out, then pushed the next loaded car back to the job site. When the ballast became firm 'n' level, they laid the crossties then placed the rails in position. They sang 'n' worked together with rhythm 'n' perfect timin'. The final steps were securin' the rails with spikes, levelin', 'n' finally usin' their linin' bar (gandy pole), they lined them.

Come along with me to the Gandy Dancer job site, let's watch 'n' listen as they go about their work---there's the caller singin' out now,

"Everybody roun' man. Whoah....Lula, Lula, doncha know? Ah ain't gonna be yo' man no mo' Lula?

"Whup...We goin' back. Yeah, come on na, two steps forward one step back, dat's the way we line da track. Yeah...hup, jus' right dere..."

Most historians believe that the rhythmic motion, two steps forward one step back resembled a dance, hence the name "Gandy Dancers." Ah hope ya'll could hear um, Ah hope ya could see um, cause like me, ya won't get another chance. Gandy Dancers have faded into the pages of history only brought back to mind by folks like me that listened to their songs 'n' saw um dance.

HURRICANE BETSY

Hurricane Betsy smashed ashore near New Orlans during the night on September 9th 1965. This monster storm produced sustained winds of 135mph with wind gusts up to 150mph. Betsy completely wiped out several small fishin' towns in Saint Bernard Parish. Grand Isle and Delacroix Island were totally washed away. Houses in the lower Ninth Ward 'n' parts of Gentilly had flood waters that reached the eaves of houses. Nearly all of the drownin' victims were people in the Lower Ninth Ward. Breaches on both sides of the Industrial Canal levee caused most of the deaths. My house was only about a mile from the canal. Seventy six people died in this horrible storm, almost all of them drowned. The reason Ah say almost is because several of my co-workers told stories of people being shot. Mainly looters! Flood waters were deep enough for residents in the Ninth Ward to navigate boats on some main streets. One hundred sixty-four thousand homes were flooded durin' the ten days of floodin', leavin' thousands homeless. Betsy was the first hurricane to cost over a billion dollars.

Ah had worked a night shift the night before Betsy hit. It rained off and on throughout the night, but by the time Ah got home the sky was clear. Ah could feel a difference in the air pressure. A storm was brewin' f'sure. Ah grew up experiencin' all kinds of storms; they were a part of New Orlans life. My senses were programmed. Ah knew a storm was comin'. Ah jus' didn' know how big it would be. Ah tried to get some sleep but was too antsy. Somethin' about this storm jus' didn' feel right. Ah could feel the pressure droppin'. The hair on my arms was standin' up 'n' Ah couldn' shake the angst that had come over me. My wife 'n' children were in danger. My precious little daughter, Gina, was only about one year old, her brother Mike was four. Somethin' bad was about to happen 'n' Ah couldn' do anything about it. Ah decided to take a ride around the lakefront to check things out. First thing Ah saw was National Guard trucks movin' about. Then Ah saw waves crestin' over the sea wall. A feelin' of dread engulfed me. Ah knew there were only two bridges that crossed over the Industrial Canal in our area. If anything happened to those bridges we would be trapped in a flood zone. Ah spun my car around 'n' headed home. When Ah got there, Ah told my wife, "Pack some stuff, grab Gina 'n' Mike, 'cause we gotta get outta here." National Guard trucks were everywhere. Ah called the railroad to tell um Ah wasn' comin' in that night. The Yardmaster started givin' me a hard time. He said "ya gotta come in. We're short handed and we don't even know where the storm's gonna hit." Ah was in no mood to argue. Ah said, "Looka here! National Guard trucks are gettin' ready to evacuate my area. My first duty is to my family. You can do whatever ya want, Ah'm NOT comin' in." Ah hung up the phone, snatched my gun from the nightstand 'n' made sure all the windows had a little openin' at the bottom to allow the air pressure to balance.

At this point Ah feel compelled to give ya'll a li'l insight into what happens when our normal social order breaks down. Storms, riots, 'n' terrorist attacks are just a few examples of what can cause a societal breakdown. If you find yourself in the midsts of disaster of any kind, here's some suggestions for ya. First of all, don't panic. You have to understand you're gonna have to fend for yourself 'n' your loved ones. You need to be able to think outside the box 'n' maybe do some some off the wall stuff.Ya might even hafta break a few laws. The most important thing that you will need is a GUN! Ah don't care what laws ya havta break, have a gun with you at all times. Don't think that a knife, baseball bat, or your black belt will protect you; they won't. There will be armed groups of scumbags roamin' around. Low life vermin seem to thrive when a societal breakdown occurs.

Oh yeah, ya might need some warm clothes, water, and food as well. Ah went outside, whistled for my son's dog hopin' he would respond. He didn'. Ya see, our dog was a canine street rat. He roamed the streets with his friends all night long checkin' out da ladies. Go figure. Ah left some food and water for him on my front porch, loaded everyone into the car then sped across the Industrial Canal bridge towards Pop's house. When Ah got there Ah found the whole family glued to the television set watchin' the latest hurricane updates. Ma was worried. My young brother Gerard wasn' too interested 'cause he hadn' experienced a serious hurricane yet. That was about to change. Pop wasn' troubled at all. He'd been through several storms with us 'n' he always managed to keep us safe. All the news reporters were urgin' people in low lyin' areas to seek shelter on higher ground. Ah wondered, where the hell is higher ground? The whole city is below sea level. When Ah heard reports that Betsy had wind gusts of 150 mph Ah suggested that we get to a safer buildin'. Pop asked "Why? We're doin' okay. We have food, a tub full of water, 'n' the electricity is still on."

About 8:00 PM rain began poundin' Pop's house 'n' strong gusts of wind rattled the windows. Betsy's leadin' edge was hittin' us with fierce winds 'n' poundin' rain. Betsy was here deliverin' everything the newscasts had predicted. She pounded on us for at least an hour. Suddenly the wind quieted and the rain stopped. We were in the storm's eye. If we were gonna leave we had to do it now. Pop still didn' want to leave. Ma and I kept tryin' to get him go to a shelter, but he wouldn' budge. We hem-hawed around for an hour or so. One of the news stations urged people in Chalmette, Arabi, St. Bernard, 'n' Gentille (we were in Gentille), to go to shelters. The reportor listed shelters that were open. Ah saw my old high school on the list, 'n' shouted. We can go to Nicholls; it's a solid buildin' 'n' not very far from here. Pop didn' respond until the electricity went off. This convinced him. He finally agreed to leave. Pop, Ma, Gerard, 'n' their two dogs got in Pop's pickup truck. Ah hustled my family into my car 'n' breathed a sigh of relief. Time was of the essence. We were backin' out of the driveway when Gerard noticed an injured owl in our neighbor's hedges. Pop stopped his truck, got out, went back in the house, 'n' brought out a towel. He covered the owl. Then he put it in his enclosed patio shed. Ah couldn' help thinkin,' "Isn't that just like Pop. In the midst of a Category 3 hurricane he takes the time to rescue an injured owl." Disasters bring out evil in some people 'n' good in others. The owl survived 'n' remained with Pop for many years. When he was set free, he made his home in a nearby tree.

We had only driven about a mile when the back end of Betsy banged into our little convoy. Hugh tree limbs were flyin' around us like leaves in the wind. Whole trees were uprooted. Snappin' power lines were flauntin' a bizarre sort of light show. In some spots Ah had to swerve around fallen trees. In others ah had to drive on the neutral ground (median) to avoid sparkin' power lines that were whippin' around like a snake with it's tail on fire. Drivin' in these conditions was a crucial test of my drivin' skills. We were in a life threatenin' situation. Ah had to rely on everything Ah ever learned about drivin'. Ah had to put it all together right there on that street at that moment in time. Lives depended on it.

We made it to the shelter, but still had a problem. Wind gusts were so strong we couldn' walk. Two big guys rushed out of the buildin' 'n' helped my wife get Gina into the buildin'. Ah held onto lil' Mike as Ah fought my way into my old school. We managed to secure a spot near an exit, close to the restrooms. There was no electricity. Flashlights cut through the darkness showin' glimpses of frightened faces. This was troublin' 'cause frightened people are unpredictable. They panic 'n' usually do dumb things. Some people comin' in told us Arabi 'n' Chalmette were floodin' and the Industrial Canal was overflowin' it's banks. A hush fell over the crowd. They became restless 'n' kinda jumpy. Sure enough, when wind gusts blew several windows out, sounds of the breakin' glass caused some to panic. They started a stampede towards the exits. Thank God, some veteran storm people were there. They shouted, "STOP! Calm down. That was jus' some windows breakin'. We're still okay."

We spent the followin' night at the shelter, then decided to make our way back to Pop's house. The drive back was challengin' to say the least. We were in the Lower Ninth Ward where most of the streets were flooded. We had to wind our way through neighborhoods, drive over lawns, and maneuver around downed trees 'n' power lines. We managed to find ways around flooded streets and finally made it to Gentilly. For a moment Ah thought we had a clear path to Pop's house, but my enthusiasm was short lived. When Ah got to the underpass on Gentilly Boulevard Ah found the street flooded with about four feet of water. There was no way Ah could drive through it. We were within walkin' distance to Pop's, however, walkin' wasn' an option. All of us were mentally and physically worn out. Ah made my way up an embankment to the railroad tracks above. From my vantage point Ah saw a car makin' it's way across the tracks at an abandoned crossin'. Ah came down 'n' told Pop, "Follow me, Ah a way o-va' the tracks."

Ah didn' have any trouble findin' the crossin' cause Ah kinda knew the neighborhood. We cautiously crossed over the tracks; this was not the time to get in a hurry. Once our vehicles cleared both sets of tracks Ah knew we were home free. Ah felt my muscles relax a little as Ah drove the last mile to Pops house. When we finally got there we found everything intact. In fact the electricity was already back on. Pop was right after all. We shoulda' stayed right there.

My family was safe at Pop's house. We had survived the most destructive hurricane ever to hit New Orlans, up to that time. Decades later Hurricane Katrina caused more damage than Betsy and killed more people in New Orlans than any other hurricane in history.

Ah was a little uneasy as Ah drove back across the Industrial Canal towards my house. Ah didn' know if it had been damaged, looted, or even if it was still there. As Ah turned off Chef Highway onto Downman Road, the street leadin' to my house, my heart sank. The street had about a foot of water coverin' it. Low places on the roadside had at least two feet of water. Not a good sign 'cause my house was only two blocks away. Ah maneuvered my car to the highest part of the road and drove slow, dryin' my brakes all the while. Every old school New Orlans driver knew how to dry their brakes back then. Barmaids from a nearby bar frolickin' around in the flood waters seemed oblivious to the devastation around them. When Ah reached my house Ah waded through knee deep water to my front porch. Ah climbed the three steps up to the porch where Ah was given a hearty welcome by my dog. It only took a few minutes to walk straight through my shotgun style house. Everything was intact. Nothin' was taken or damaged by looters. Fortunately my house was owned by a New Orlans Police Captain that investigated internal affairs. A lot of cops owed him favors. Anytime my house needed maintenance or repairs, four or fav' cops always "volunteered" to do the work on their own time. That's the way it works in New Orlans. Looters woulda been hunted down 'n' givin' a li'l tough love. My backyard and laundry shed didn' do so well. Flood waters ruined my washin' machine, winter clothes, 'n' my kid's toys.

Ah don't remember how long Ah stayed at Pop's, but eventually Ah went home, back to work and tried to get back to some sort of normal life. In New Orlans normal life can be a contradictory term. Ah managed to secure a 1.57% hurricane disaster loan, replaced some of my damaged stuff, then vowed to myself that as soon as Ah had enough money, Ah would relocate my family to California. Often while workin' in a pourin' rain, Ah would look up to the heavens sayin.' "One of these days um goin' to California."

Ah said this so often my co-workers nicknamed me "California."

LAY THAT PISTOL DOWN BOY

A year or so went by. Another holiday season rolled around and as usual

Ah was tryin' to get in the Christmas spirit. Ya see Ah was a lil' burned out with: workin', crabbin', crab boils, people passin' by day 'n' night, and a lot of various family functions. It seemed like we always had some sort of social obligations. So Ah wasn' very excited about my in-laws Christmas party. We decided to make a full night of it anyway. Sylvia asked her sister if the kids could spend the night. Ah made plans with Ma for Sylvia 'n' I to spend the night at her house so we could spend some time with her and Pop. Ah knew it would be a late night 'cause cause we were gonna'meet up with a childhood friend of mine after the Christmas party. Ronnie was by far, the most fun person Ah ever met. We grew up together. Ah knew him my whole life. After a four year stint in the Marine Corps, Ronnie went through the State Police academy 'n' became a Louisiana State Trooper. He knew the right people. In a short time Ronnie was promoted to a powerful position. People outside of Louisiana have no idea how prominent State Troopers are. Ah carried his card in my wallet. That little card afforded me privileges you wouldn' believe. Ah could do anything short of murder.

The Christmas party turned out to be a lot of fun, complete with a Santa 'n' lots of presents for the kids. But Ah was kinda glad when Sylvia told her relatives that we were meetin' Ronnie at twelve-thirty 'n' we had to leave. It was almost one o'clock before we met up with Ronnie at an all-night roadside cafe out on Chef Highway. Ronnie was workin' narcotics under-cover so he didn' want to hang out in places where he was workin'. We had a great time jokin' around and listenin' to excitin' cop stories. By the time we left it was around 2:30 AM. My car 'n' the one behind me were the only cars on the road. Ah was drivin' along talkin' about events of the night when Ah casually looked in my rear-view mirror 'n' noticed a car really close behind me. Naturally Ah thought he wanted to pass, so Ah changed lanes. He changed lanes also. Then he rolled right up close to the back of my car again. Ah said, "That car's followin' us!" Sylvia replied, "Yeah Ah know Ah been watchin' it. Do ya have ya gun?" Ah didn' have it. Ah had left it on the night table at Ma's. Ah didn' think Ah'd need my gun at a Christmas party. Ah changed lanes a few more times to make sure he was followin' us. He definitely was. Ah thought this guy may have seen us with Ronnie 'n' thought we had drugs to sell. Ah picked up speed then made a quick turn into Ma's subdivision. Ah still couldn' get this guy off my tail. Ah told Sylvia, "When we get to Ma's house, get out quick, Ah'll stay between you 'n' him. Go in and get my gun."

Ah pulled in the driveway behind Pop's car. Sylvia jumped out runnin'. By the time she got to the door, Ma was already there. Ah don't know how she did it, but Ma could always sense trouble. Sylvia rushed in, got my gun, 'n' handed it to me. Then she went back in 'n' called the cops. In the meantime the guy drove a little past the house, then swung around 'n' parked his car about thirty feet from me. Ah ducked behind Pop's car, 'n' tried to scare him off by wavin' my gun around so he could see it. Ah even pointed it at him. He didn' even move. Ah expected him to duck down or drive off, but he just sat there. Then he drove around the block, came back, parked 'n' sat there starin' at me. Ah crept up to the front of my car 'n' aimed my gun again. This time Ah saw him reach down on the seat next to him. He had a gun! Ah hit the ground still aimin' at him from a prone position. He pulled his head back, but didn' do anything else. Ah made sure Ah was out of hiss line of fire 'n' waited for him to make the next move. He just sat there starin' at me. Thank God two cop cars came before any shots were fired. One cop car pulled up behind him, the other blocked him in from the front. They got him!

After they handcuffed the bad guy, one of the cops came over to explain things to me. It turns out the cop was an ol' friend of mine from way back in the third grade. Ah met this guy in a kinda unusual way. Vernon sat right behind me in class. One day he was tryin' to annoy me for some reason. He kept tappin' me on the shoulder, makin' me turn around. About the third time he did this, Ah turned around 'n' punched him right in the face. We eventually became friends. Not close friends, but friends jus' the same.
Vernon told me the guy was drivin' around lookin' for his cheatin' wife. He saw Sylvia and I leavin' the diner, thought Sylvia was his wife, but wasn' sure. He followed us tryin' to get a better look at her before shootin' us. He told the police he intended to kill both of us with the 45-caliber pistol he had on his front seat. Vernon hung around awhile sharin' some old stories, then he left. Ah have no idea what happened to our stalker 'n' really didn' care. The danger was over.

Ah'd say it ended up bein' a pretty excitin' night after all. Wouldn' you? Hurricane Betsy, almost gettin' shot, coupled with risin' crime in the city, solidified our decision to leave New Orlans.

Leavin' family, friends, and a secure high payin' railroad job wouldn' be easy. But if my family was gonna' have a chance for a better life, we had to make the move. Besides Ah was ready for another adventure. We gave most of our big stuff to my fisherman friend Johnny. Then Ah rented a small u-haul trailer, hooked it up to my 1965 Datsun station wagon, 'n' loaded it with clothes 'n' kids toys. Ah had to tie two bikes on the outside of my trailer. We musta' looked like The Beverly Hillbillbillies. Early the next mornin' we left. Once again Ah found myself on the open road, but this time Ah had a family to look out for.

LOOKA HERE!

You've probably heard the theory that life's a big circle. That it moves in cycles.That there's an ebb and flow, an inevitable push and pull, to things. Ah believe this to be true. Indeed, my life has unfolded that way. Ah've always been compelled to seek excitement and adventure. Been pushed forward by some unseen force towards the unknown. At the same time, Ah felt a strong tug. Even as Ah ventured to the other side of the world, Ah was bein' pulled by the forces of family and home. Take it from this ol' coonass who's bin dere and dun dat, there's nothin' wrong with chargin' ahead. Jus' don't forget who you are and where ya came from!

This is my family Coat of Arms. DiGiovanni is Italian for *of John*. I had my good friend Jim Wagner design this modern version for me.

This is me at 80-years-young. A life of martial arts training, yoga, eating right, and trusting in God kept my body, mind, and soul strong.